CU00670938

Table of Contents

2J

About the Writers

Julia Olson got her start teaching piano in Utah, where she also taught preschool at a private school that emphasized learning through music. Since then, she has taught private piano lessons as well as early childhood music and group piano classes in California and Illinois. She is a member of the National Music Teachers Association and the Early Childhood Music and Movement Association. In addition to maintaining a piano studio with children of all ages, Julia directs children's choirs in her community.

Kevin Olson is an active pianist, composer, and member of the piano faculty at Utah State University, where he teaches piano literature, pedagogy, and accompanying courses. In addition to his collegiate teaching responsibilities, Kevin directs the Utah State Youth Conservatory, which provides weekly group and private piano instruction to more than 200 pre-college, community students. Before teaching at Utah State, he was on the faculty at Elmhurst College near Chicago and Humboldt State University in northern California.

He also writes and edits music for The FJH Music Company, which he joined as a writer in 1994. Many of the needs of his own piano students have inspired a diverse collection of books and solos he has published of original music and instructional material. Kevin received his bachelor's and master's degrees in music composition and theory from Brigham Young University, and holds a Doctorate of Education from National-Louis University.

Kevin and Julia live in Logan, Utah with their four children: Skyler, Casey, Aubery, and Wesley.

A few things to remember about music...

Beat and Tempo

Music makes you want to tap your feet because it has a beat, like a beating drum. Listen to the beat in all the music you hear. See if you can clap or tap to the beat. The beat in music can be fast, slow, or in the middle. This is called *tempo*. A metronome can help you set a tempo for your music. You might want to purchase a metronome for practice at home.

Tempo Settings

There are many different words to describe tempo settings in music. Some of the more common tempo settings are *largo, andante,* and *allegro*. Set your metronome to these tempo settings and clap to the beat.

Largo
40–60

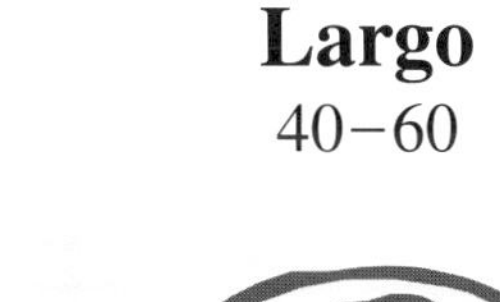

Slow, like a tired turtle

Andante
76–108

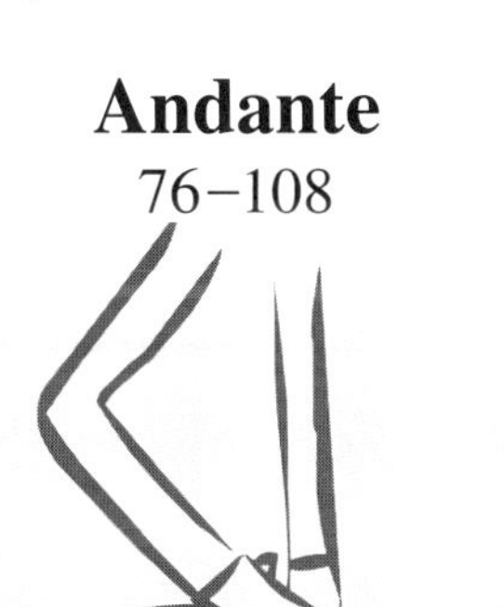

Neither fast nor slow, like walking sneakers

Allegro
120–168

67

Fast, like a race car

Dynamic Markings

Music can be soft, loud, or in the middle. There are words to describe how soft or loud you can play. These words are called *dynamics*. Play some keys on the piano to make them sound soft, loud, or in the middle.

p is for *piano*

Soft, like a mouse

m is for *mezzo*

mp ***mf***

Moderately soft or moderately loud (in the middle)

f is for *forte*

Loud, like thunder

A few things to remember about counting...

Notes and Note Values

In music, there are many different types of notes. Some notes are held for a short amount of time and others are held longer. To play music, you will need to know how many beats each note is worth.

Quarter Note
1 Beat
Clap and say 1

Half Note
2 Beats
Clap and HOLD
say 1 2

Dotted Half Note
3 Beats
Clap and HOLD
say 1 2 3

Whole Note
4 Beats
Clap and HOLD
say 1 2 3 4

Rests and Rest Values

Sometimes in music, we take a short break before we play again. This is called a *rest*. There are different types of rests and rest values as well.

Quarter Rest
1 Beat of Silence
say 1

Half Rest
2 Beats of Silence
say 1 2

Whole Rest
3 or 4
Beats of Silence
say 1 2 3 or 1 2 3 4

Bar Lines and Measures

To keep music notes and rests organized, there are lines called *bar lines*. The beats between the bar lines make up *measures*. At the end of a song, you will see a *double bar line*. The bar lines and measures help us count our music. You will count the beats in each measure and start over on beat 1 each time you come to a bar line or a new measure.

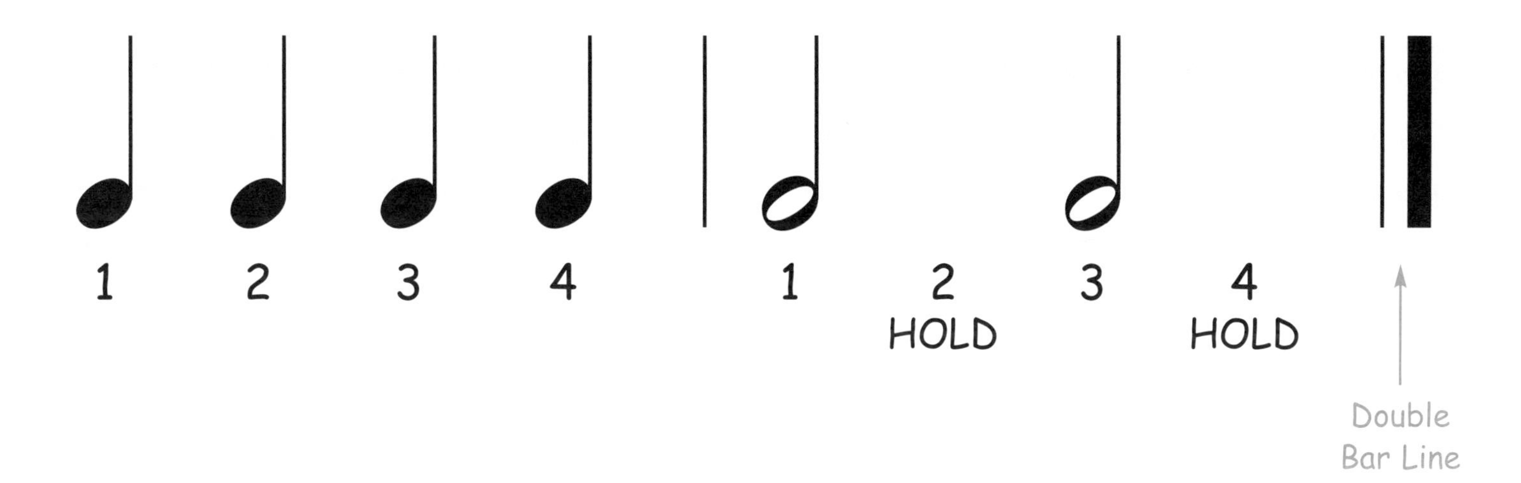
1 2 3 4
1 2 3 4
HOLD
HOLD
Double
Bar Line

Time Signature

At the beginning of your music you will find a *time signature*. The time signature has a top number and a bottom number. The top number tells you how many beats are in each measure and the bottom number tells you the type of note that gets the beat. (For now, it will usually be the quarter note.)

2 Beats
per measure
Quarter Note
gets the beat
3 Beats
per measure
Quarter Note
gets the beat
4 Beats
per measure
Quarter Note
gets the beat

A few things to remember about playing the piano...

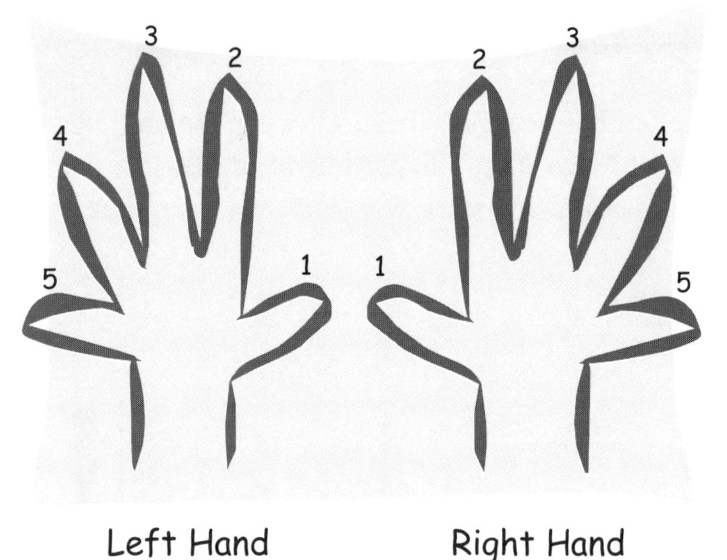
3
2
4
5
1
2
3
4
1
5
Left Hand
(L.H.)

Right Hand
(R.H.)

Finger Numbers

Each of your fingers has a number assigned to it for playing the piano.

Thumb is finger number 1.
Pointer finger is finger number 2.
Tall finger is finger number 3.
Ring finger is finger number 4.
Pinky is finger number 5.

Wiggle each of your fingers and mix it up for review.

The Piano Keyboard

The piano keyboard is made up of many keys, with high notes to the right and low notes to the left. There are both white keys and black keys. The black keys are in groups of 2 and 3.

Play and count all the 2-black-key groups on your piano.

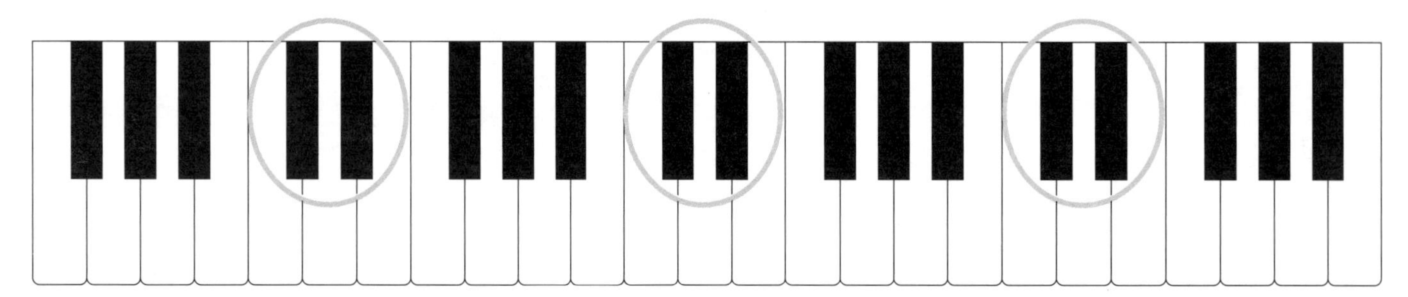

Play and count all the 3-black-key groups on your piano.

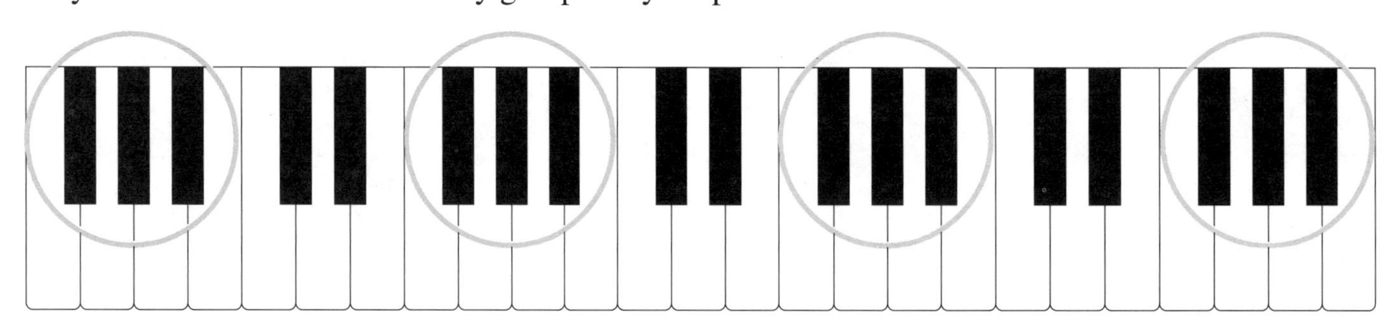

The Musical Alphabet

The musical alphabet is different than the regular alphabet. The musical alphabet goes up to G but then starts all over at A again, like this:

A B C D E F G A B C D E F G A B C etc.

The White Keys

The musical alphabet is repeated over and over on the white keys. Play all the white keys starting with the first one on the left, which is A. Sing the musical alphabet as you play.

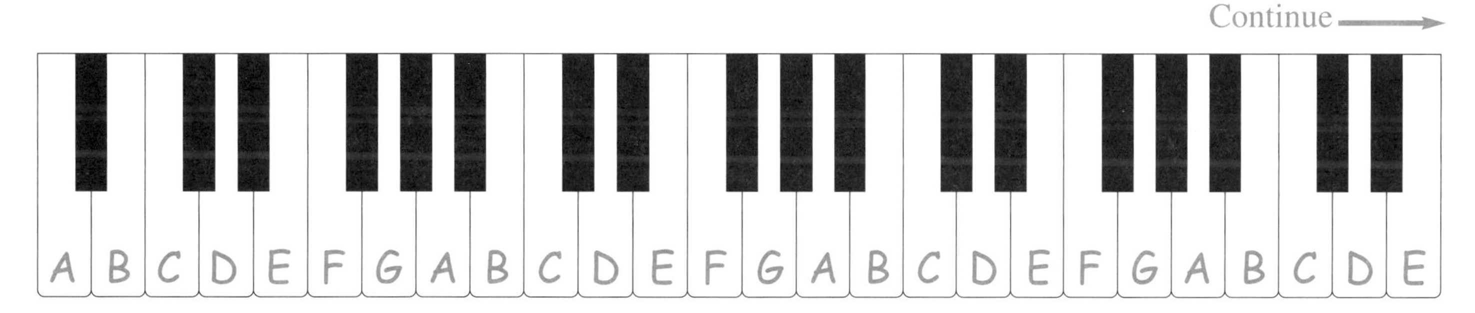
Continue
A B C D E F G A B C D E F G A B C D E F G A B C D E

Because there are *so* many white keys, it helps to look at the 2-black-key groups to learn them. Below each 2-black-key group you will always find CDE, and below each 3-black-key group you will always find FGAB.

C D E
F G A B

Octave

Every 8 notes, a key is repeated. This is called an *octave*. For example, look at all of the C's on the keyboard below. These C's are different octaves but they are all C's. The C's to the left are the lower C's and the C's to the right are the higher C's.

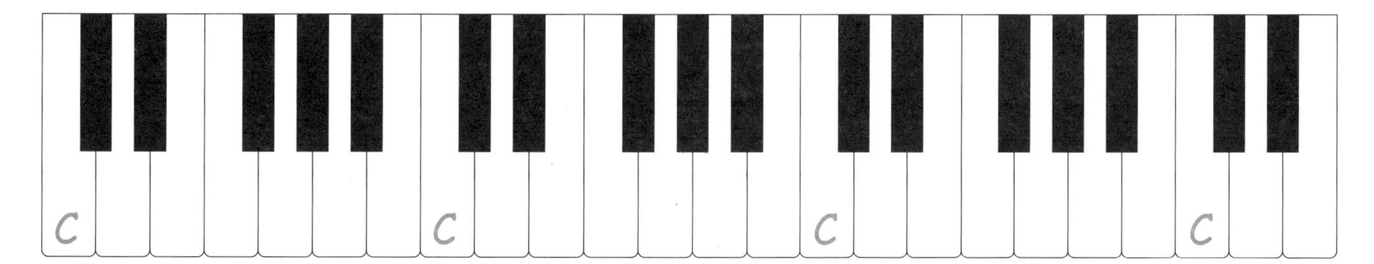
C
C
C
C

A few things to remember about note-reading...

The Grand Staff

Music notes are written on a group of lines and spaces called a *staff*. A staff has 5 lines and 4 spaces. Piano music is written on two staves (staffs) grouped together called the *grand staff*. The top staff is called the treble staff and the bottom staff is called the bass staff.

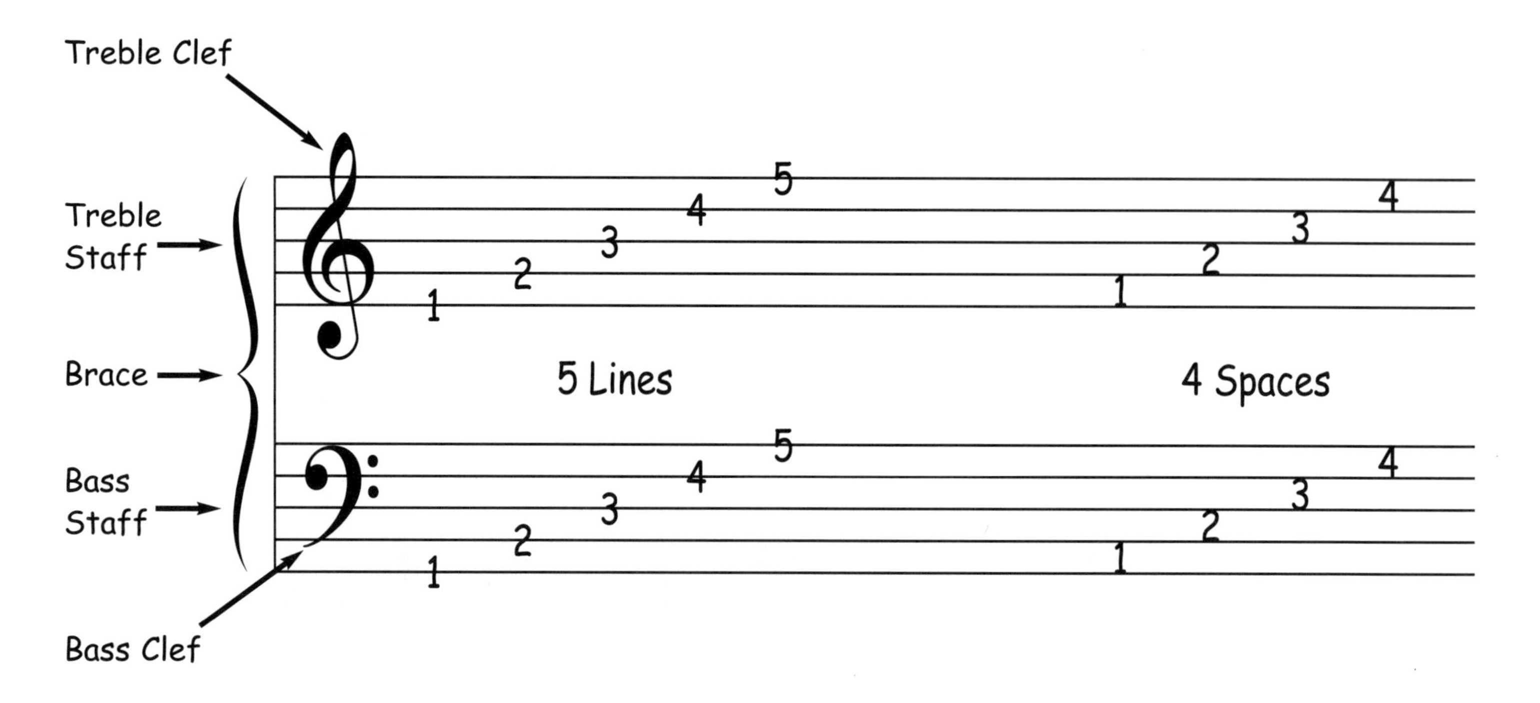
Treble Clef
Treble Staff
Brace
Bass Staff
Bass Clef
5 Lines
4 Spaces
1 2 3 4 5
1 2 3 4

The Musical Alphabet on the Staff

Right hand usually plays all the notes that are written on the treble staff.
Left hand usually plays all the notes that are written on the bass staff.

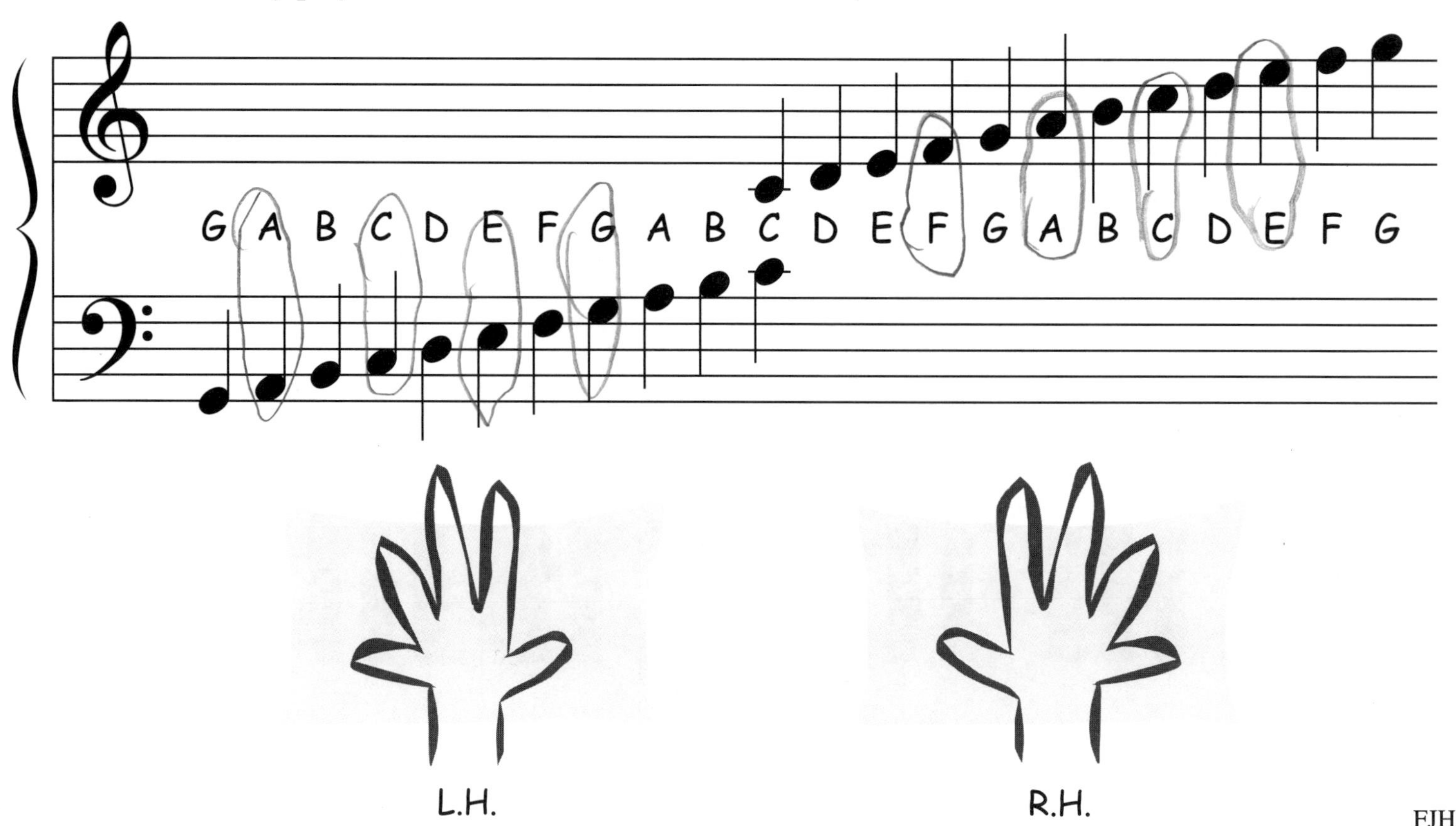
G A B C D E F G A B C D E F G A B C D E F G
L.H.
R.H.

Middle C Hand Position*

The notes in this book are in the Middle C Position. To play in Middle C Position, place both thumbs on the C that is in the middle of the piano. Place the rest of your fingers as indicated in the note guide below.

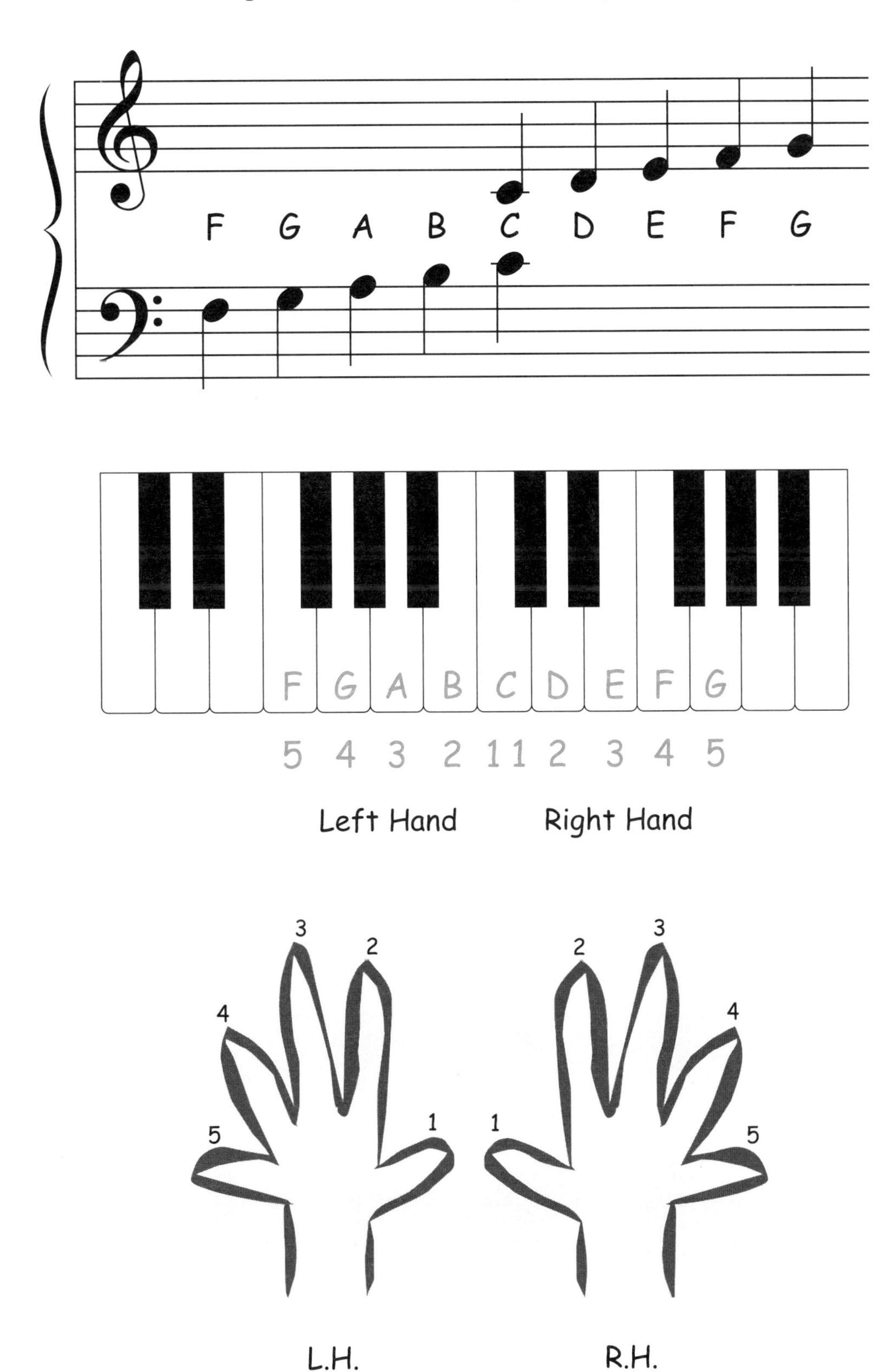

F G A B C D E F G
F G A B C D E F G
5 4 3 2 1 1 2 3 4 5
Left Hand
Right Hand
3 2 4 1 5
2 3 4 1 5
L.H.
R.H.

*Hand Positions are only "guides." They help you feel comfortable learning new notes. Once you are comfortable, you should explore your pieces further by starting on a different finger.

Unit 1 Middle C and D on the Keyboard

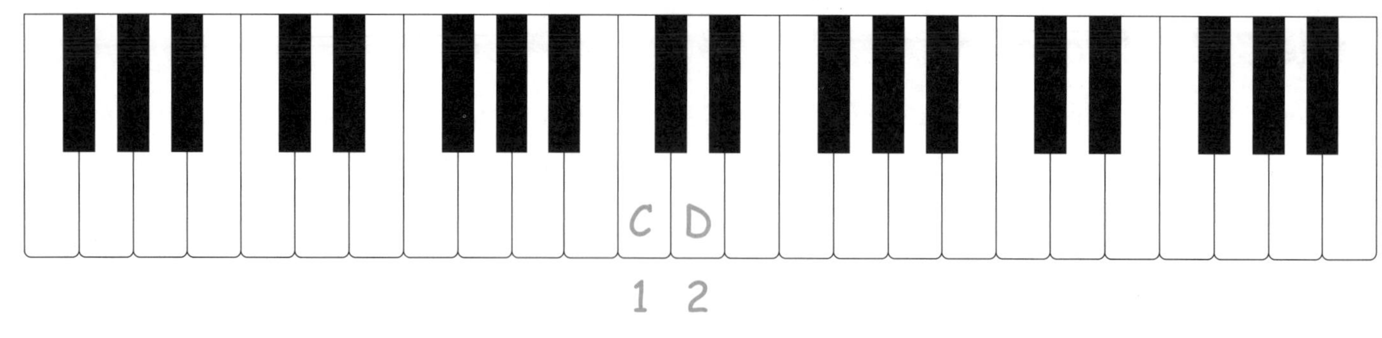
C D
1 2

Right Hand

Remember that hand positions are just guides. When you are comfortable with the pieces in this unit, explore using different fingers.

Middle C and D on the Staff

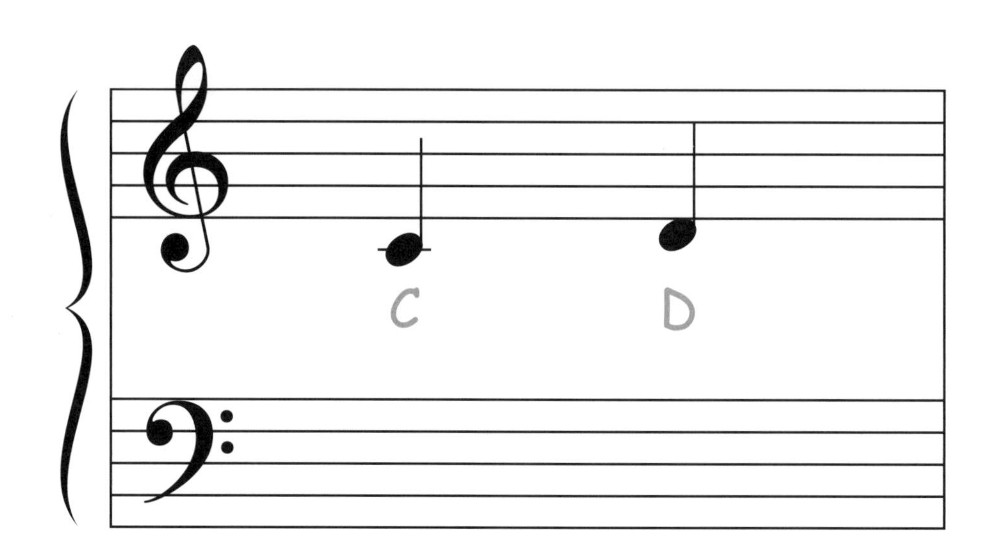
C
D

Play the example below, keeping your eyes on the music.

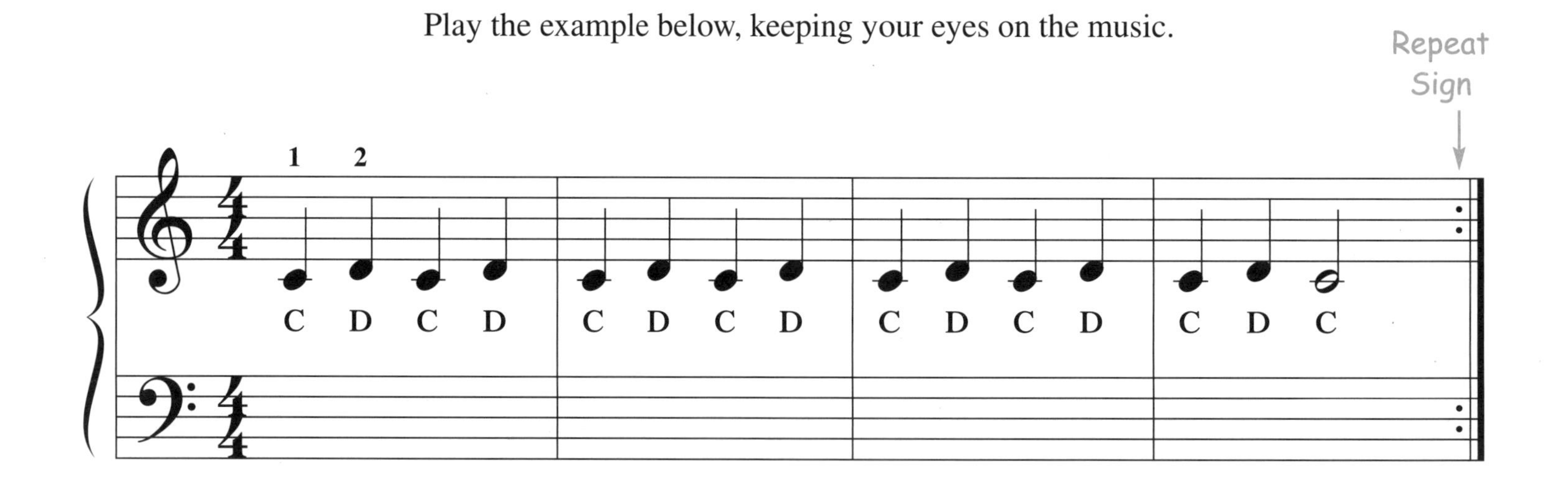
Repeat Sign
1 2
C D C D
C D C D
C D C D
C D C

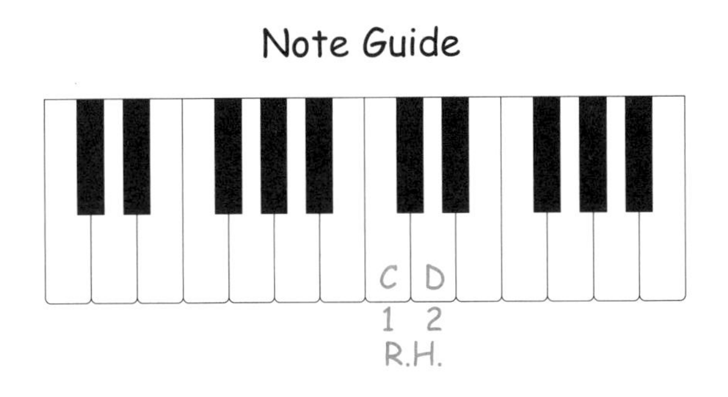
Note Guide
C D
1 2
R.H.

Watching Ocean Waves

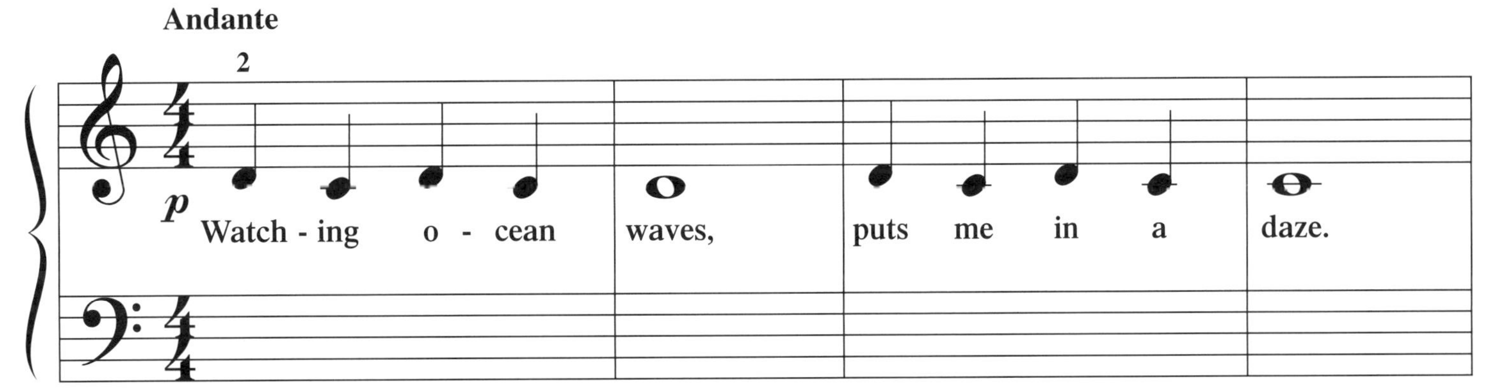
Andante
2
p
Watch - ing o - cean waves, puts me in a daze.

When played as a solo, press the right (damper) pedal for the entire piece.

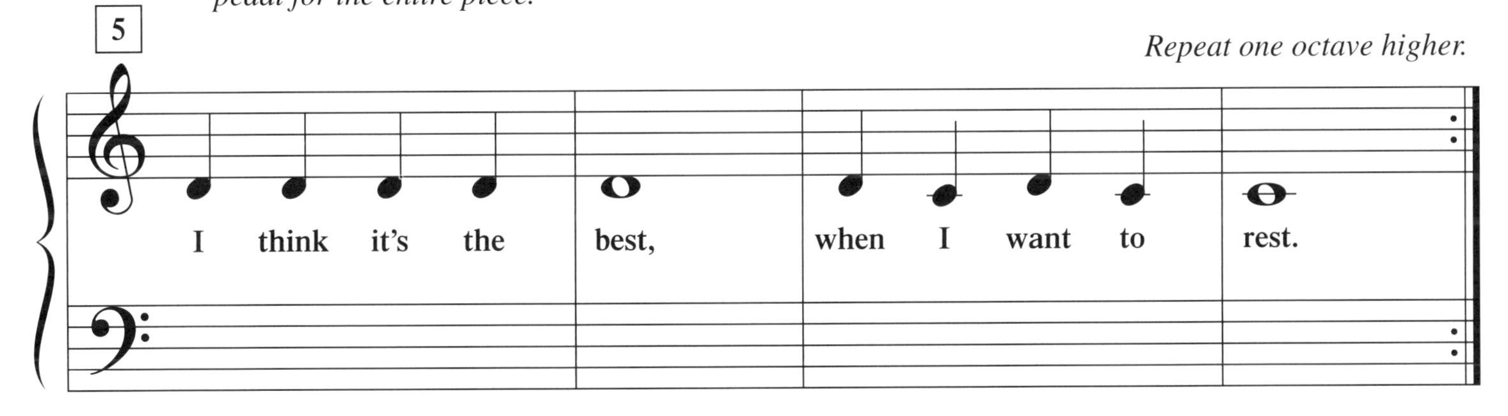
5
Repeat one octave higher.
I think it's the best, when I want to rest.

After you are comfortable with this piece, try playing with **R.H.** finger **3** on **D.**

Teacher Duet: Student plays as written.

R.H.
L.H.
pp
with pedal
5

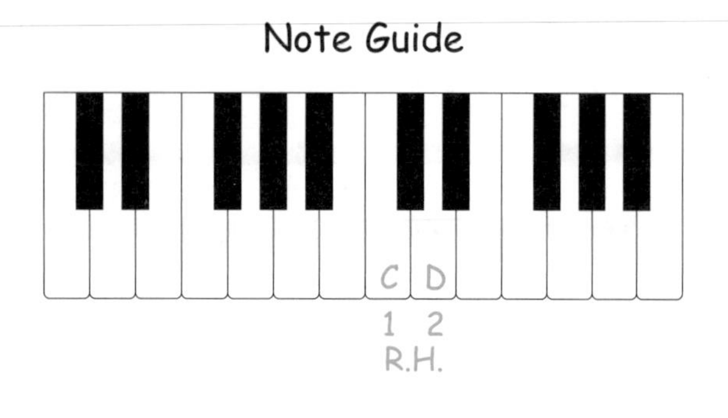
Note Guide
C D
1 2
R.H.

Can't Remember How to Fly

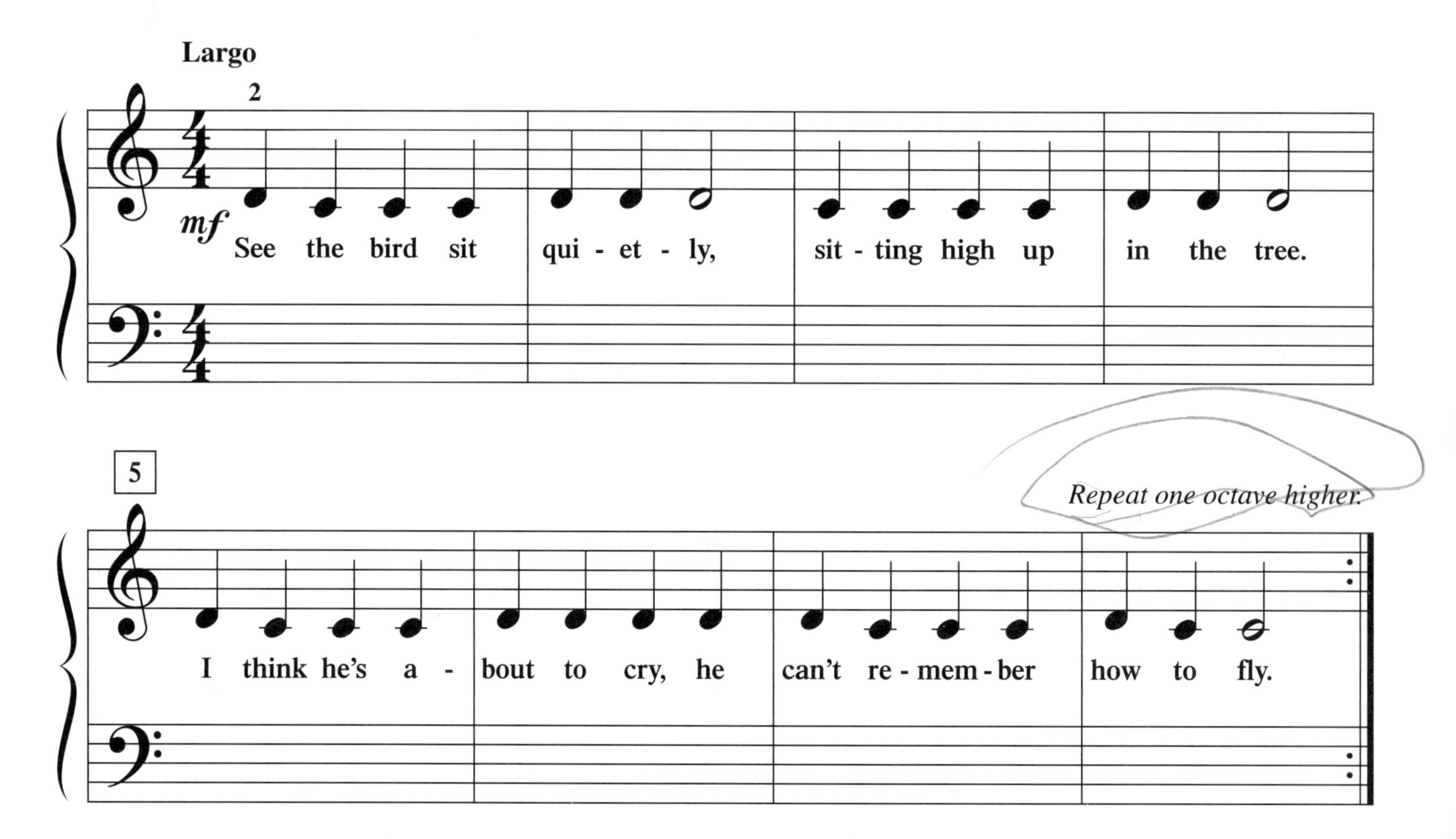
Largo
2
mf
See the bird sit qui - et - ly, sit - ting high up in the tree.
5
Repeat one octave higher.
I think he's a - bout to cry, he can't re - mem - ber how to fly.

After you are comfortable with this piece, try playing with **R.H.** finger **3** on **D.**

Teacher Duet: Student plays as written.

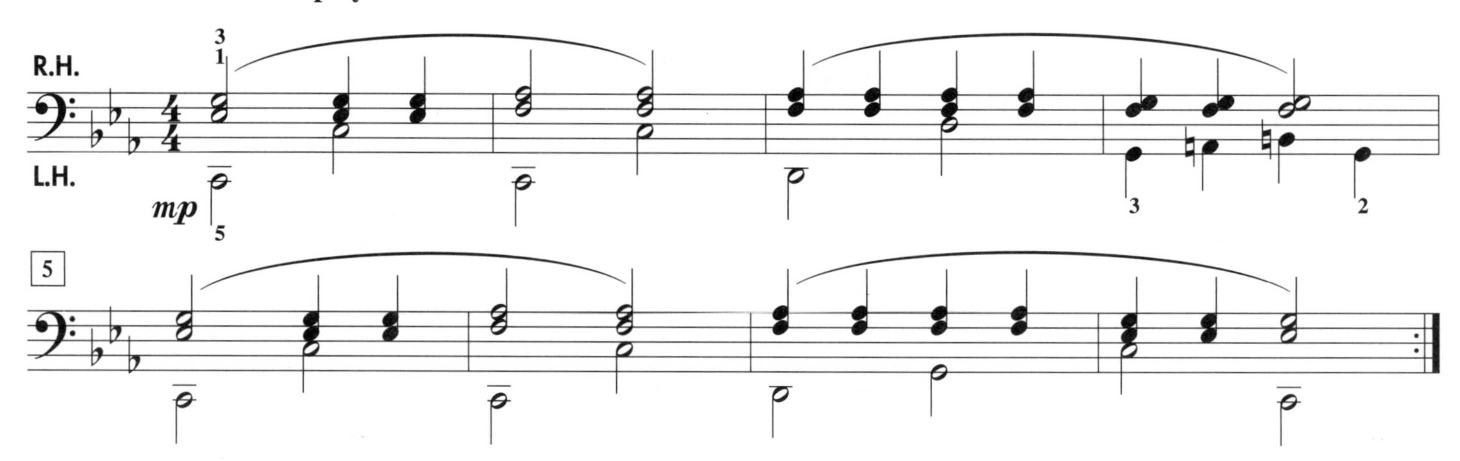
R.H.
L.H.
mp
5

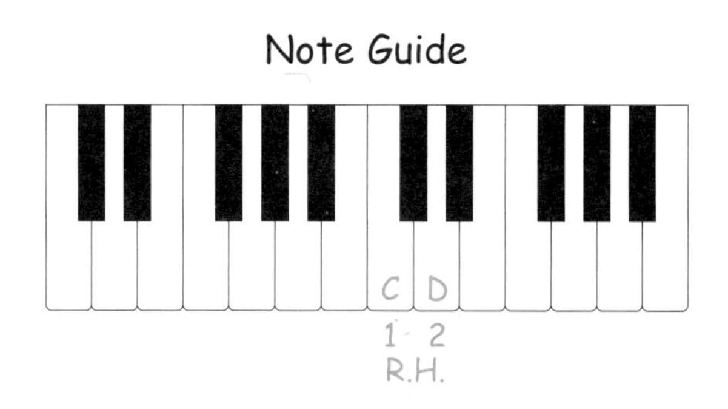
Note Guide
C D
1 2
R.H.

New Shoes

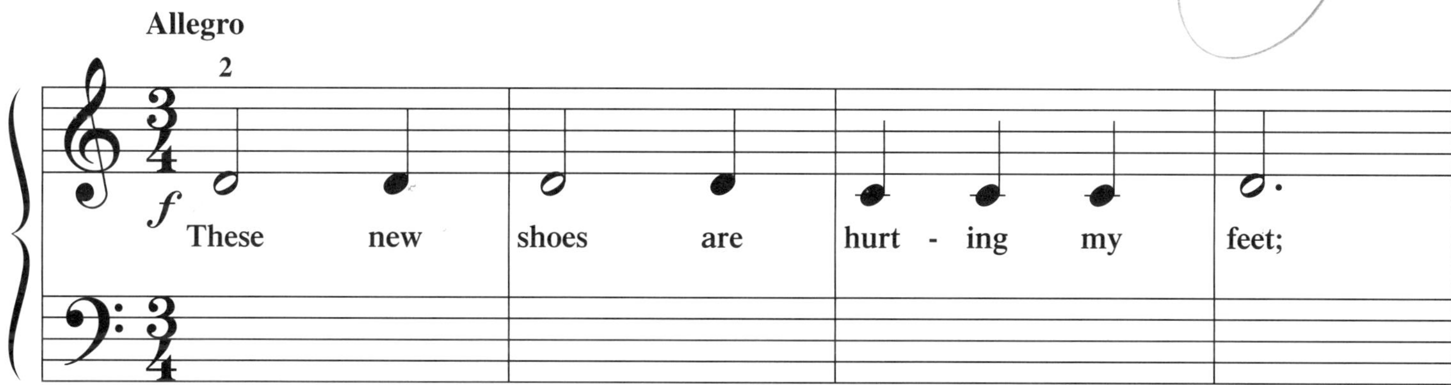
Allegro
2
f
These new shoes are hurt - ing my feet;

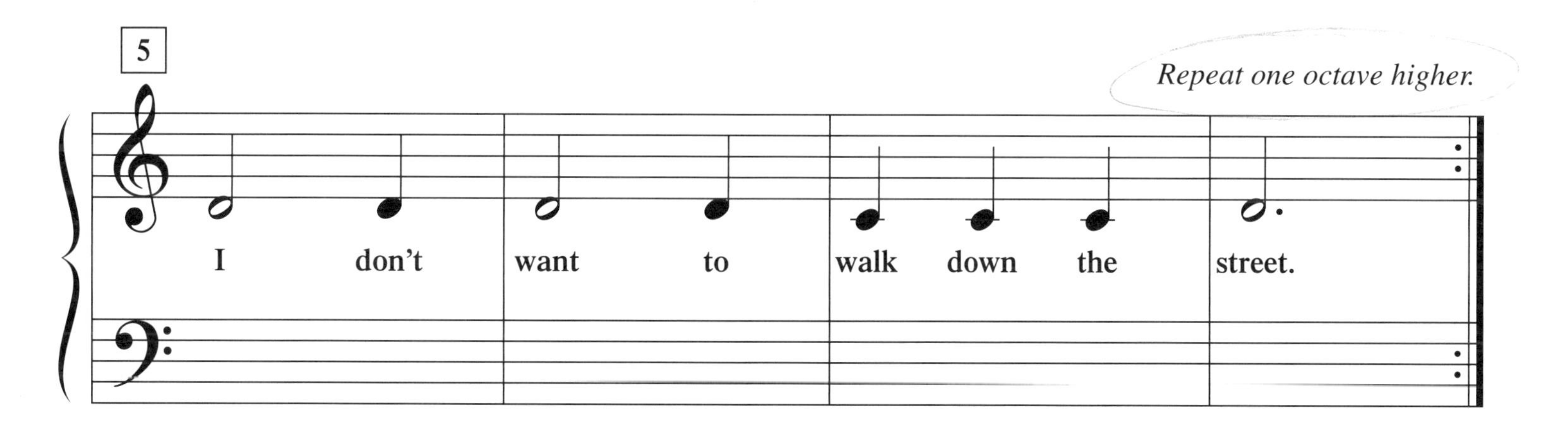
5
Repeat one octave higher.
I don't want to walk down the street.

After you are comfortable with this piece, try playing with **R.H.** finger **3** on **D.**

Teacher Duet: Student plays as written.

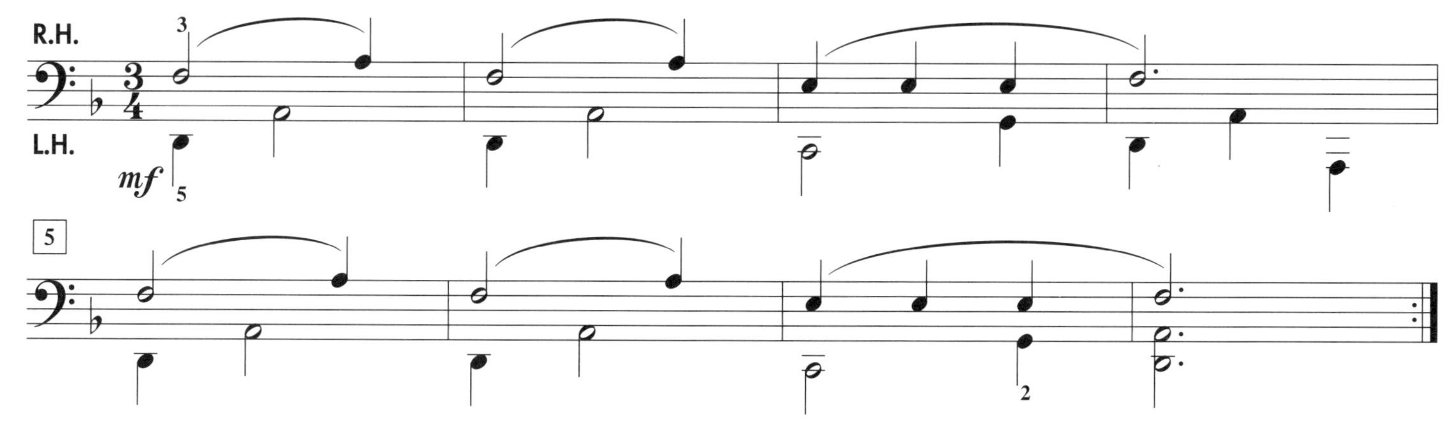
R.H.
L.H.
mf
5

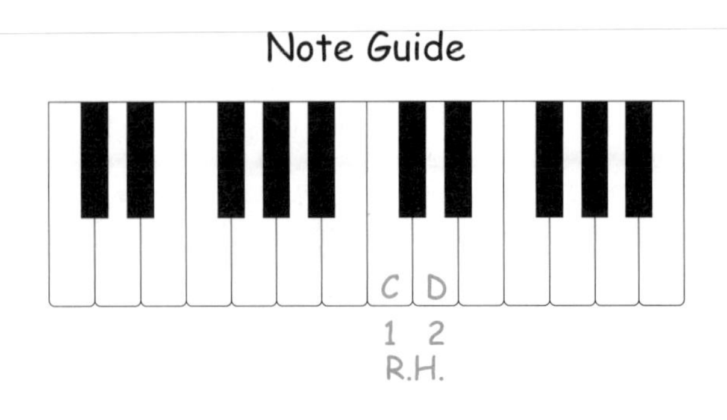
Note Guide
C D
1 2
R.H.

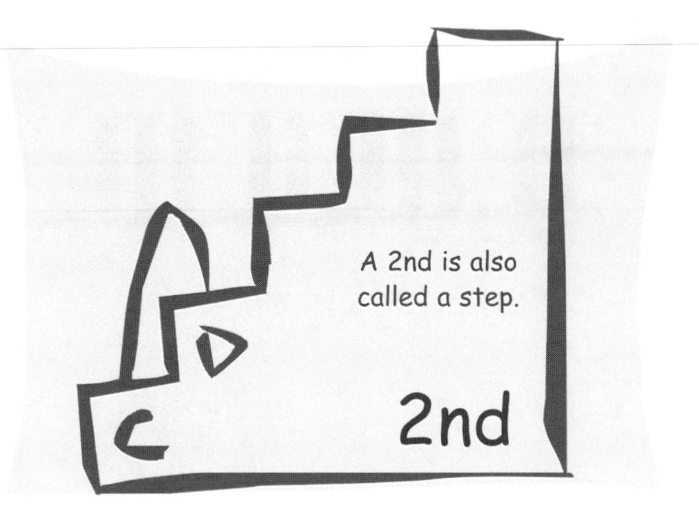
A 2nd is also called a step.
D
C
2nd

Step and Hop with C and D

An interval is the distance between two notes.

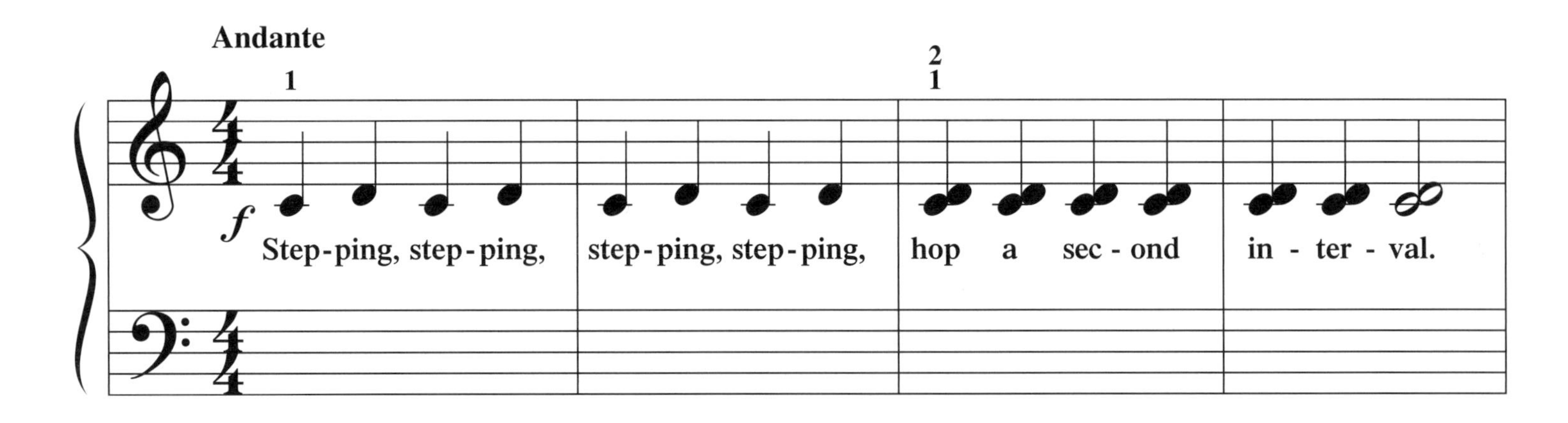
Andante
1
2
1
f
Step-ping, step-ping, step-ping, step-ping, hop a sec-ond in-ter-val.

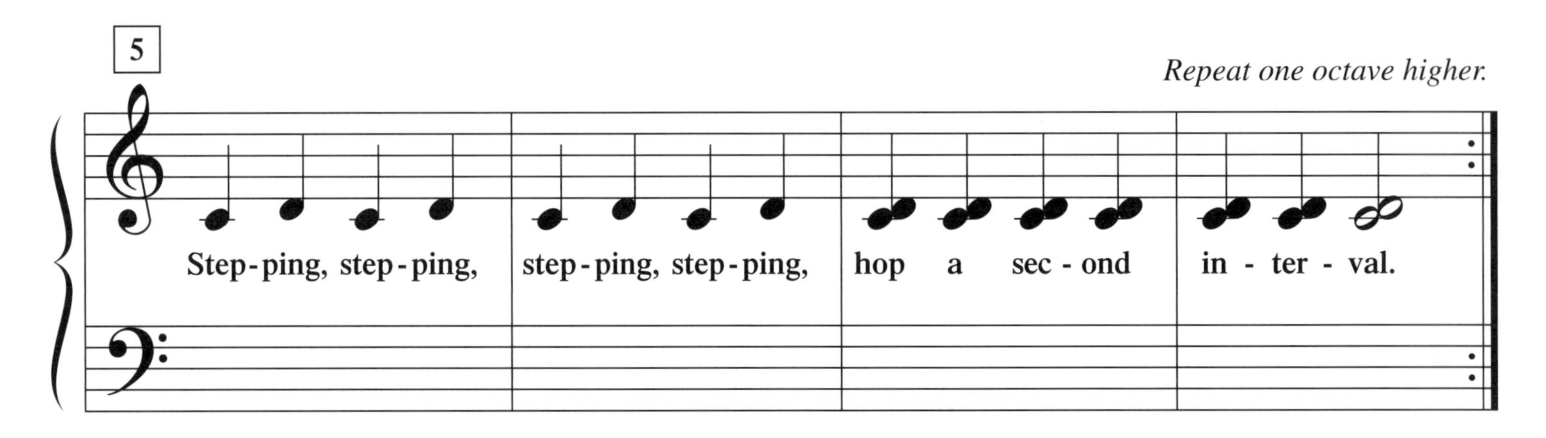
5
Repeat one octave higher.
Step-ping, step-ping, step-ping, step-ping, hop a sec-ond in-ter-val.

After you are comfortable with this piece, try playing with **R.H.** finger **2** on **C.**

Teacher Duet: Student plays one octave higher.

R.H.
L.H.
mp
3
5
5

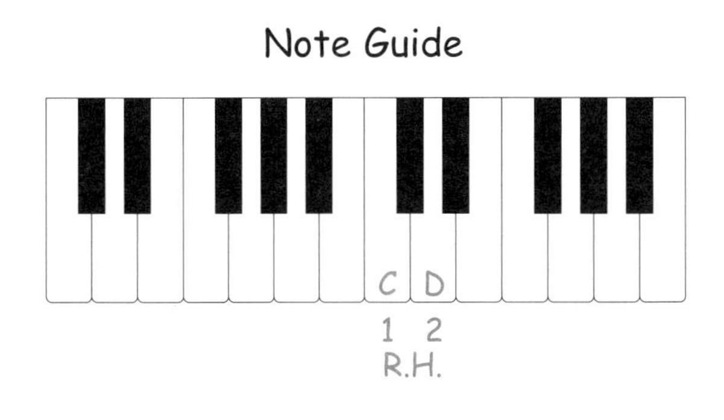
Note Guide
C D
1 2
R.H.

Pop, Pop, Pop

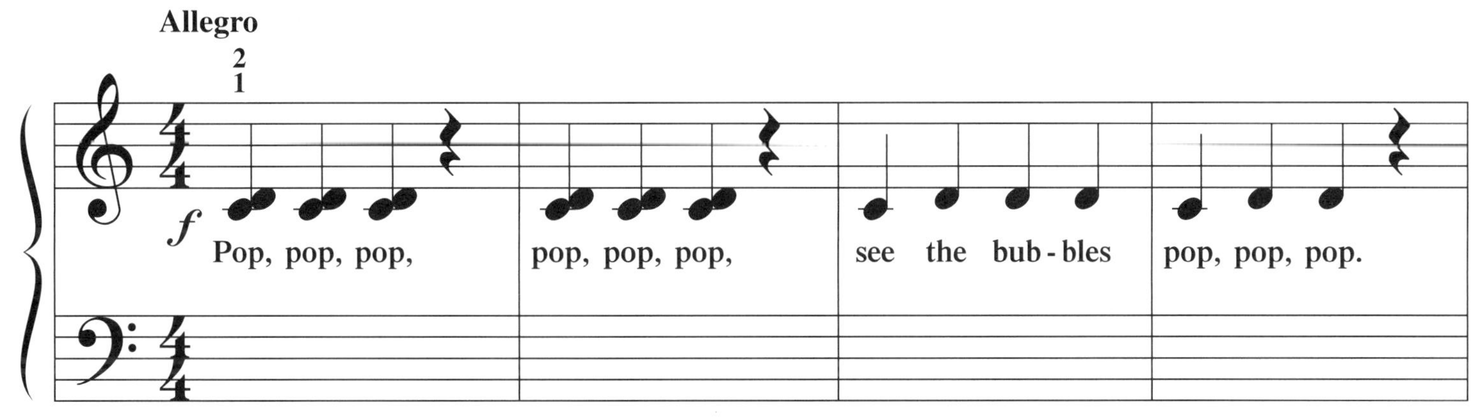
Allegro
Pop, pop, pop,
pop, pop, pop,
see the bub - bles
pop, pop, pop.

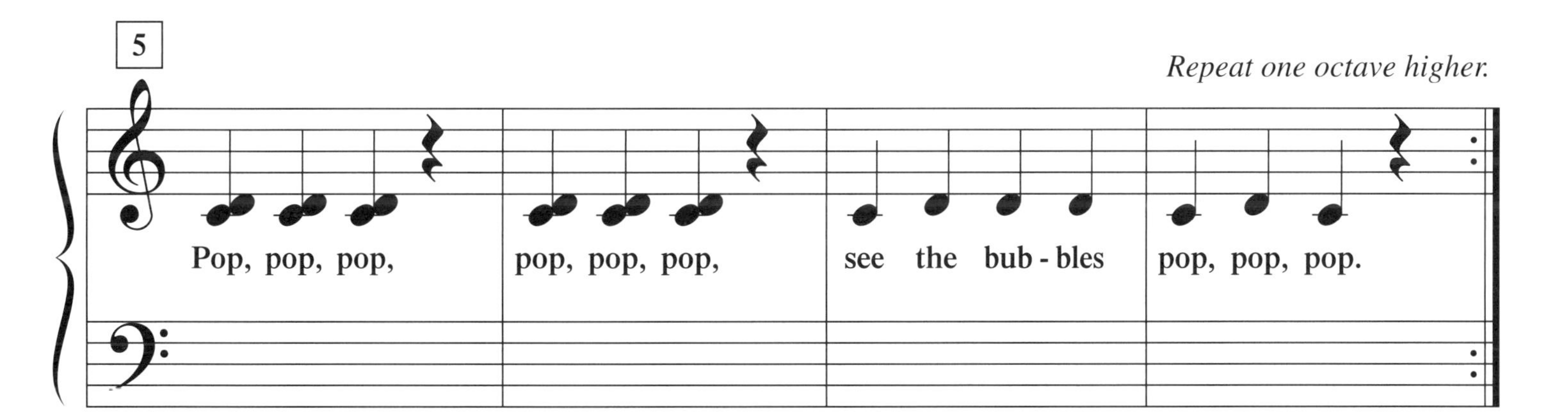
5
Repeat one octave higher.
Pop, pop, pop,
pop, pop, pop,
see the bub - bles
pop, pop, pop.

After you are comfortable with this piece, try playing with **R.H.** finger **2** and **3** on **C** and **D.**

Teacher Duet: Student plays as written.

R.H.
L.H.
5

Unit 2

E on the Keyboard

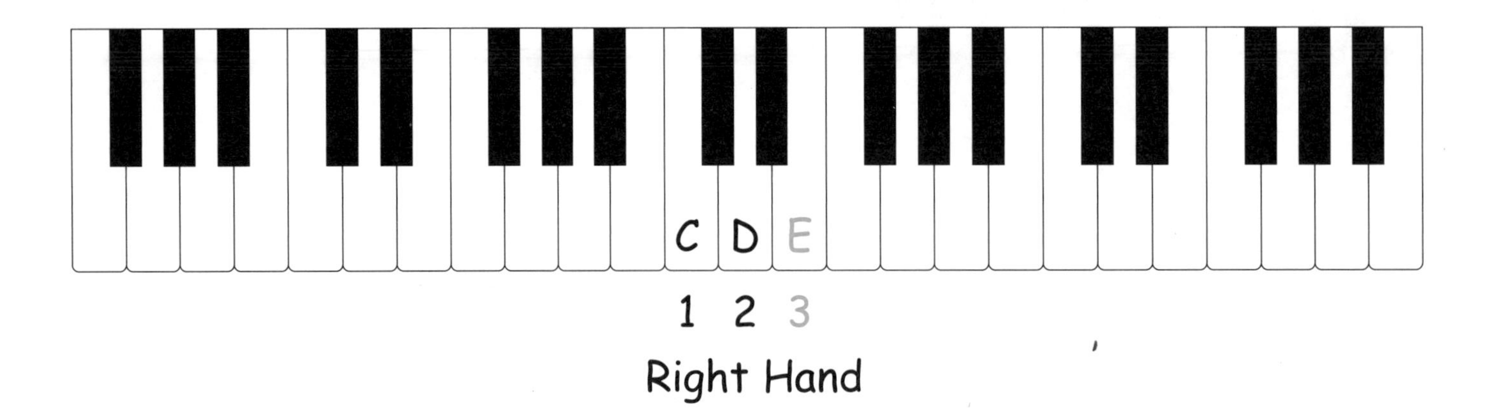
C D E
1 2 3
Right Hand

Remember that hand positions are just guides. When you are comfortable with the pieces in this unit, explore using different fingers.

E on the Staff

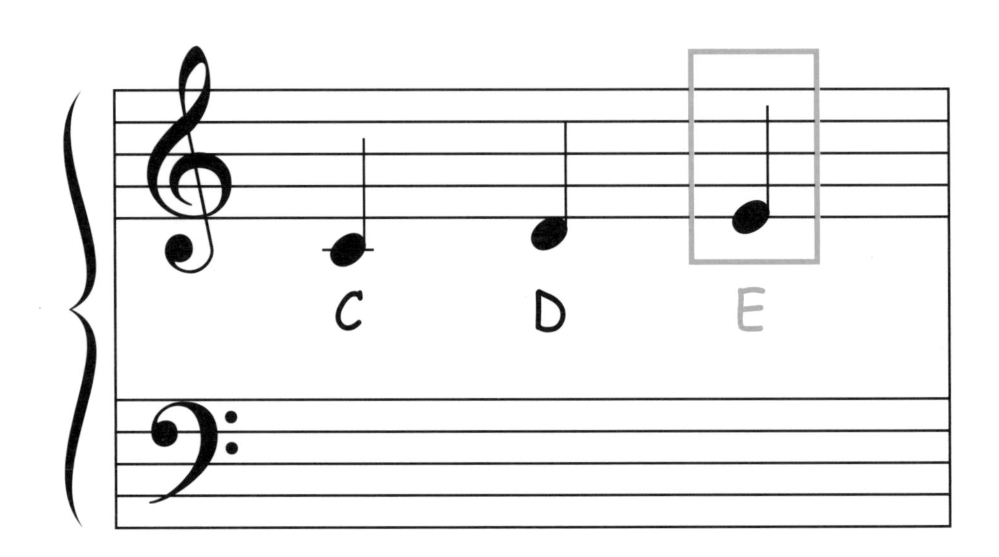
C D E

Play the example below, keeping your eyes on the music.

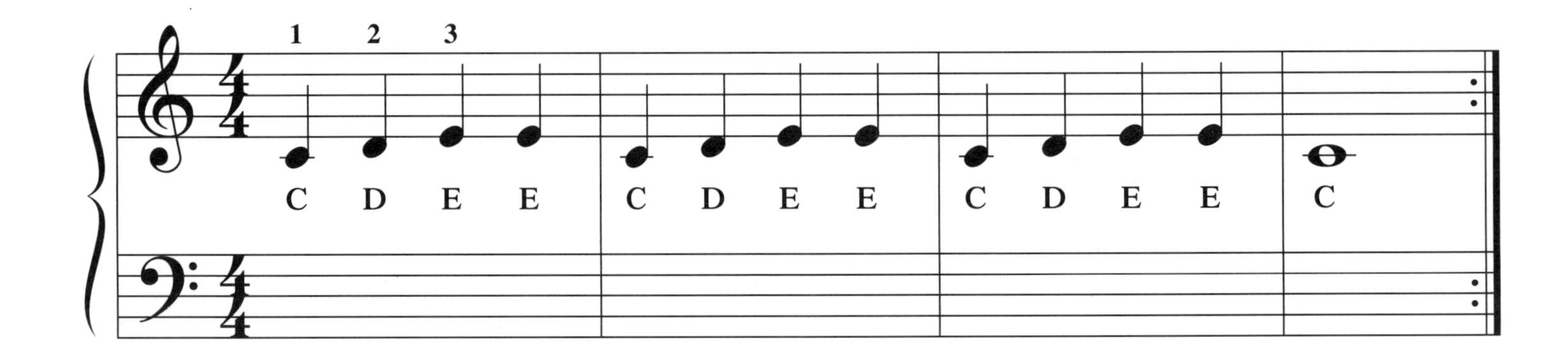
1 2 3
C D E E C D E E C D E E C

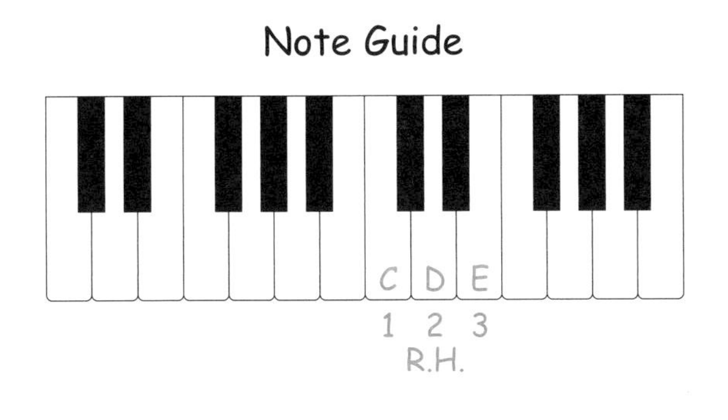
Note Guide
C D E
1 2 3
R.H.

I Am Tall

Allegro
1
f
I am tall, I am tall; I am ver - y, ver - y tall.

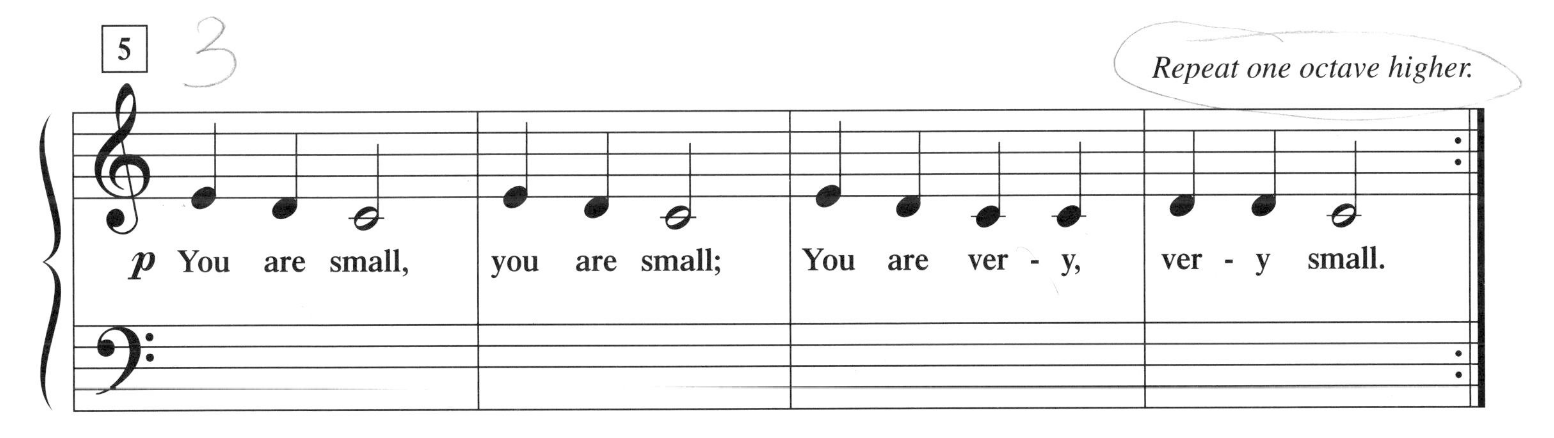
5
Repeat one octave higher.
p
You are small, you are small; You are ver - y, ver - y small.

After you are comfortable with this piece, try playing with **R.H.** finger **2** on **C.**

Teacher Duet: Student plays as written.

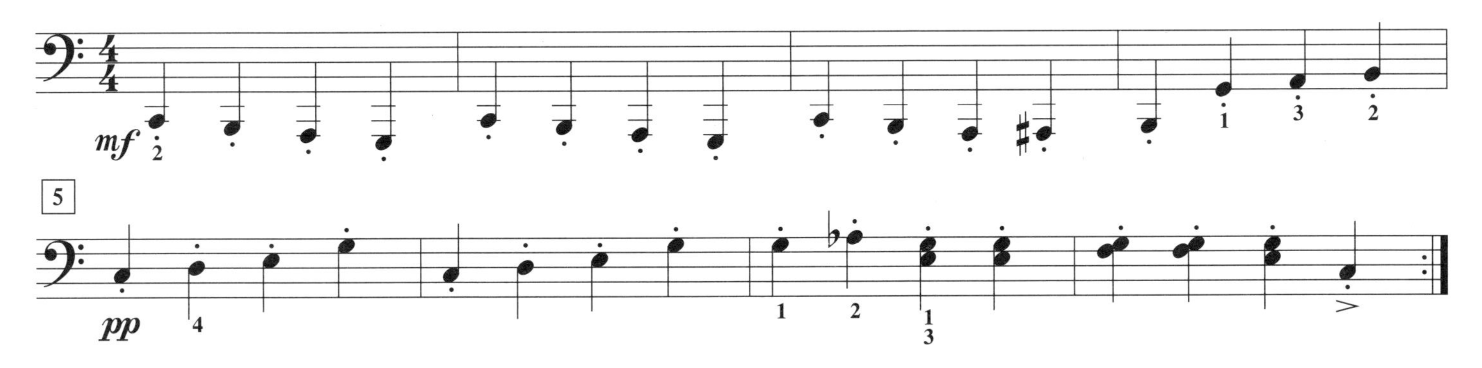
mf
pp
5

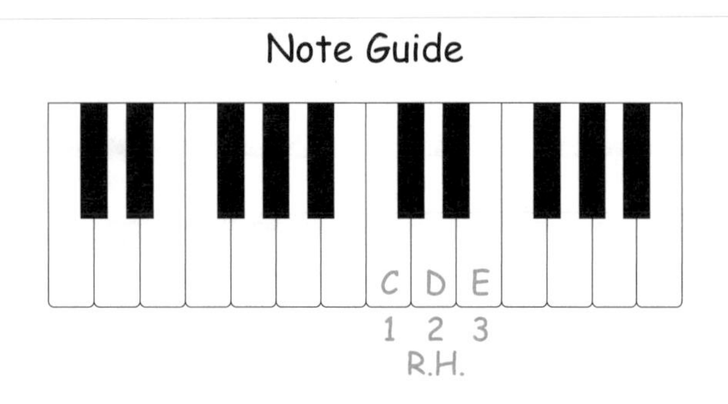
Note Guide
C D E
1 2 3
R.H.

The World Keeps on Turning

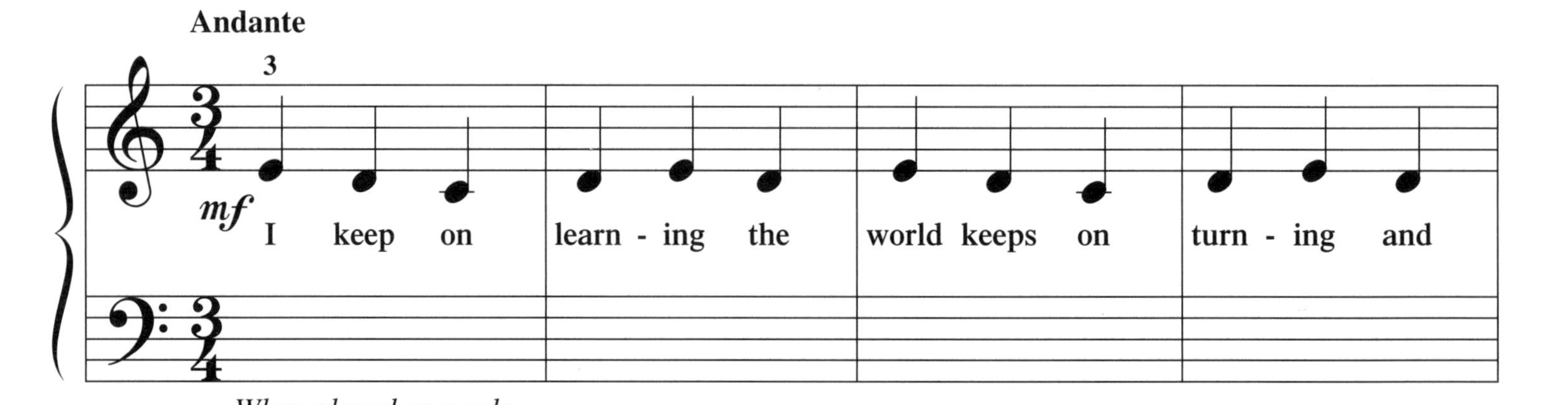
Andante
3
mf
I keep on learn - ing the world keeps on turn - ing and

When played as a solo, press the right (damper) pedal for the entire piece.

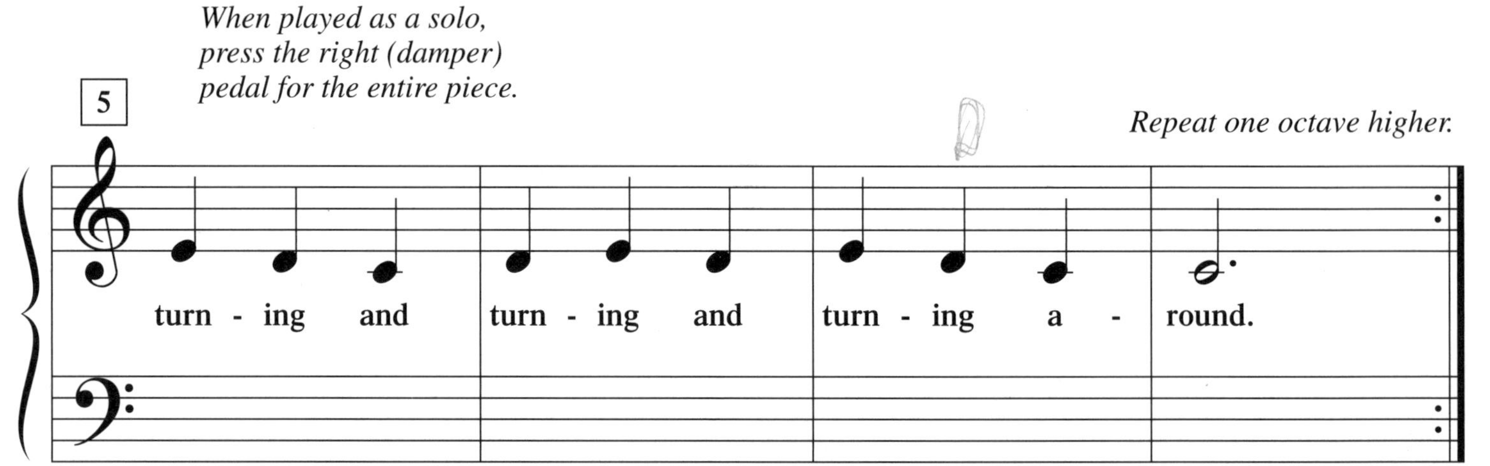
5
Repeat one octave higher.
turn - ing and turn - ing and turn - ing a - round.

After you are comfortable with this piece, try playing with **R.H.** finger **4** on **E.**

Teacher Duet: Student plays as written.

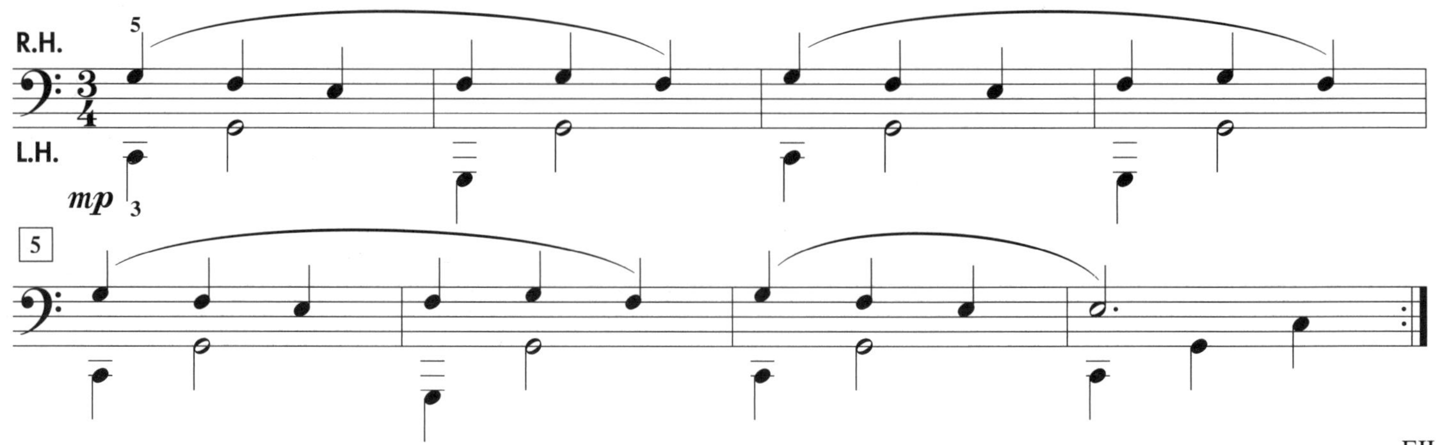
R.H.
L.H.
5
mp
3
5

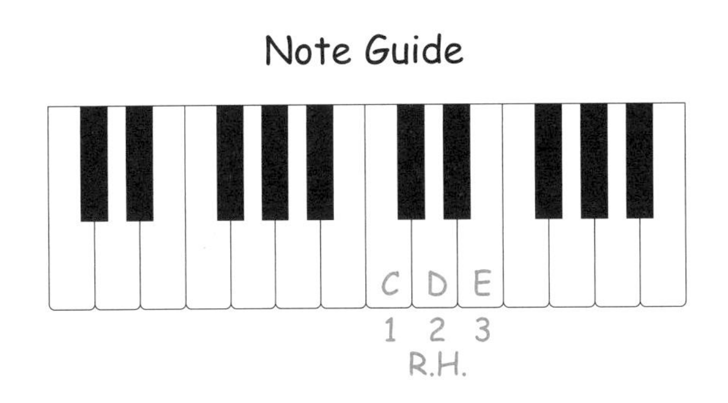
Note Guide
C D E
1 2 3
R.H.

One Blade of Grass

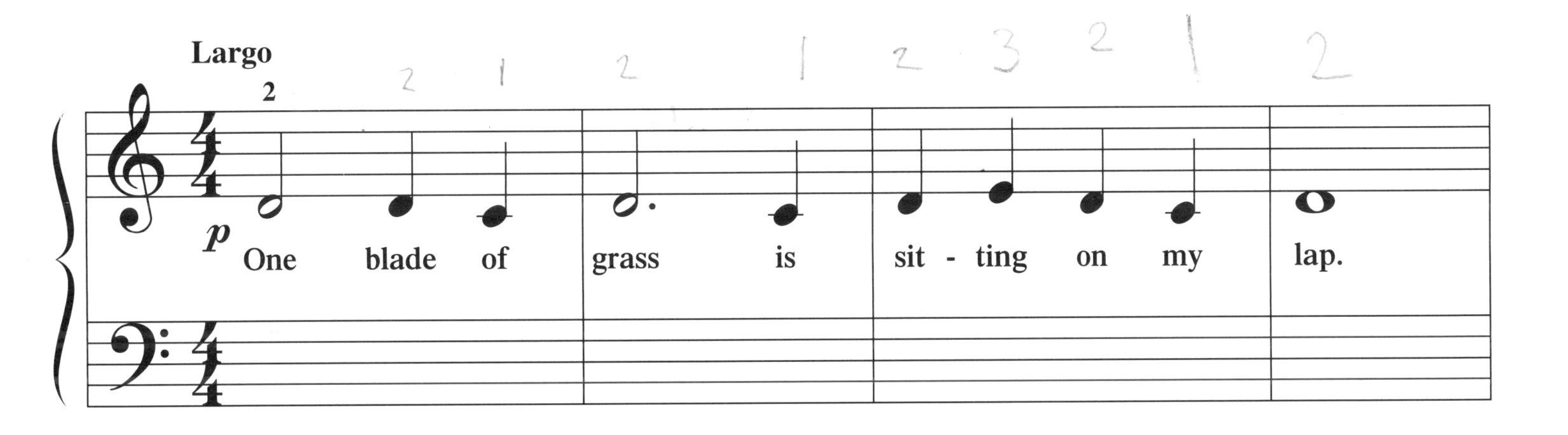
Largo
2
p
One blade of grass is sit - ting on my lap.

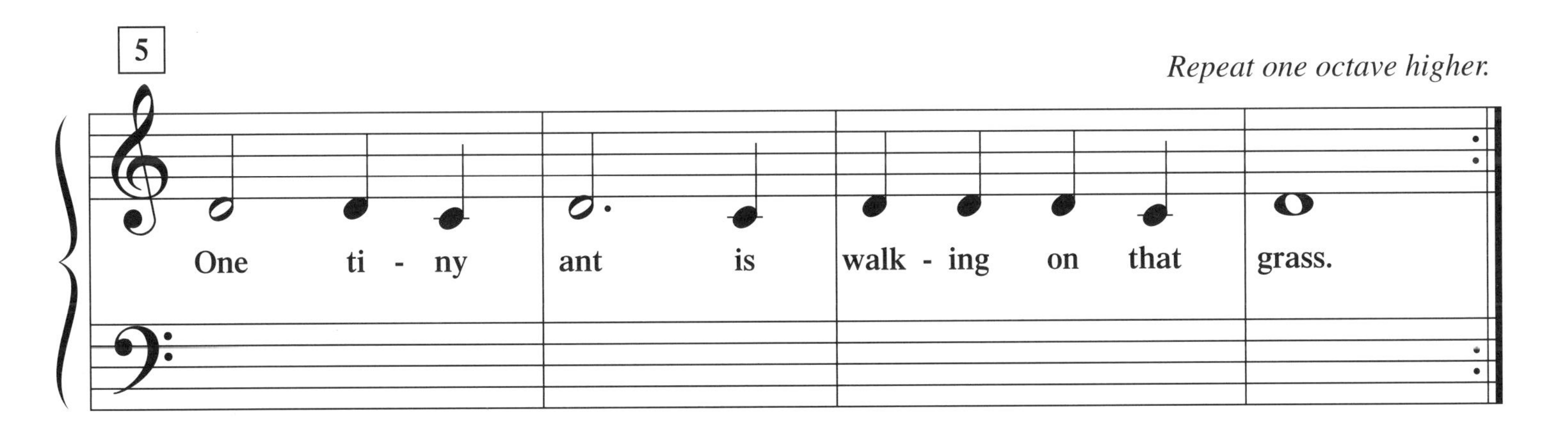
5
Repeat one octave higher.
One ti - ny ant is walk - ing on that grass.

After you are comfortable with this piece, try playing with **R.H.** finger **3** on **D.**

Teacher Duet: Student plays as written.

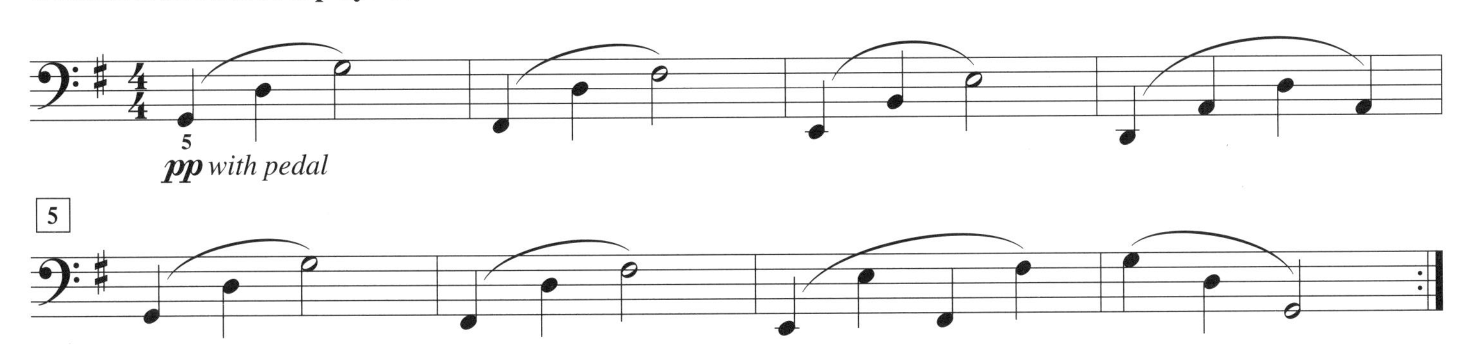
5
pp with pedal
5

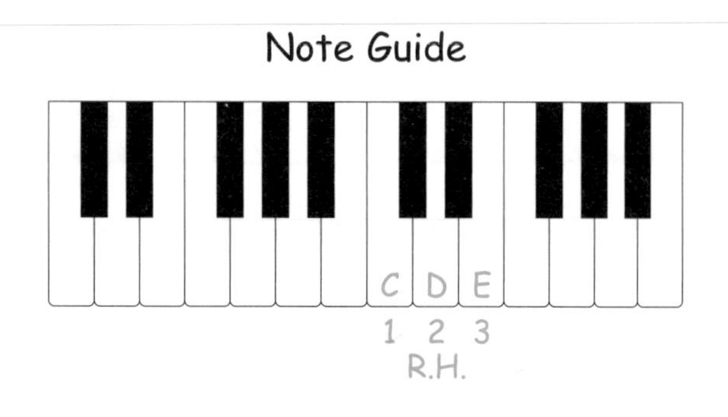
Note Guide
C D E
1 2 3
R.H.

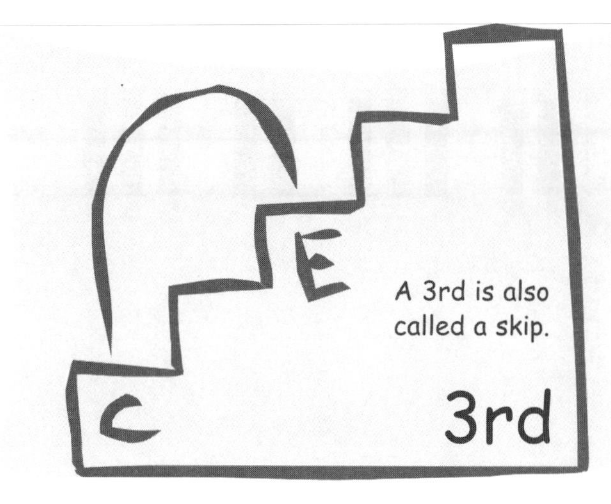
E
A 3rd is also called a skip.
C
3rd

Skip and Hop with C and E

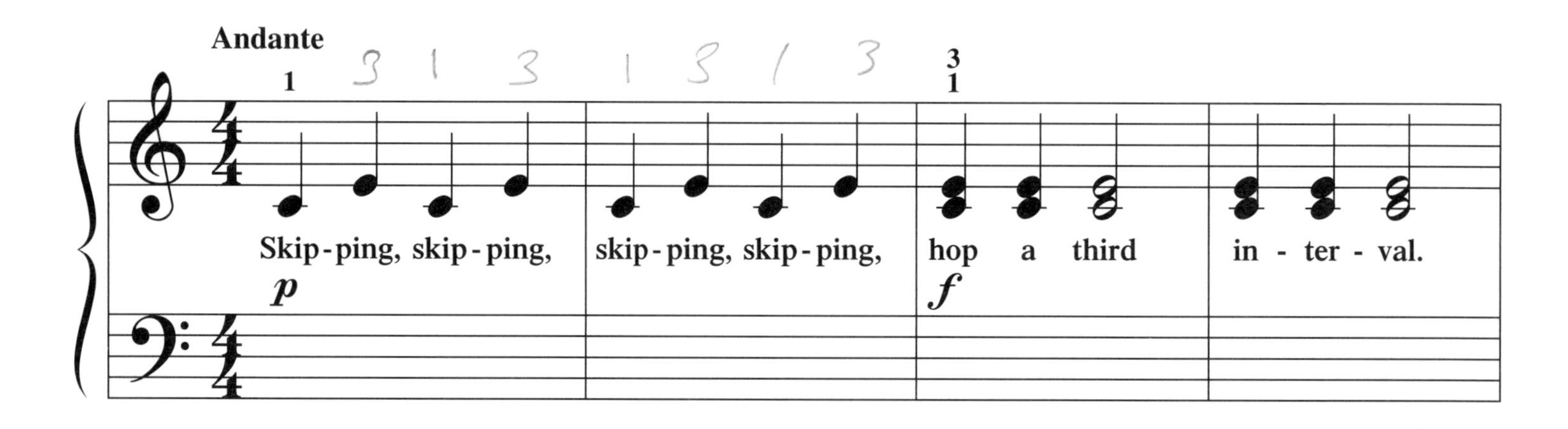
Andante
Skip-ping, skip-ping, skip-ping, skip-ping, hop a third in-ter-val.

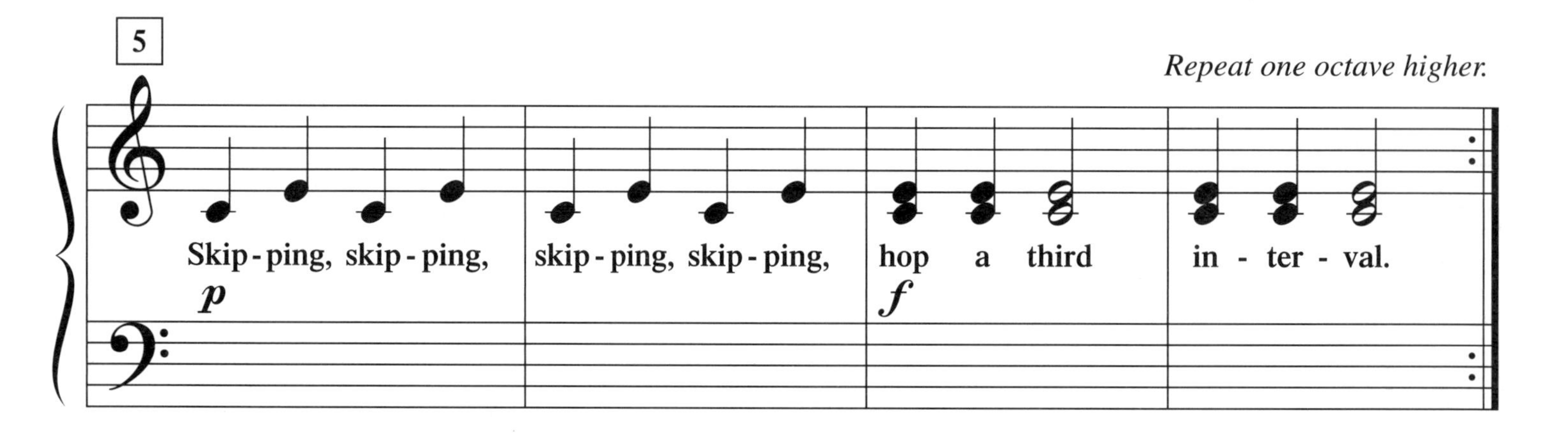
5
Repeat one octave higher.
Skip-ping, skip-ping, skip-ping, skip-ping, hop a third in-ter-val.

After you are comfortable with this piece, try playing with **R.H.** finger **2** on **C.**

Teacher Duet: Student plays as written.

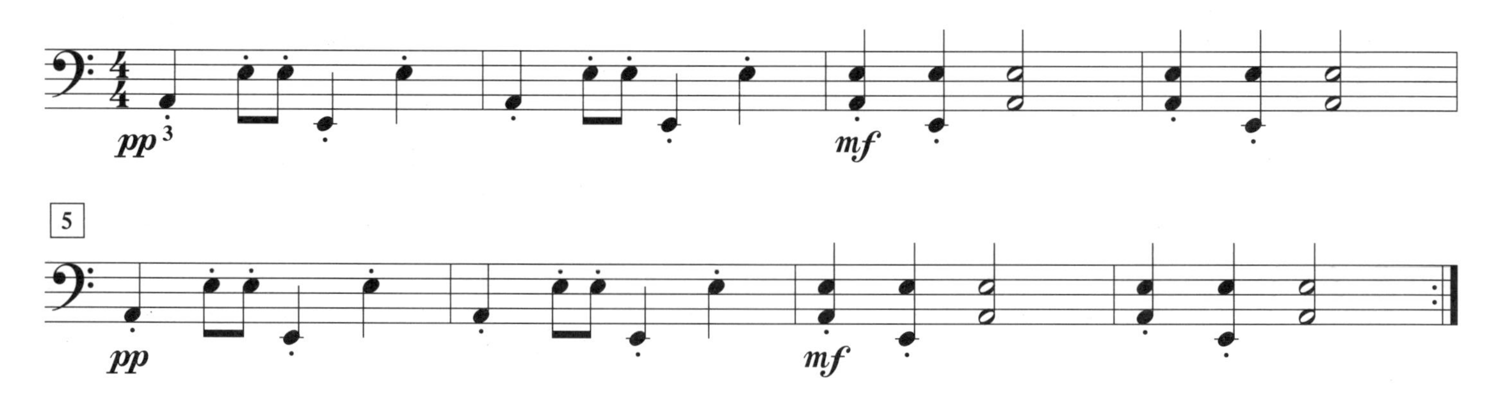

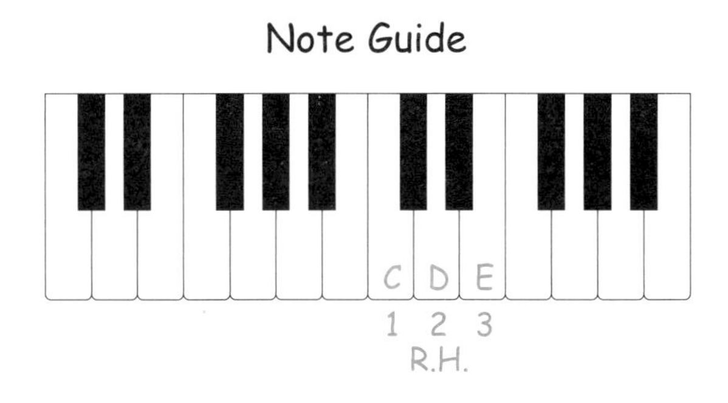
Note Guide
C D E
1 2 3
R.H.

I Love Broccoli

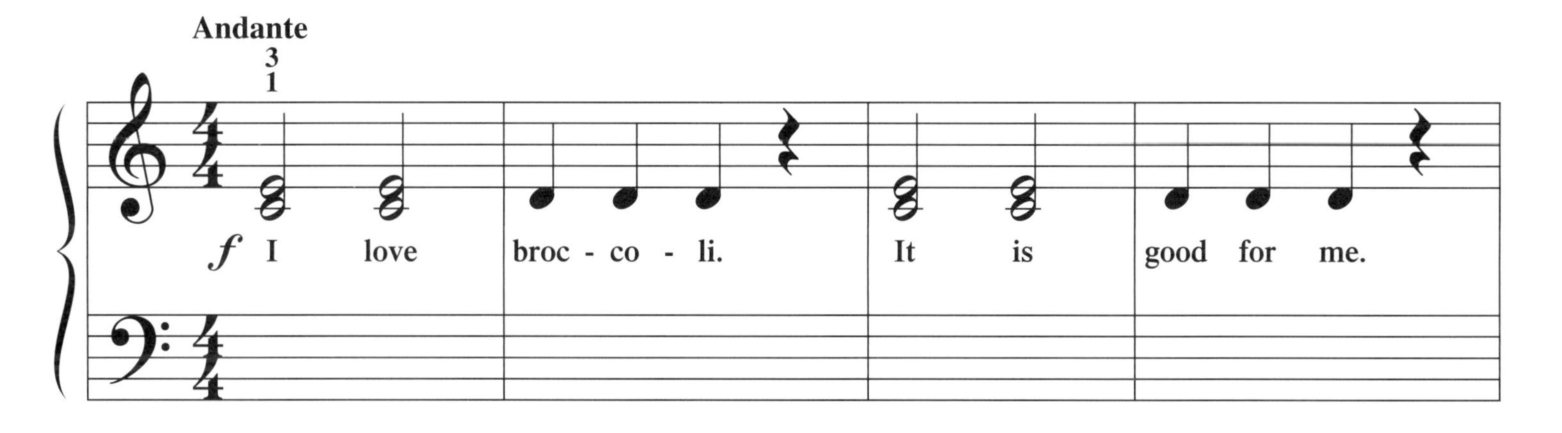
Andante
I love broc - co - li. It is good for me.

5
Repeat one octave higher.
Looks like a ti - ny tree. I love broc - co - li.

After you are comfortable with this piece, try playing with **R.H.** fingers **2** and **4** on **C** and **E.**

Teacher Duet: Student plays as written.

R.H.
L.H.
mf
5

Unit 3 Middle C and B on the Keyboard

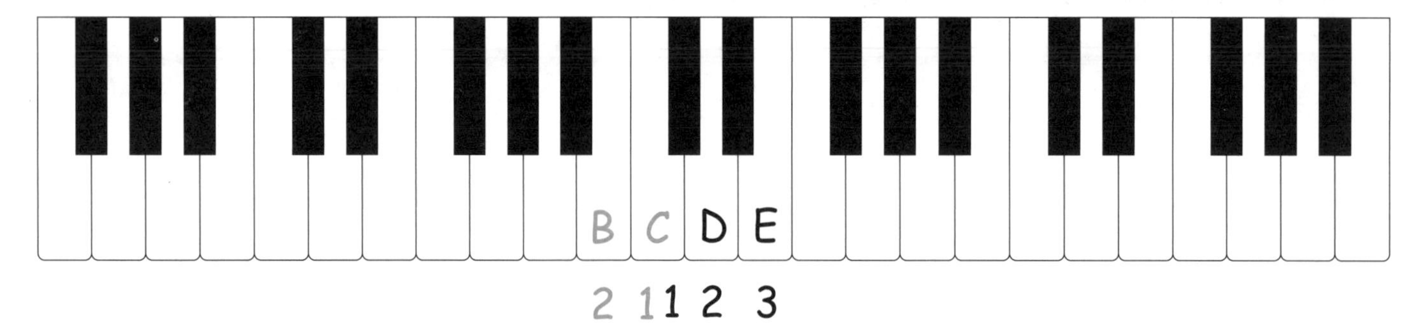
B C D E
2 1 1 2 3
Left Hand Right Hand

Remember that hand positions are just guides. When you are comfortable with the pieces in this unit, explore using different fingers.

Middle C and B on the Staff

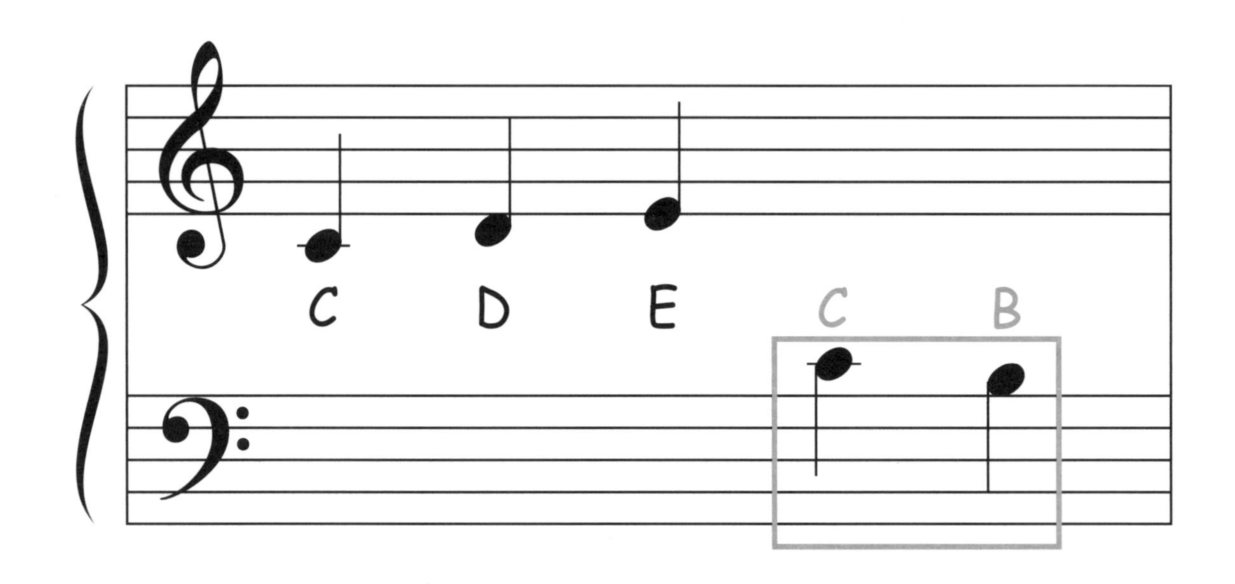
C D E C B

Play the example below, keeping your eyes on the music.

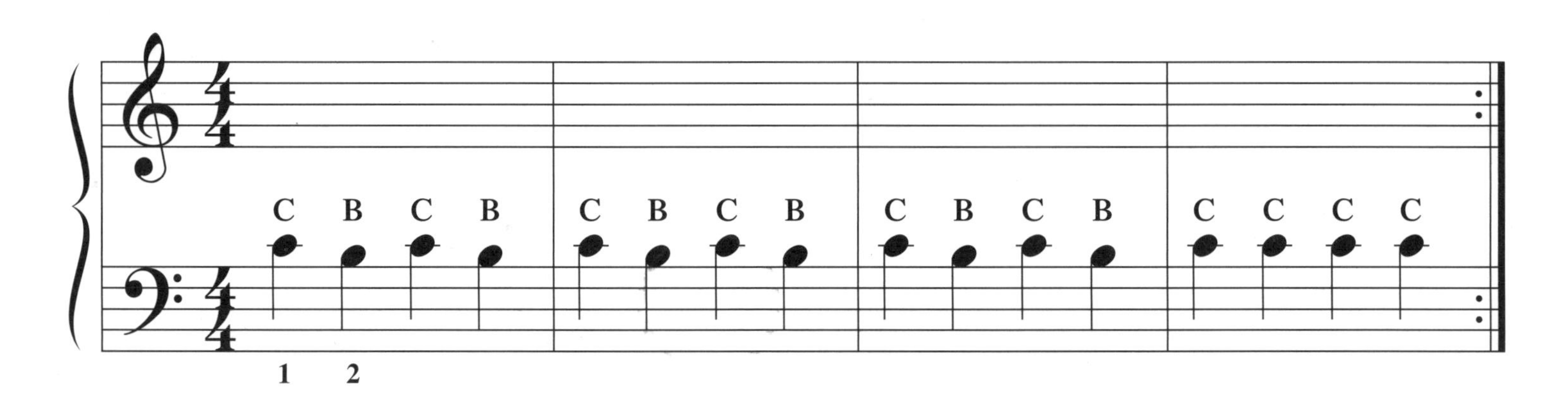
C B C B C B C B C B C B C C C C
1 2

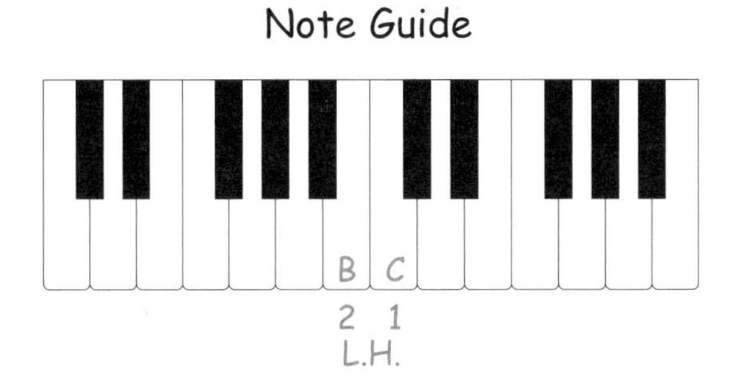
Note Guide
B C
2 1
L.H.

Have You Ever Seen a Snake?

Andante
Have you ev - er seen a snake slith - er down your street?
mf
1

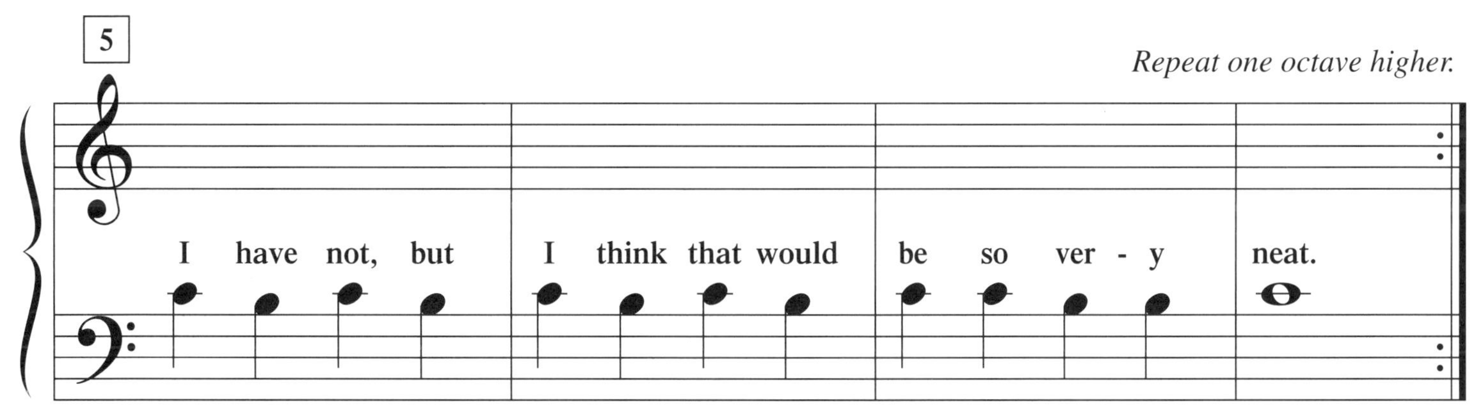
5
Repeat one octave higher.
I have not, but I think that would be so ver - y neat.

After you are comfortable with this piece, try playing with **L.H.** finger **2** on **C.**

Teacher Duet: Student plays one octave higher.

R.H.
L.H.
mp
5

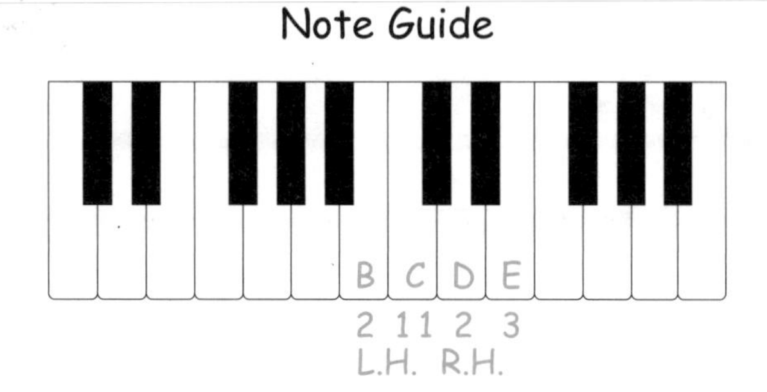
Note Guide
B C D E
2 1 1 2 3
L.H. R.H.

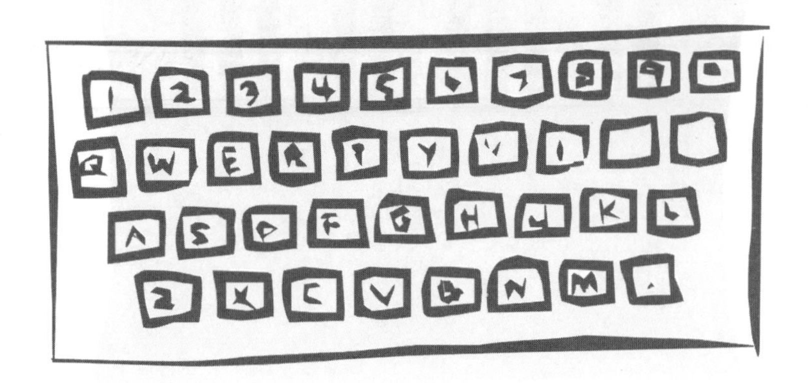

Every Time I Try to Type

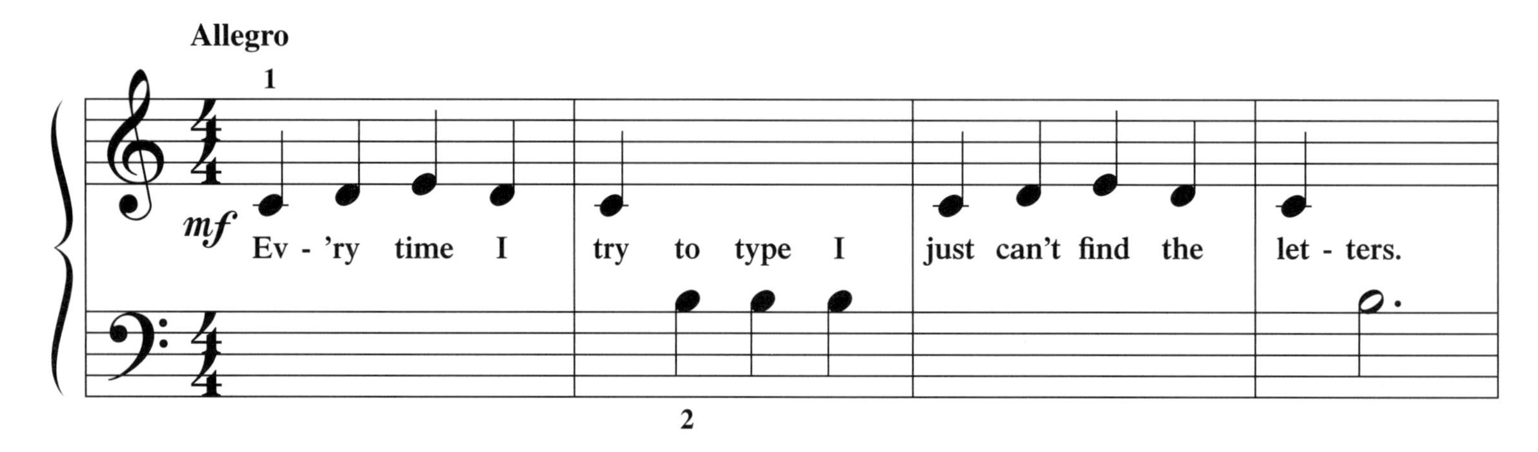
Allegro
1
mf
Ev - 'ry time I try to type I just can't find the let - ters.
2

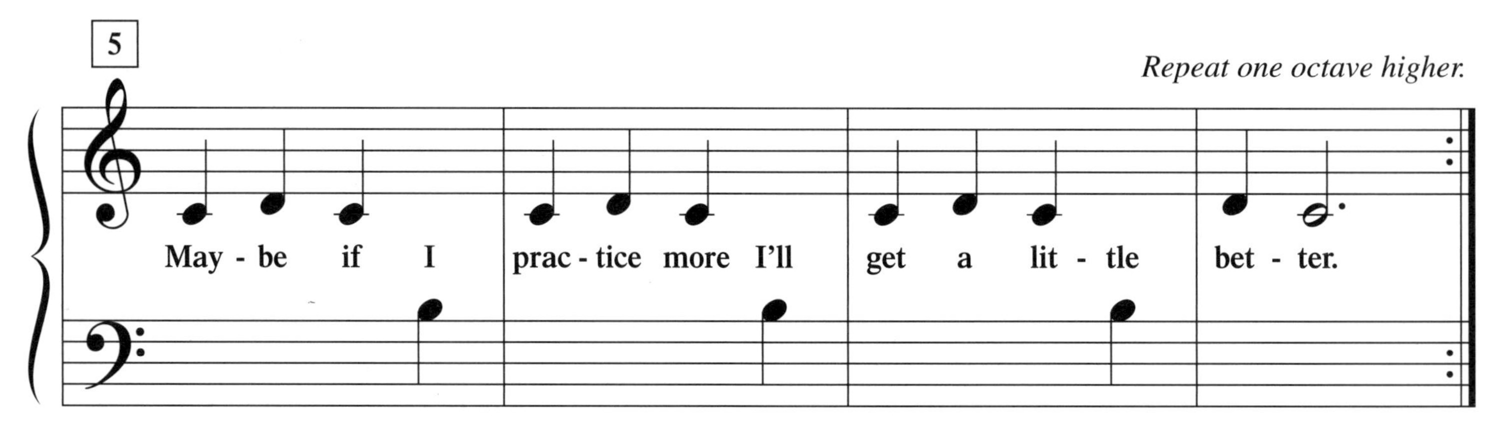
5
Repeat one octave higher.
May - be if I prac - tice more I'll get a lit - tle bet - ter.

After you are comfortable with this piece, try playing with **L.H.** finger **1** on **B.**

Teacher Duet: Student plays as written.

1
mp
5
5

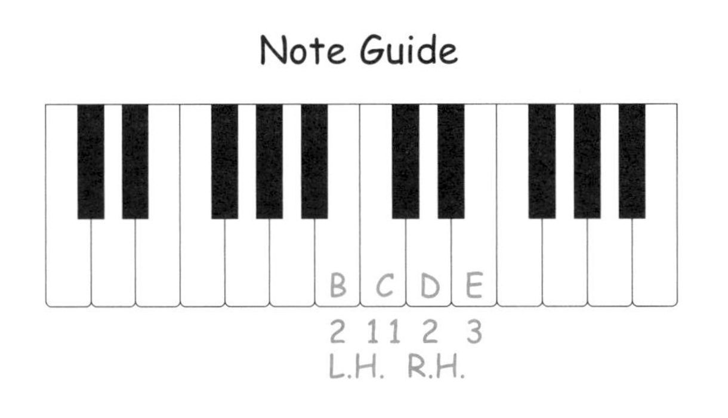
Note Guide
B C D E
2 1 1 2 3
L.H. R.H.

On a Cold and Windy Night

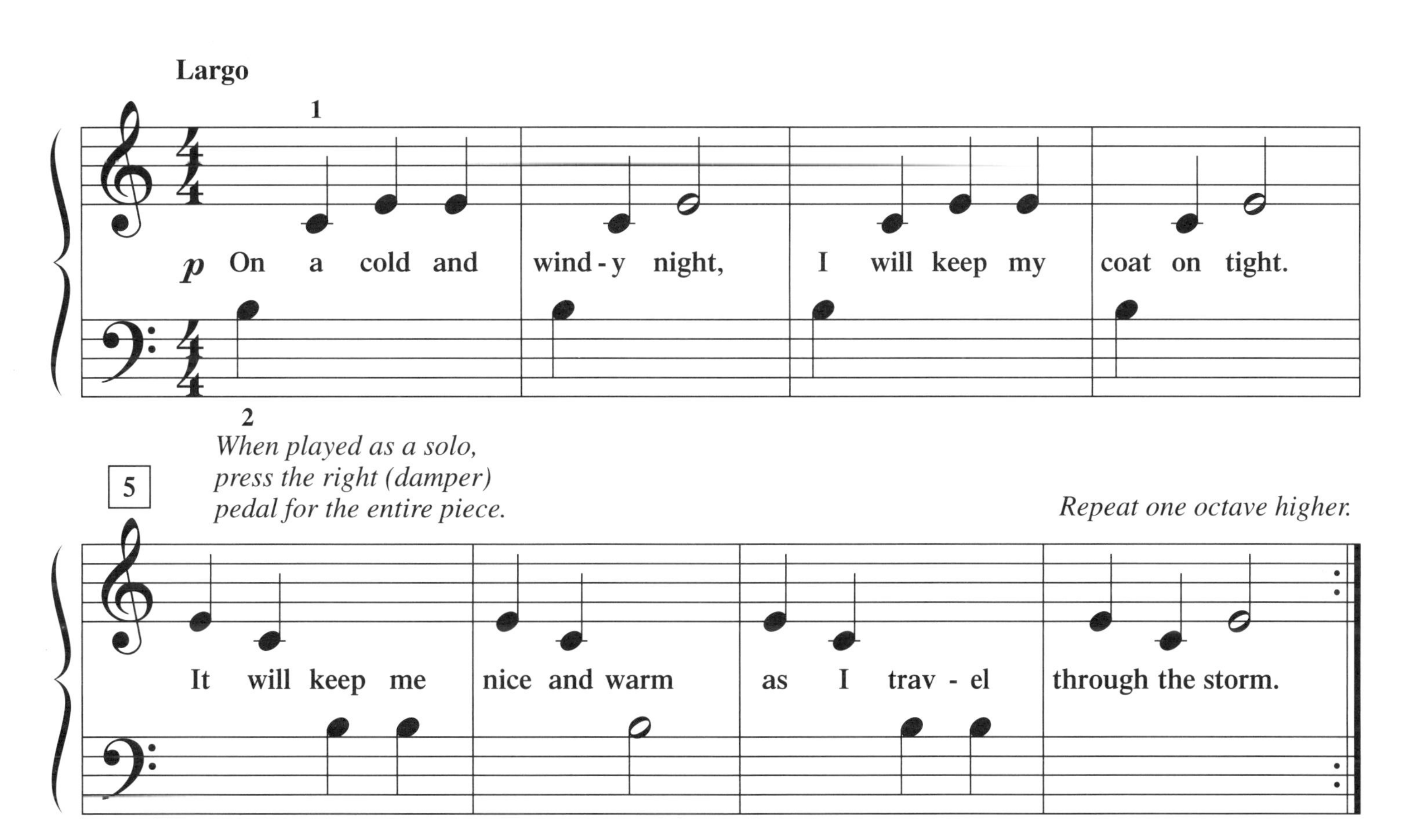
Largo
p
On a cold and wind-y night, I will keep my coat on tight.
When played as a solo, press the right (damper) pedal for the entire piece.
Repeat one octave higher.
It will keep me nice and warm as I trav-el through the storm.

After you are comfortable with this piece, try playing with **L.H.** finger **1** on **B.**

Teacher Duet: Student plays one octave higher.

pp
pp

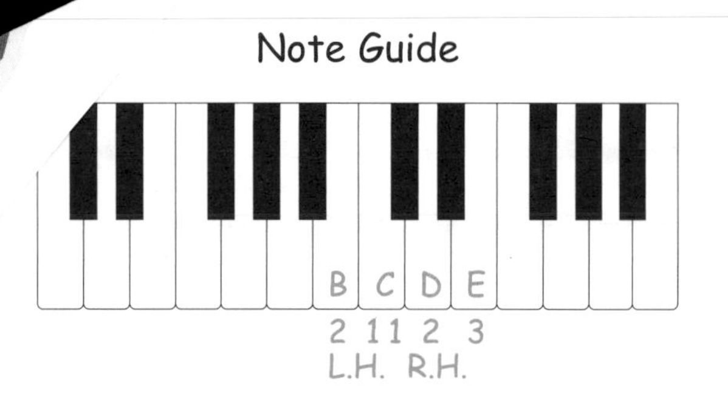
Note Guide
B C D E
2 1 1 2 3
L.H. R.H.

Slow and Steady

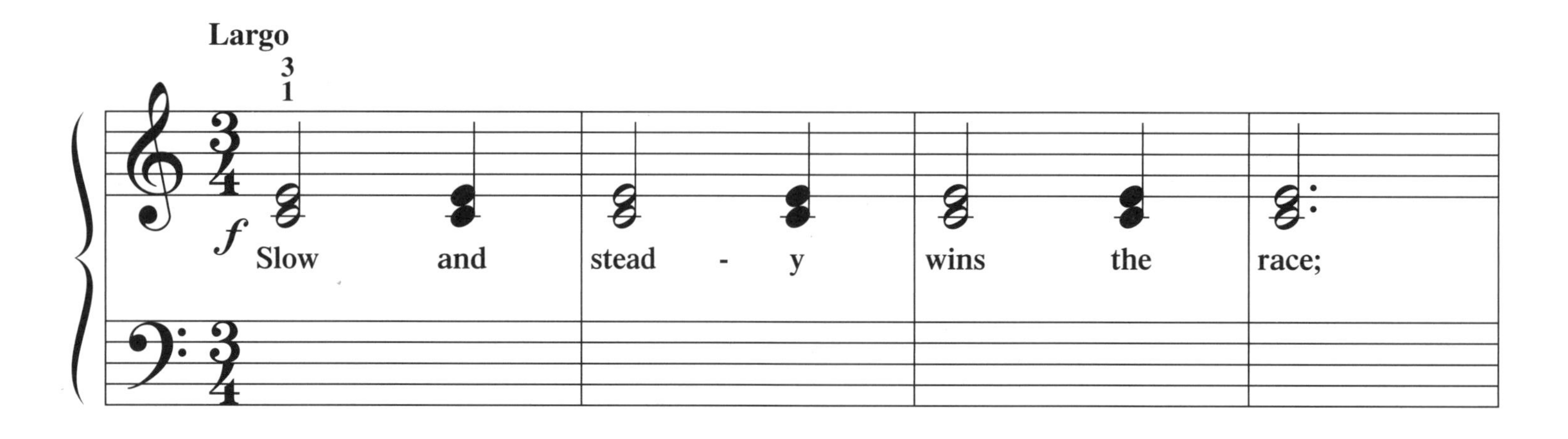
Largo
Slow and stead - y wins the race;

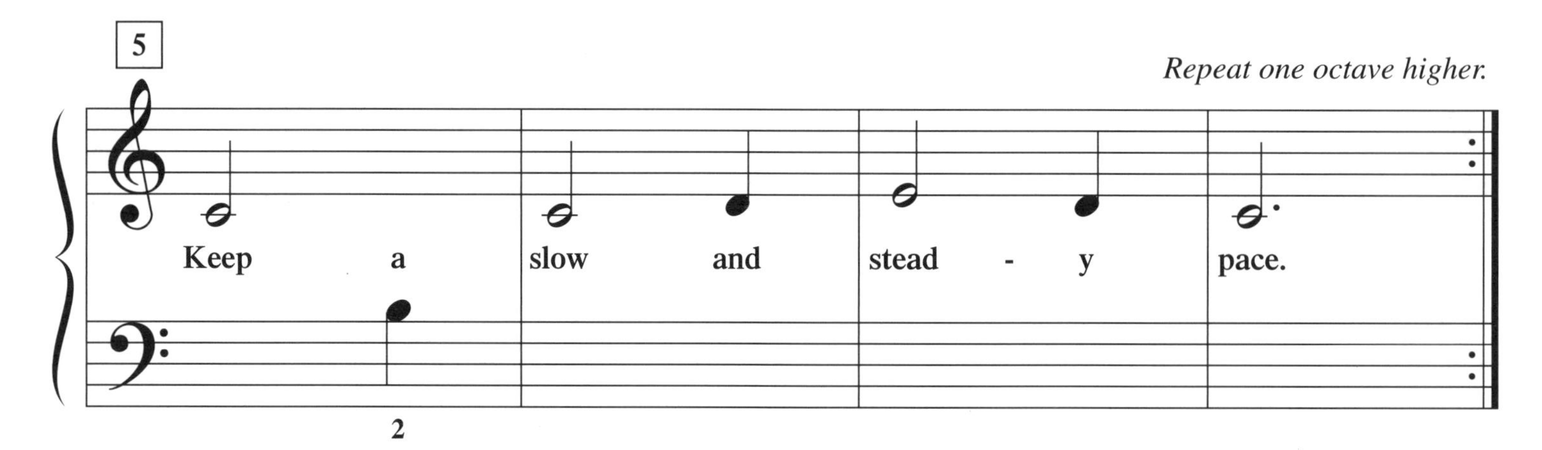
Repeat one octave higher.
Keep a slow and stead - y pace.

After you are comfortable with this piece, try playing with **L.H.** finger **1** on **B.**

Teacher Duet: Student plays as written.

R.H.
L.H.

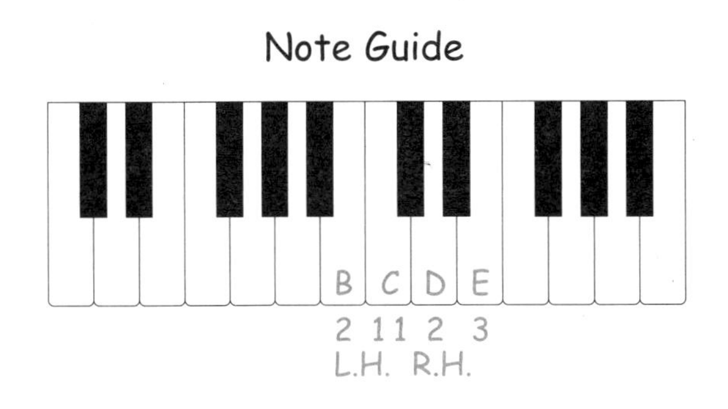
Note Guide
B C D E
2 1 1 2 3
L.H. R.H.

Seven Frogs Are Hopping

4/3/22

Allegro

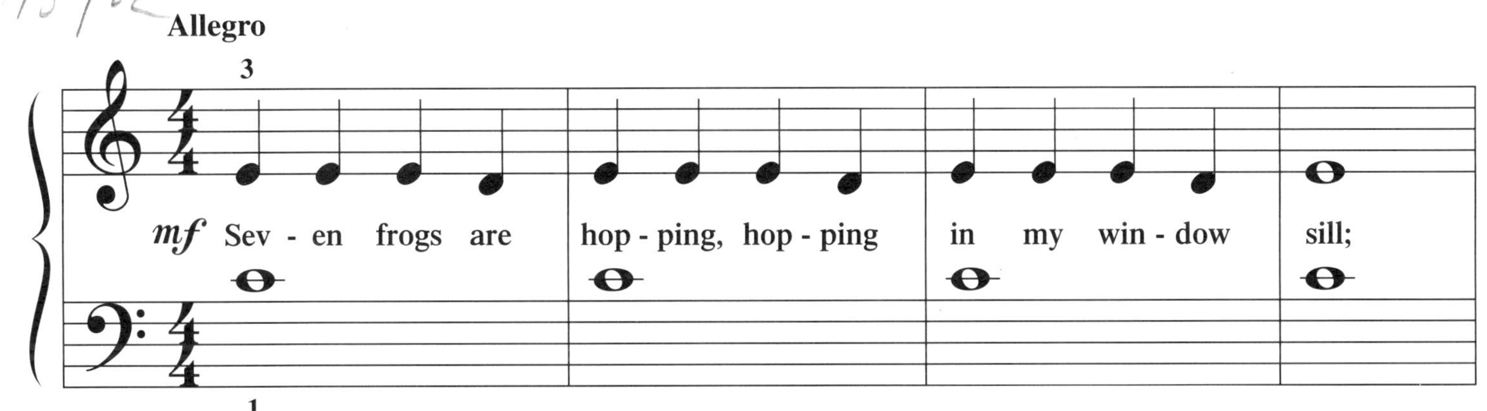
3
mf Sev - en frogs are hop - ping, hop - ping in my win - dow sill;
1

Play C and E at the same time but HOLD the C.

Repeat one octave higher.

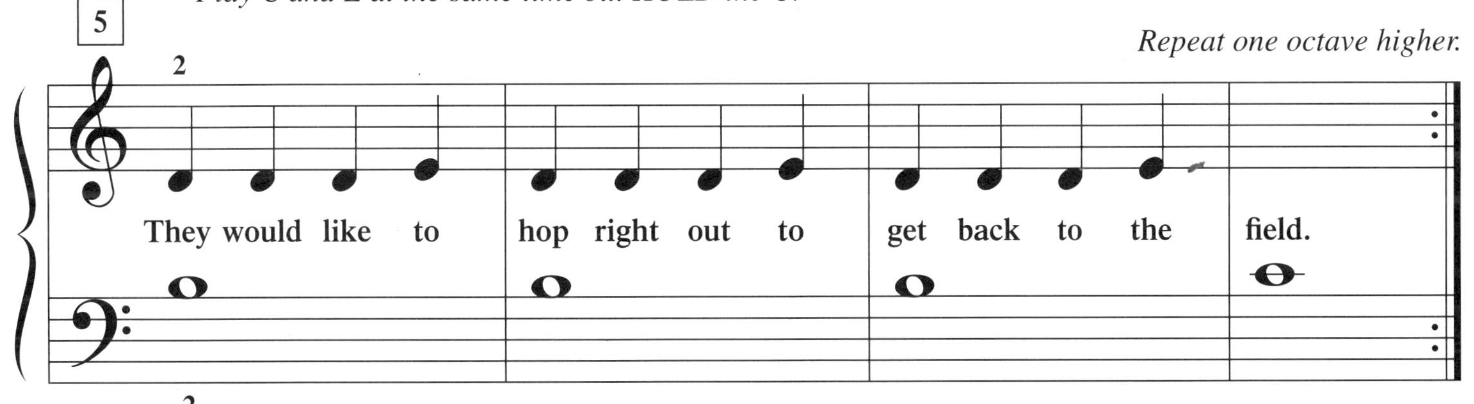
5
2
They would like to hop right out to get back to the field.
2

Play B and D at the same time but HOLD the B.

After you are comfortable with this piece, try playing with **R.H.** finger **2** on **E.**

Teacher Duet: Student plays as written.

R.H.
5
3
L.H.
mp
1
5
2
3
2
5

Unit 4

A on the Keyboard

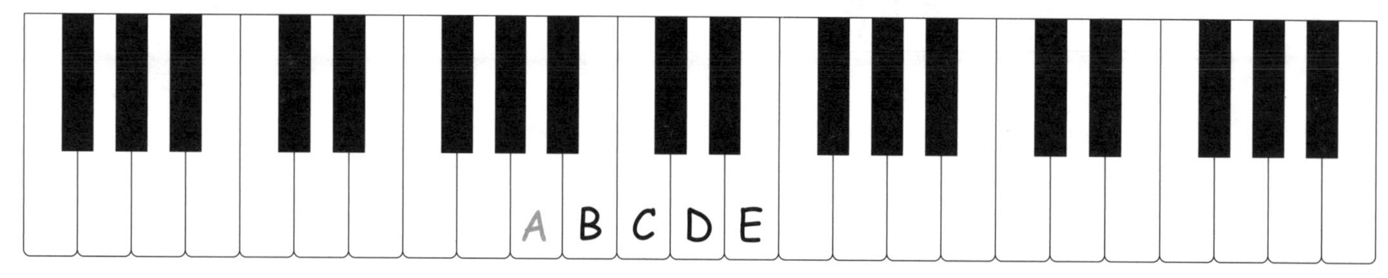
A B C D E
3 2 1 1 2 3
Left Hand Right Hand

Remember that hand positions are just guides. When you are comfortable with the pieces in this unit, explore using different fingers.

A on the Staff

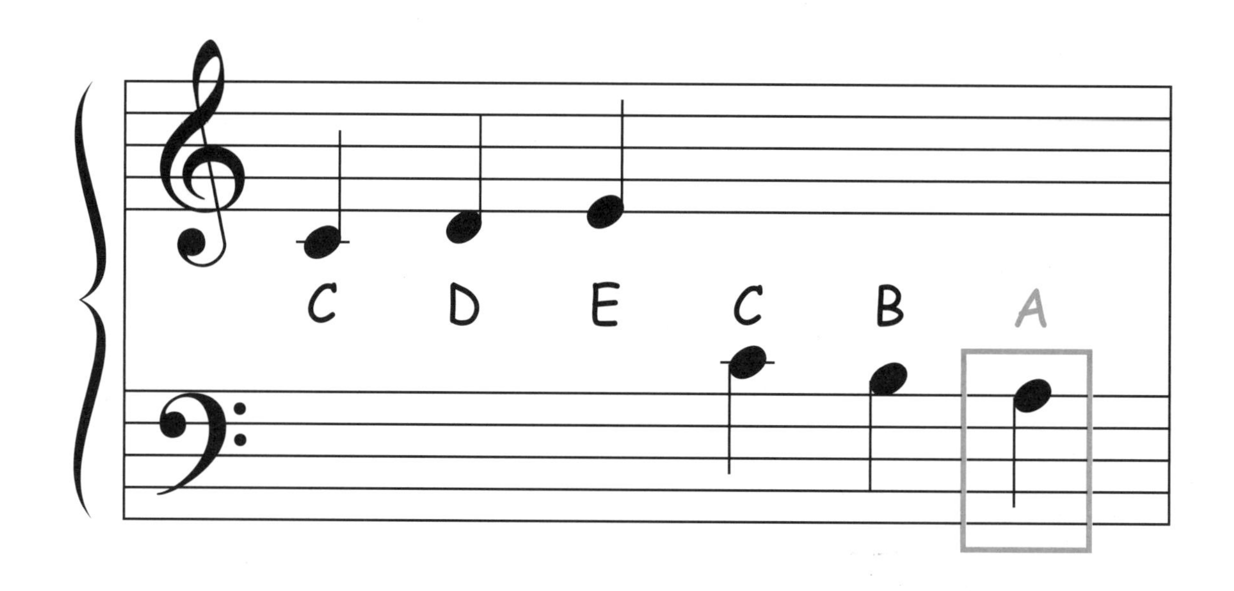
C D E C B A

Play the example below, keeping your eyes on the music.

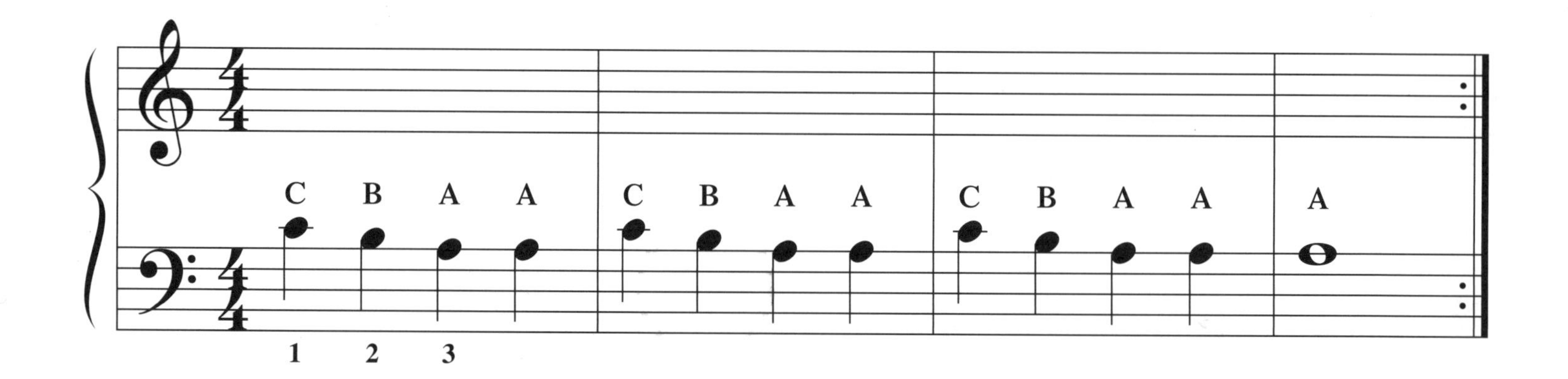
C B A A C B A A C B A A A
1 2 3

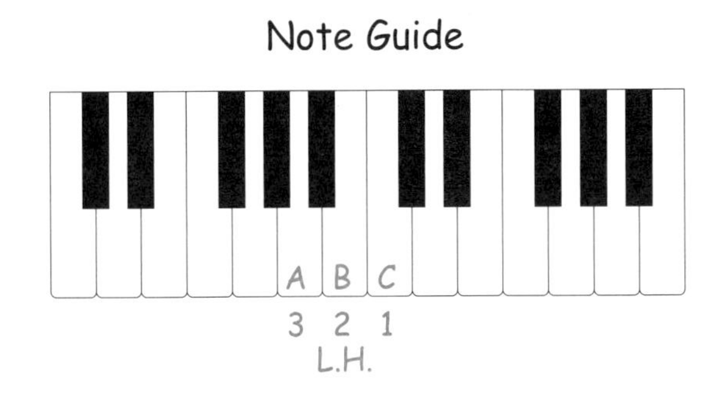
Note Guide
A B C
3 2 1
L.H.

I Have Lost My Wallet

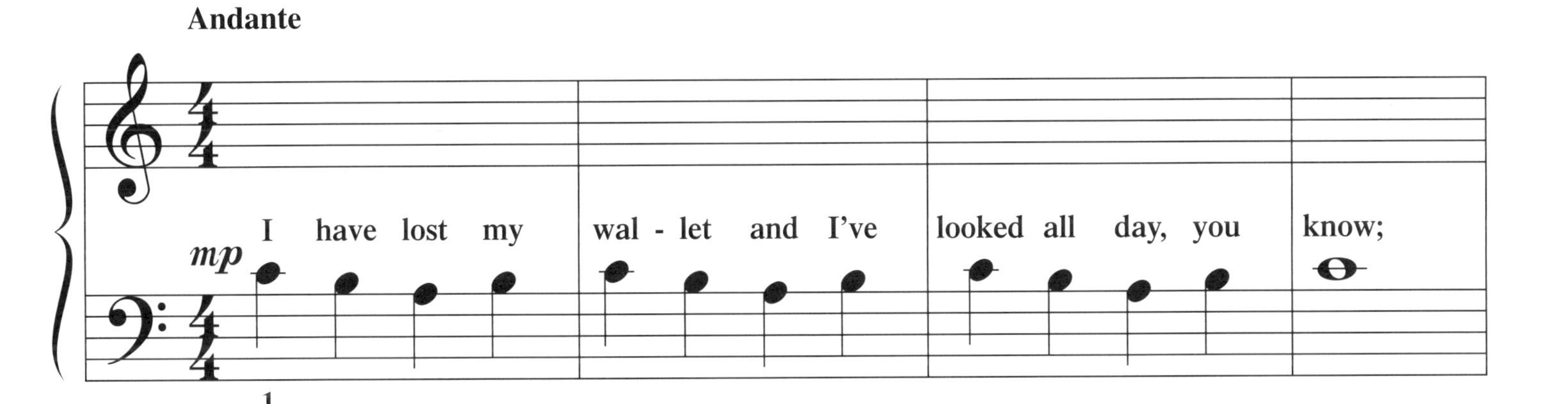
Andante
mp
I have lost my wal - let and I've looked all day, you know;
1

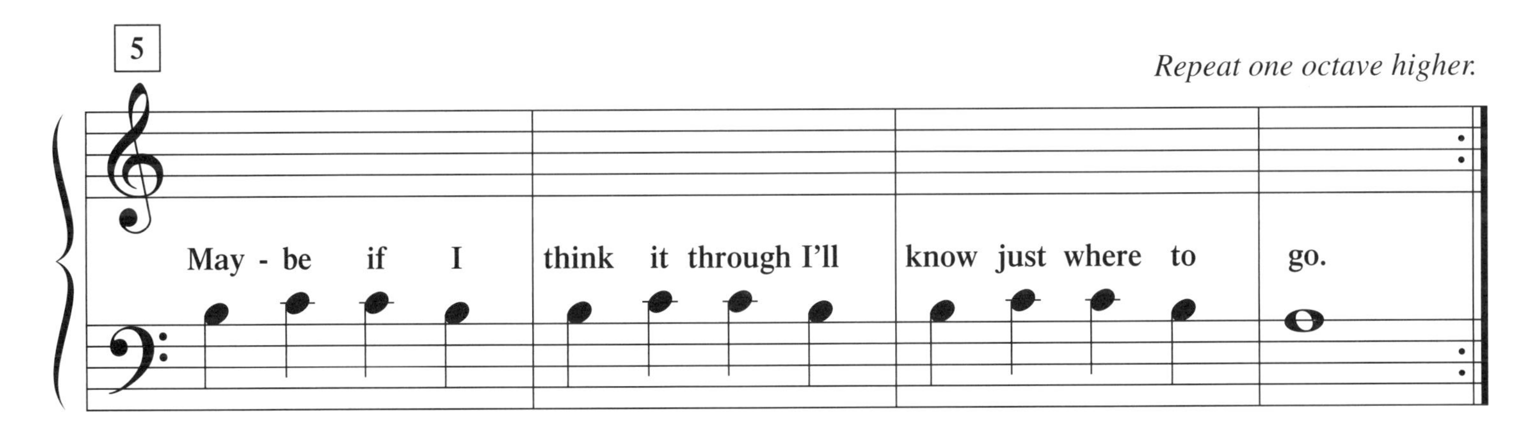
5
Repeat one octave higher.
May - be if I think it through I'll know just where to go.

After you are comfortable with this piece, try playing with **L.H.** finger **2** on **C.**

Teacher Duet: Student plays one octave higher.

p
1
5
5

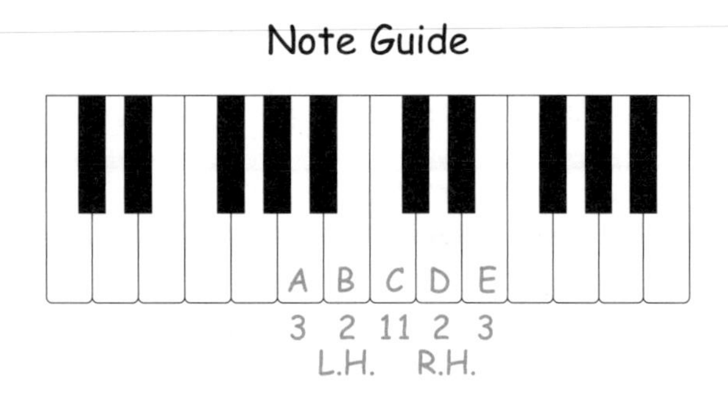
Note Guide
A B C D E
3 2 1 1 2 3
L.H. R.H.

Mister McGraff

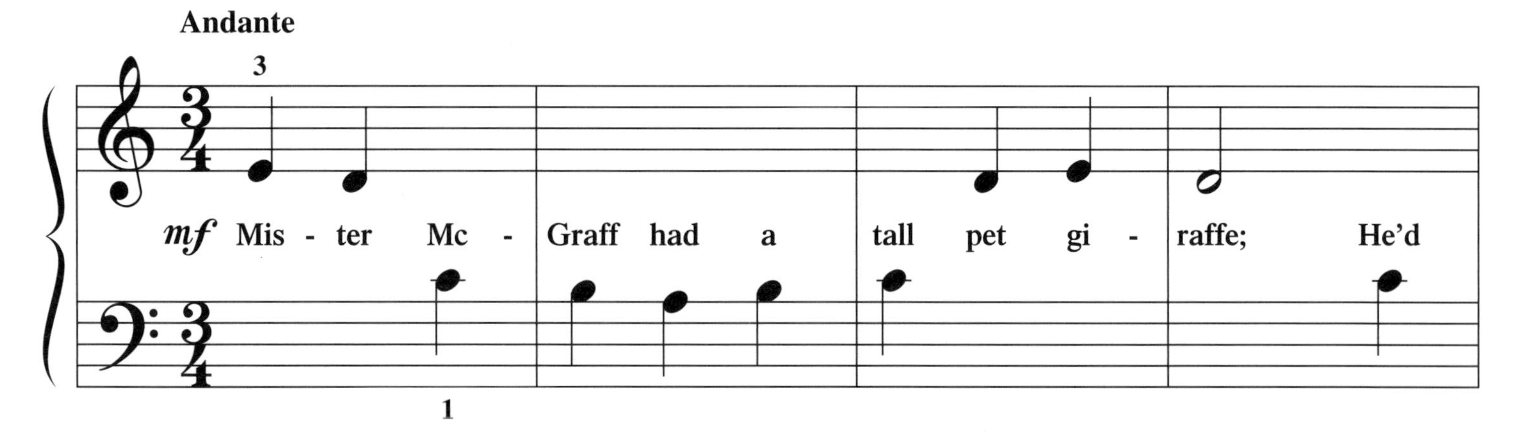
Andante
mf Mis - ter Mc - Graff had a tall pet gi - raffe; He'd

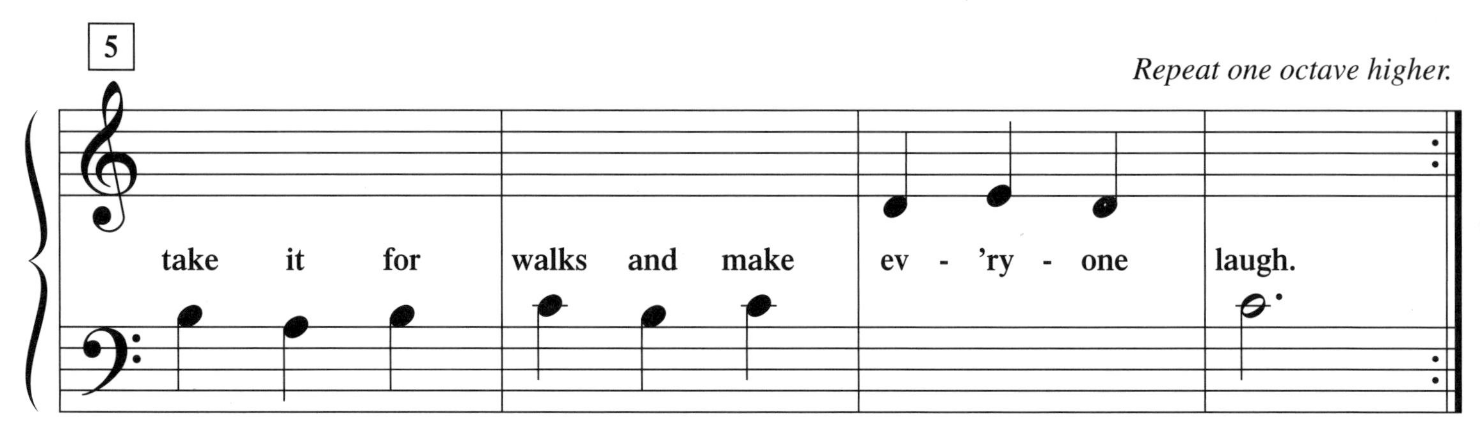
Repeat one octave higher.
take it for walks and make ev - 'ry - one laugh.

After you are comfortable with this piece, try playing with **R.H.** finger **2** on **E.**

Teacher Duet: Student plays one octave higher.

R.H.
L.H.
mp

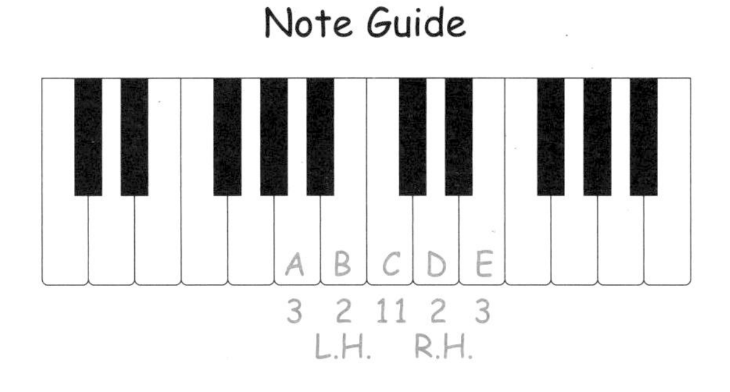

Note Guide
A B C D E
3 2 1 1 2 3
L.H. R.H.

I Like My Pillows Flat

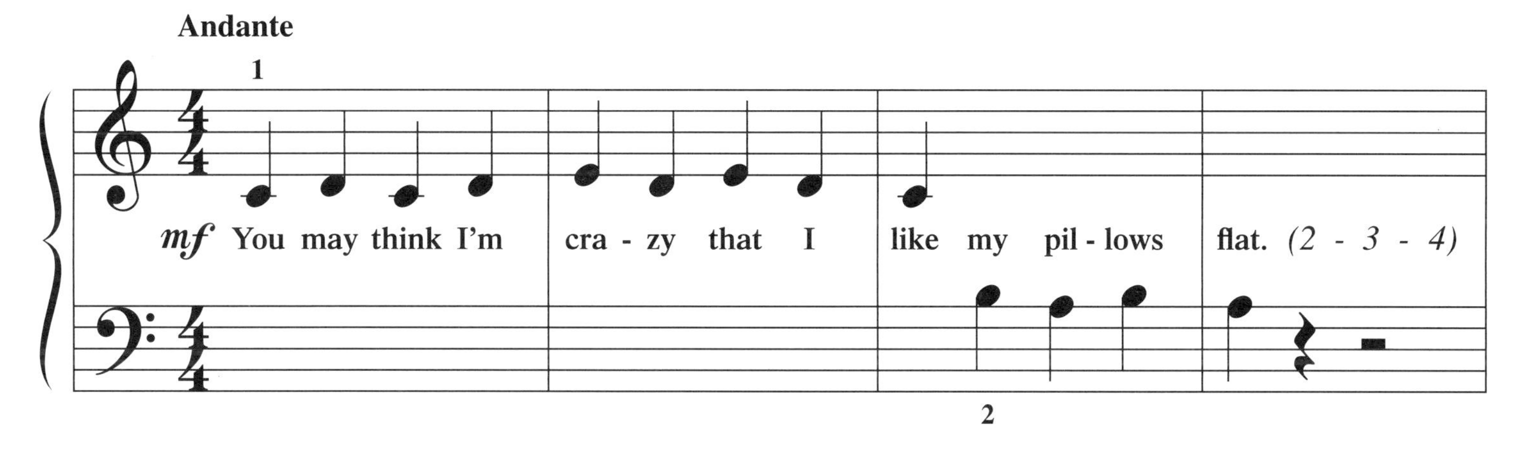

Andante
1
mf You may think I'm cra - zy that I like my pil - lows flat. (2 - 3 - 4)
2

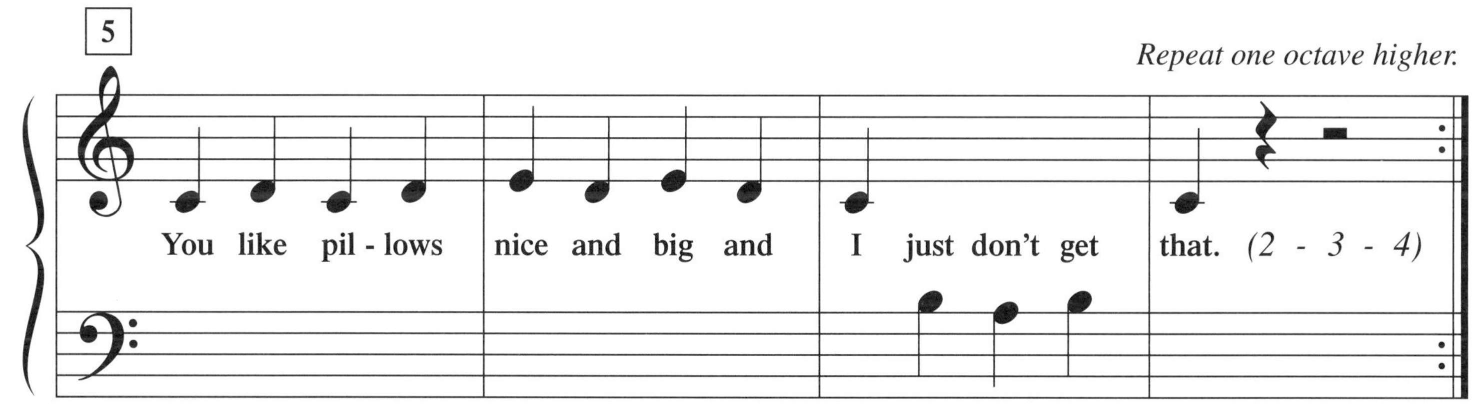

5
Repeat one octave higher.
You like pil - lows nice and big and I just don't get that. (2 - 3 - 4)

After you are comfortable with this piece, try playing with **L.H.** finger **1** on **B.**

Teacher Duet: Student plays as written.

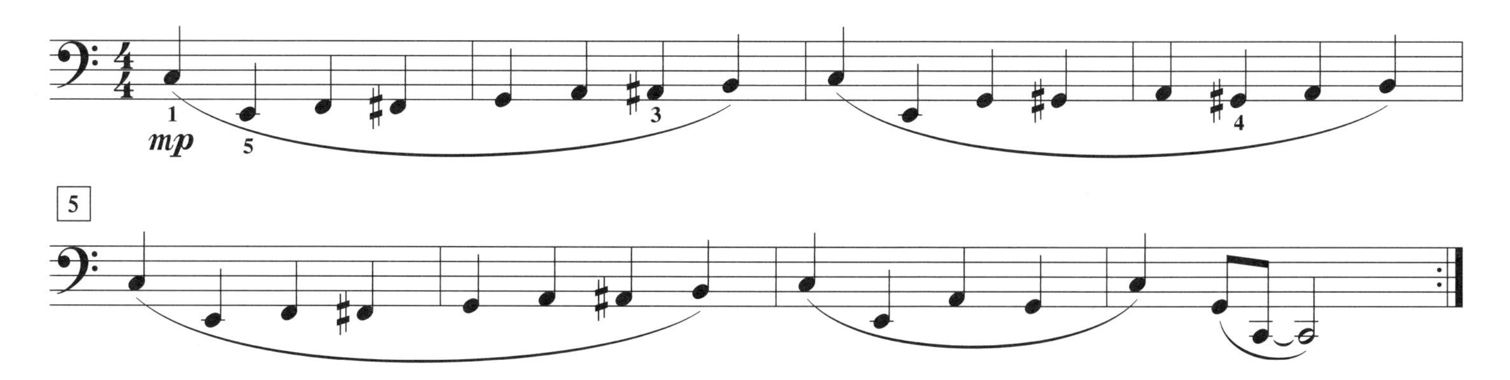

1
mp
5
3
4
5

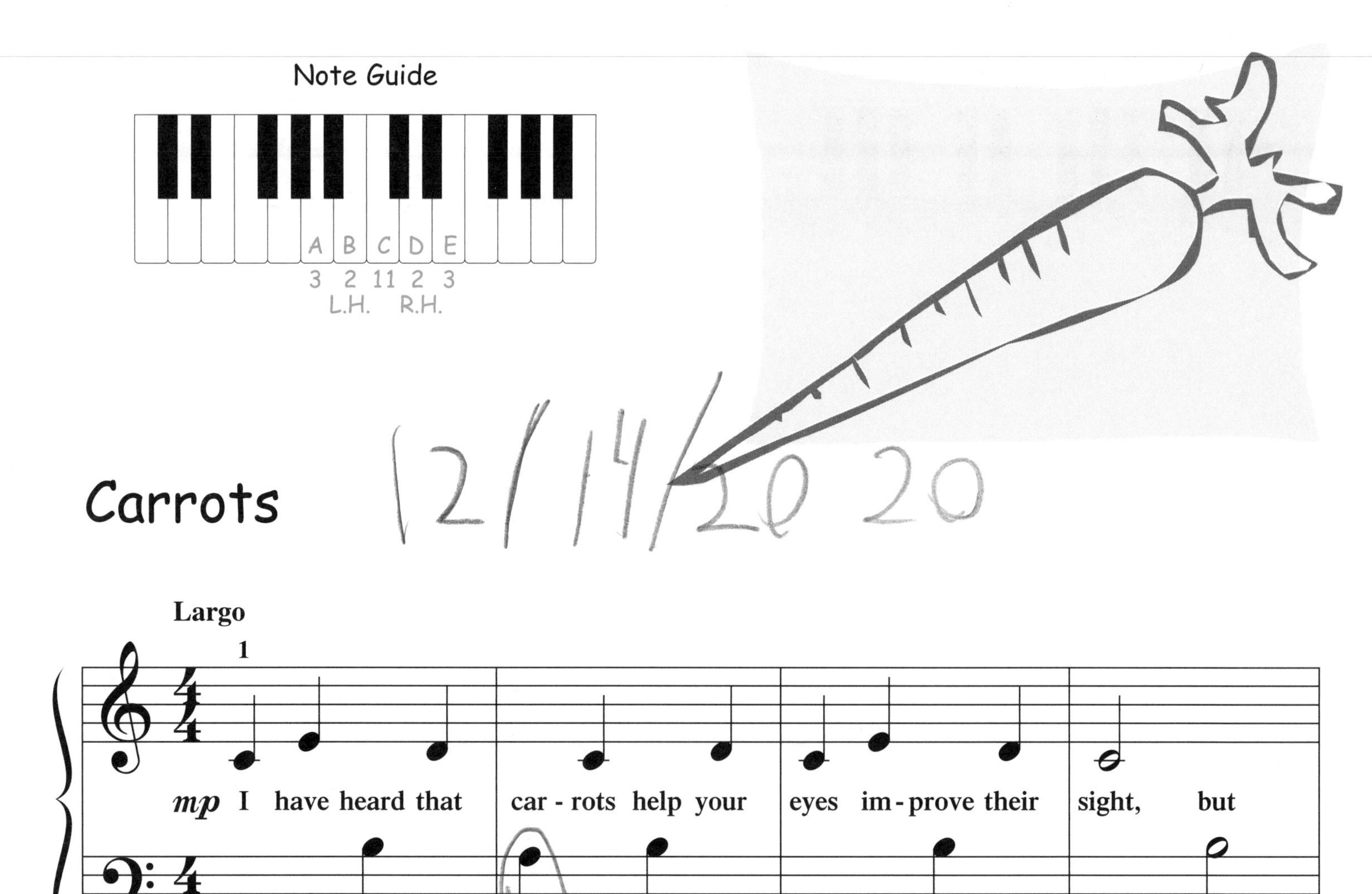
Note Guide
A B C D E
3 2 1 1 2 3
L.H. R.H.
Largo
mp I have heard that car - rots help your eyes im - prove their sight, but

Carrots

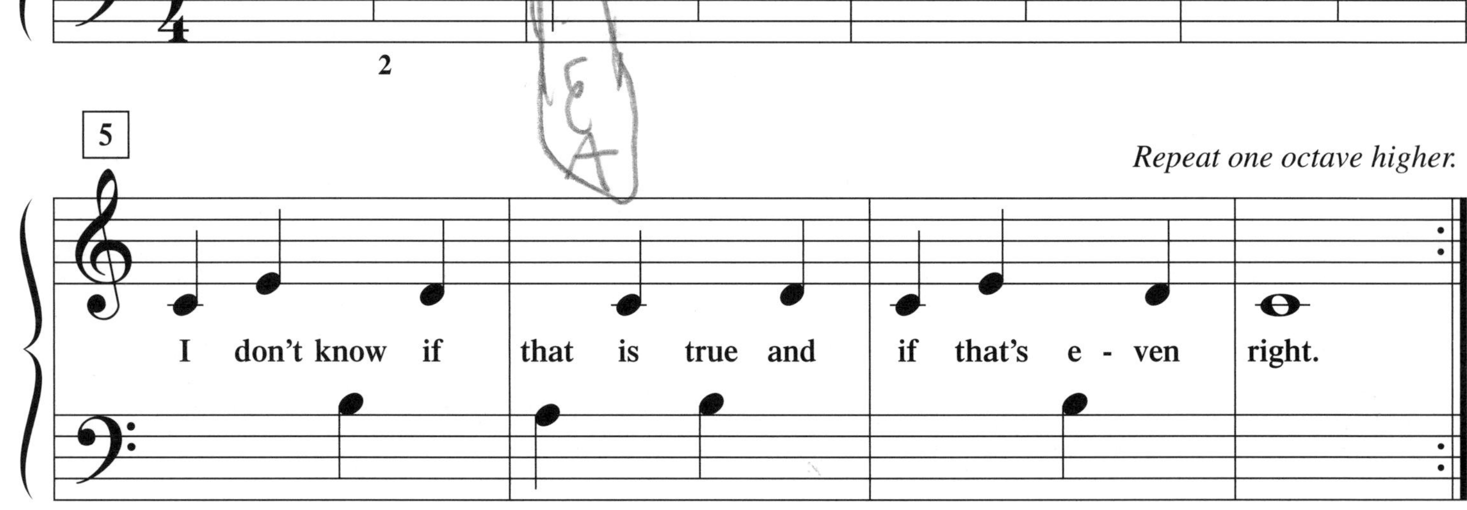
Repeat one octave higher.
I don't know if that is true and if that's e - ven right.

After you are comfortable with this piece, try playing with **L.H.** finger **1** on **B.**

Teacher Duet: Student plays one octave higher.

R.H.
L.H.

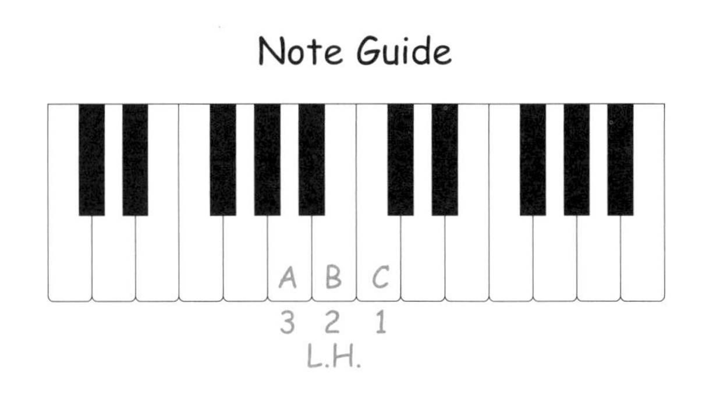
Note Guide
A B C
3 2 1
L.H.

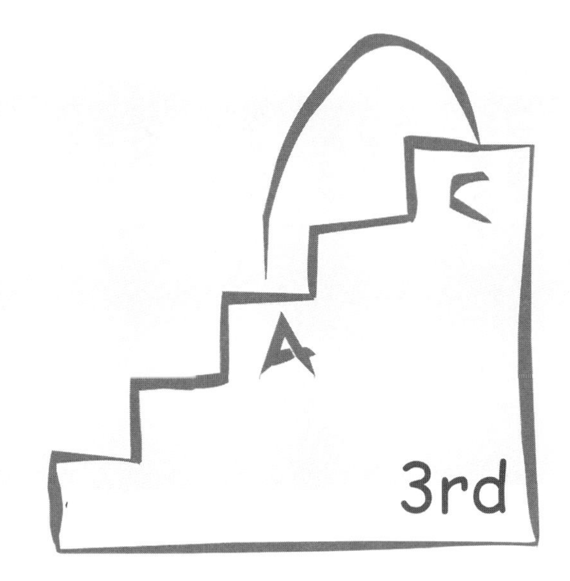
C
A
3rd

Skip and Hop with C and A

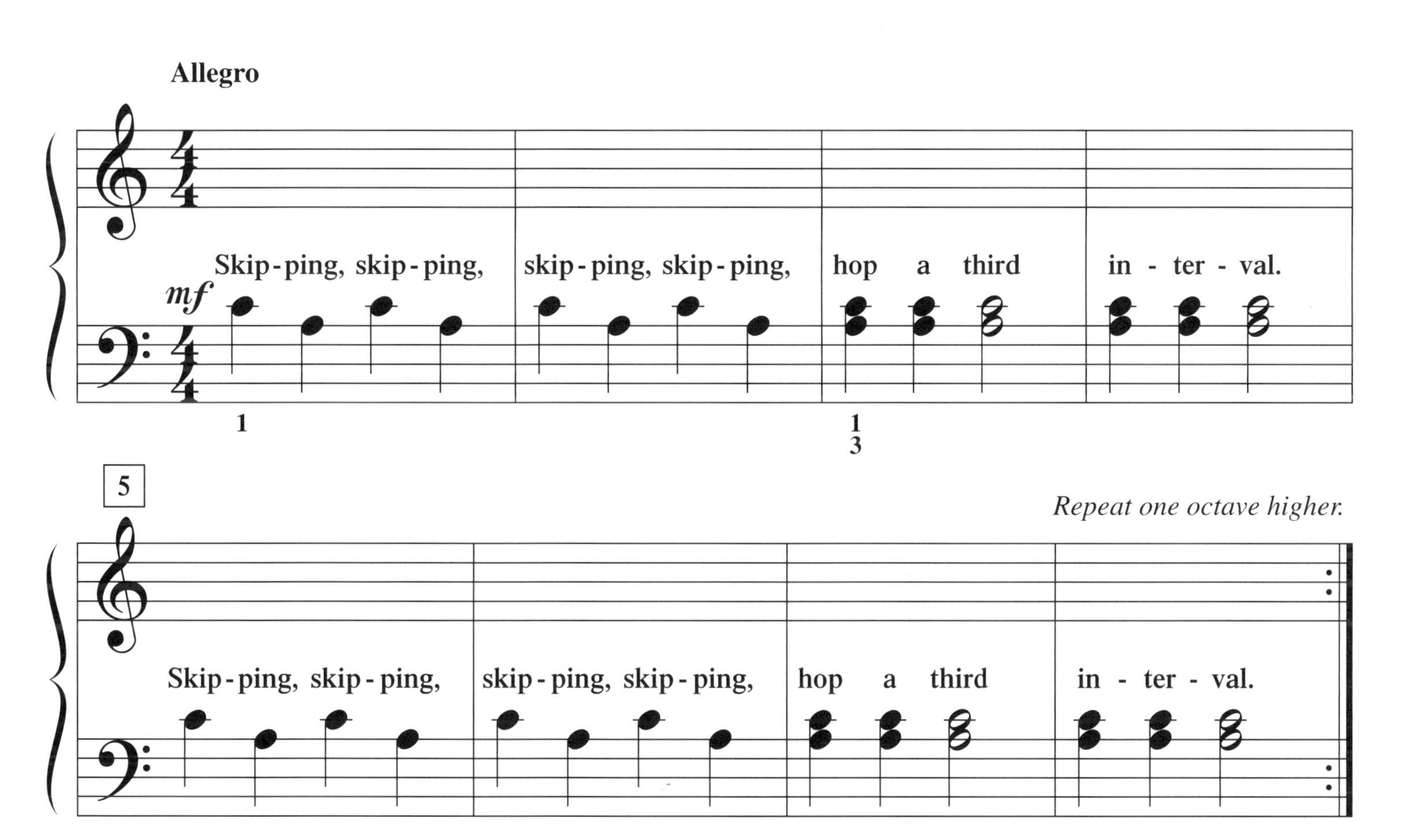
Allegro
Skip-ping, skip-ping, skip-ping, skip-ping, hop a third in - ter - val.
mf
1
1
3
5
Repeat one octave higher.
Skip-ping, skip-ping, skip-ping, skip-ping, hop a third in - ter - val.

After you are comfortable with this piece, try playing with **L.H.** finger **2** on **C.**

Teacher Duet: Student plays as written.

3
mp
5

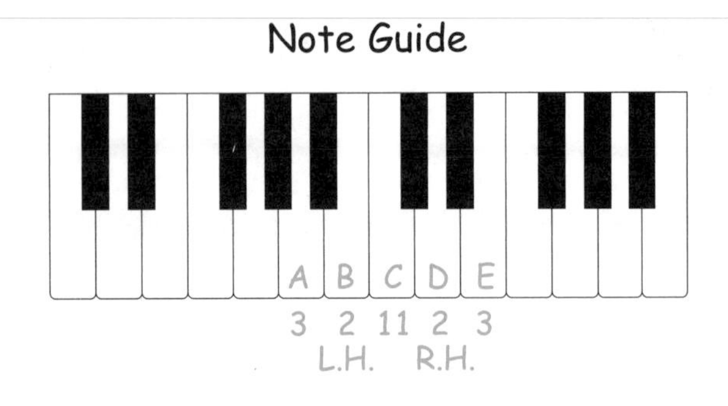
Note Guide
A B C D E
3 2 11 2 3
L.H. R.H.

You Woke Me From a Dream

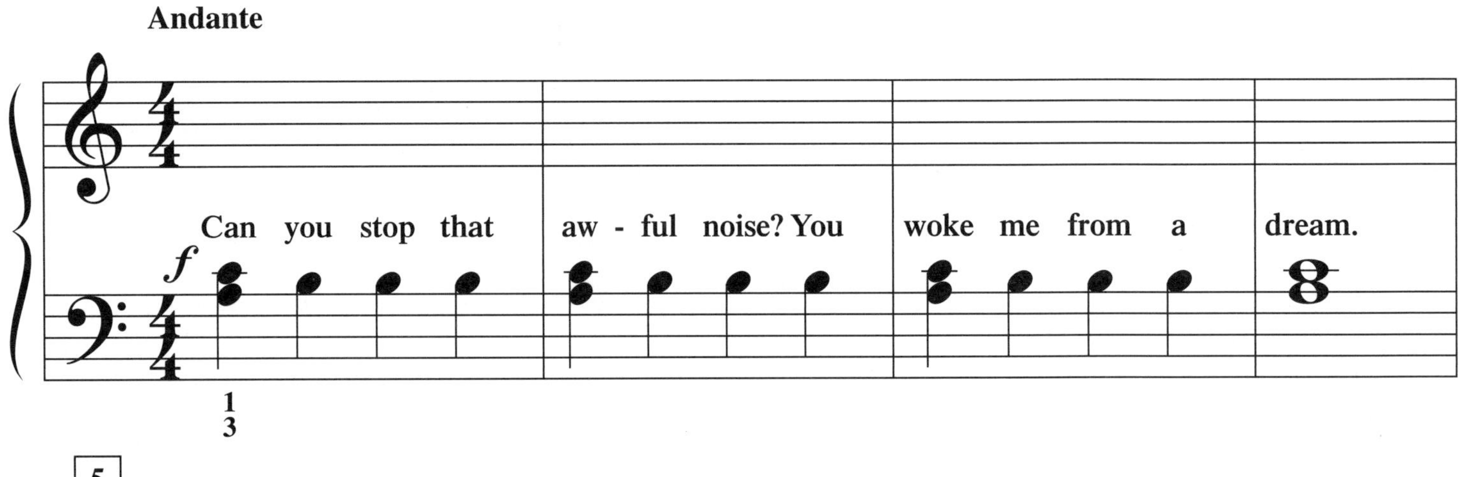
Andante
Can you stop that aw - ful noise? You woke me from a dream.
f
1
3

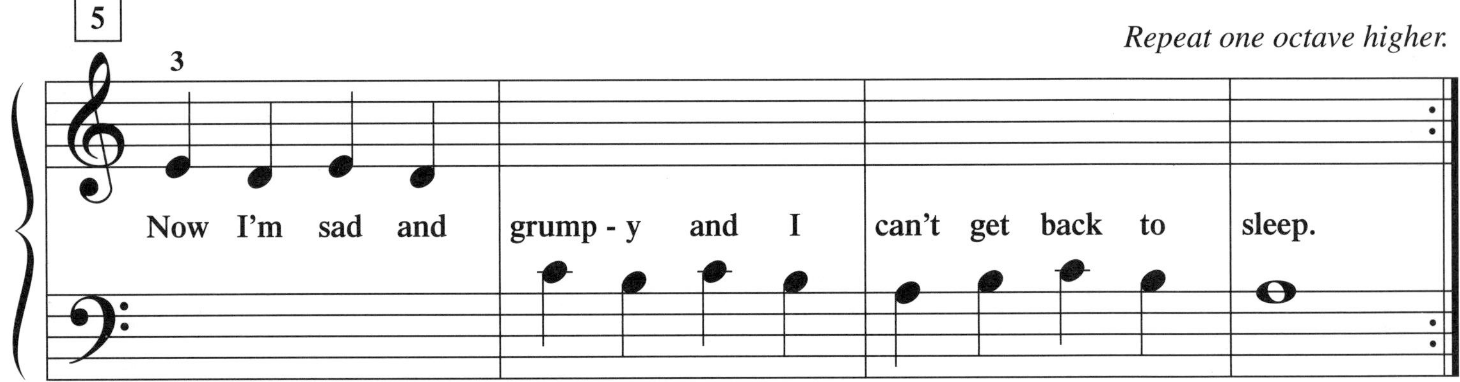
5
3
Repeat one octave higher.
Now I'm sad and grump - y and I can't get back to sleep.

After you are comfortable with this piece, try playing with **R.H.** finger **2** on **E.**

Teacher Duet: Student plays as written.

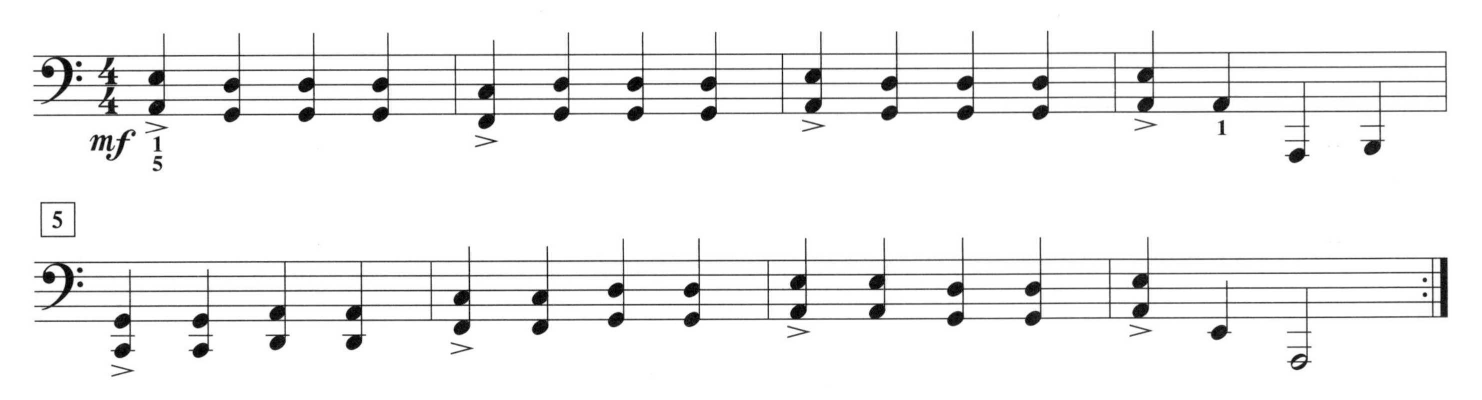
mf
1
5
1
5

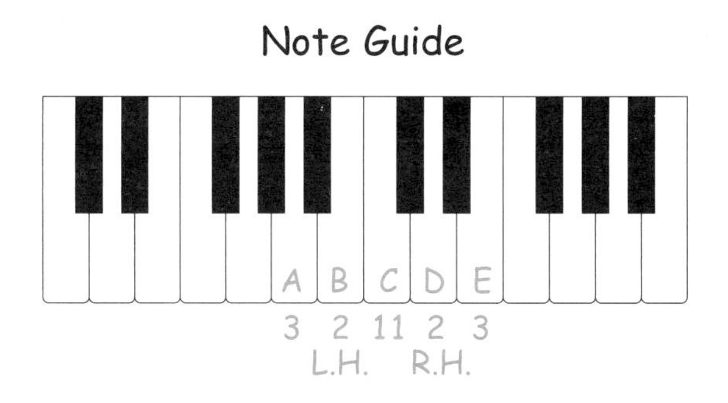
Note Guide
A B C D E
3 2 11 2 3
L.H. R.H.

I Am Very Sorry

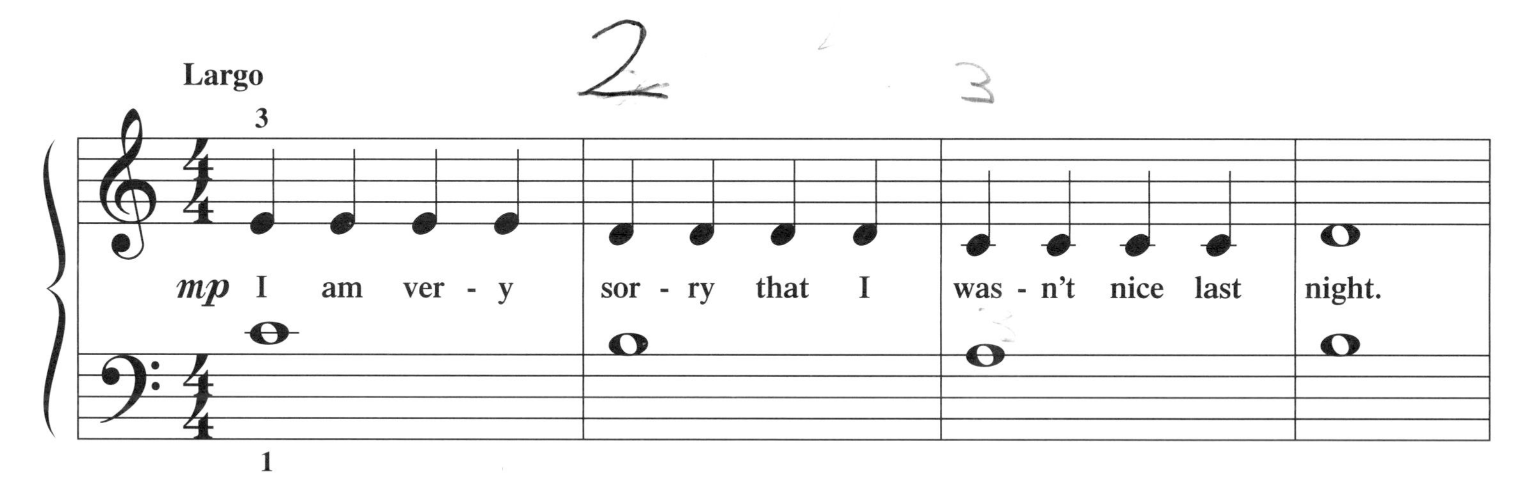
Largo
3
mp I am ver - y sor - ry that I was - n't nice last night.
1

5
Repeat one octave higher.
Can you please for - give me? I would like to make it right.

Teacher Duet: Student plays as written.

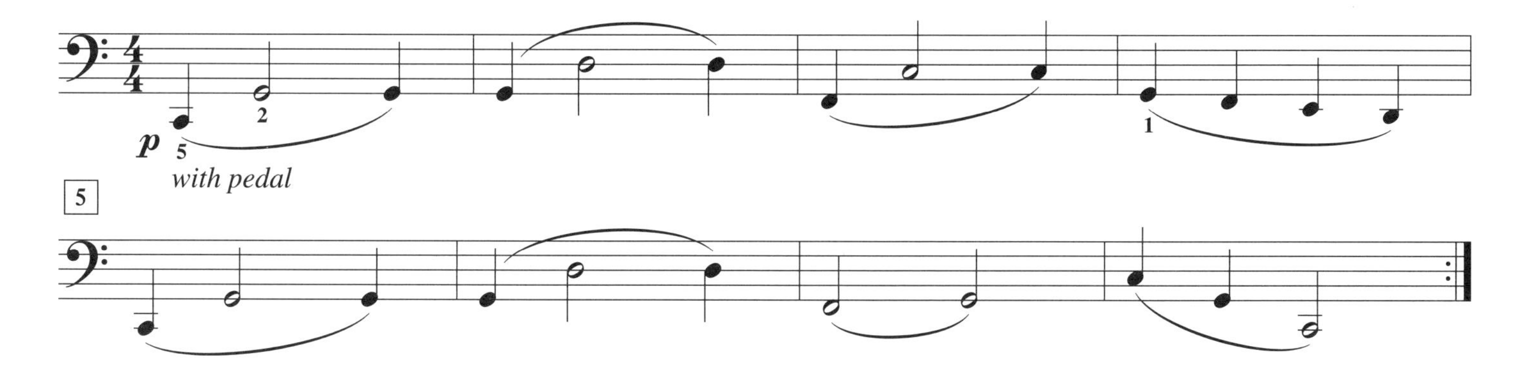
p
5
2
1
with pedal
5

Unit 5 F on the Keyboard

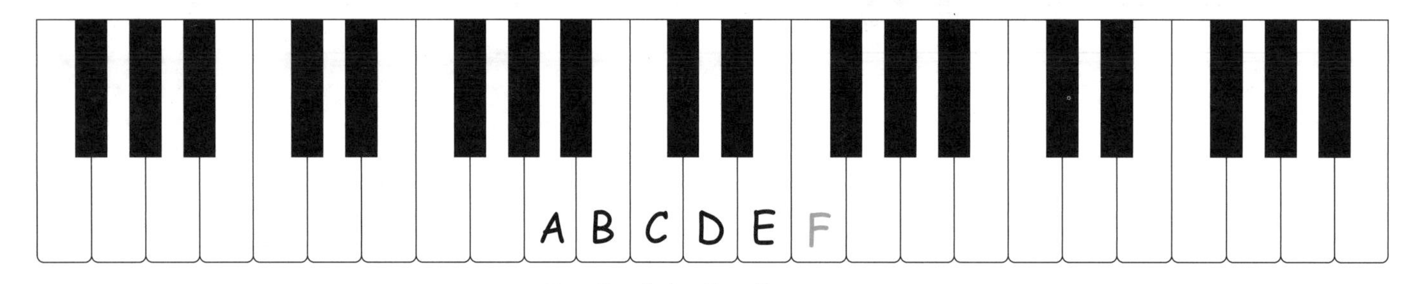
A B C D E F
3 2 1 1 2 3 4
Left Hand Right Hand

Remember that hand positions are just guides. When you are comfortable with the pieces in this unit, explore using different fingers.

F on the Treble Staff

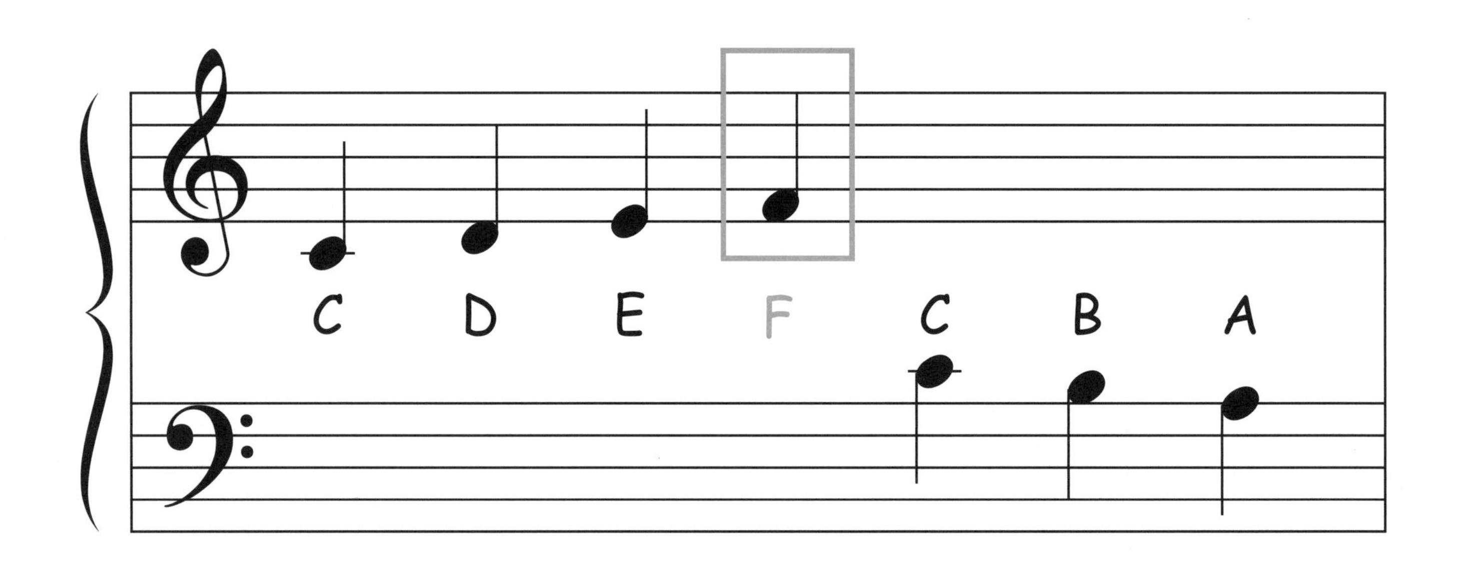
C D E F C B A

Play the example below, keeping your eyes on the music.

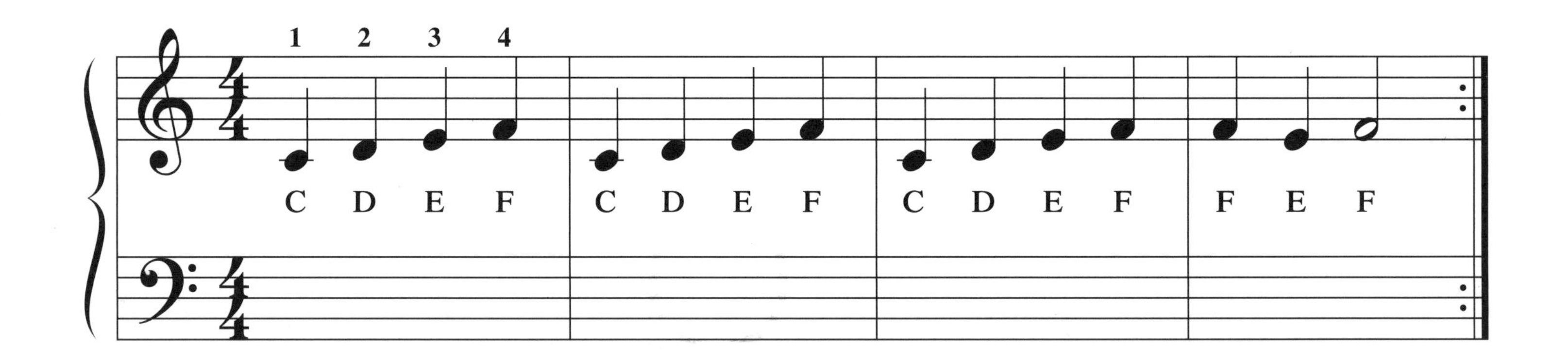
1 2 3 4
C D E F C D E F C D E F F E F

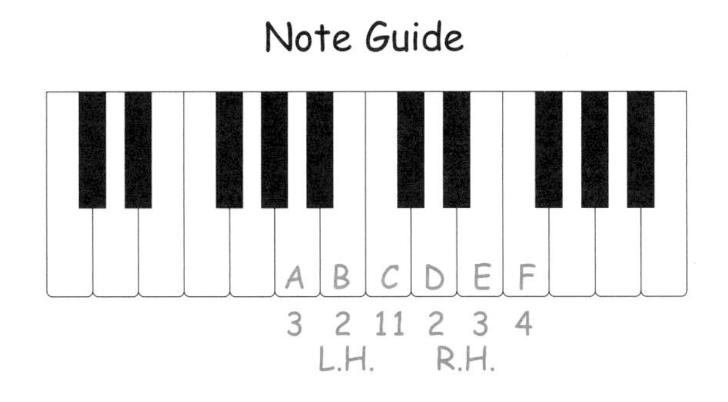
Note Guide
A B C D E F
3 2 1 1 2 3 4
L.H. R.H.

IN GOD WE TRUST

Find a Penny

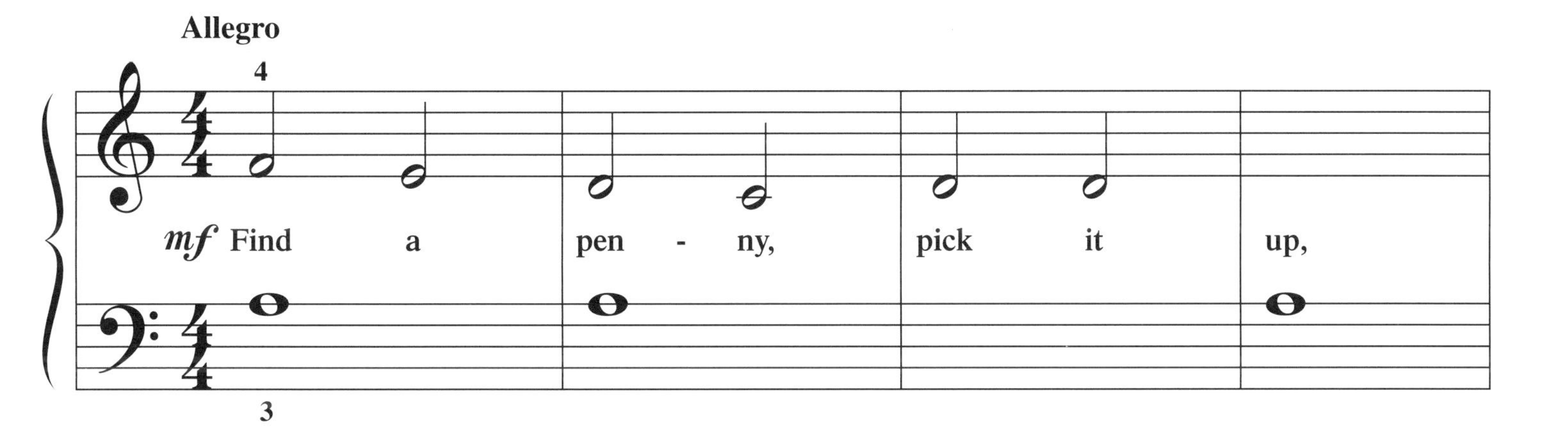
Allegro
4
mf Find a pen - ny, pick it up,
3

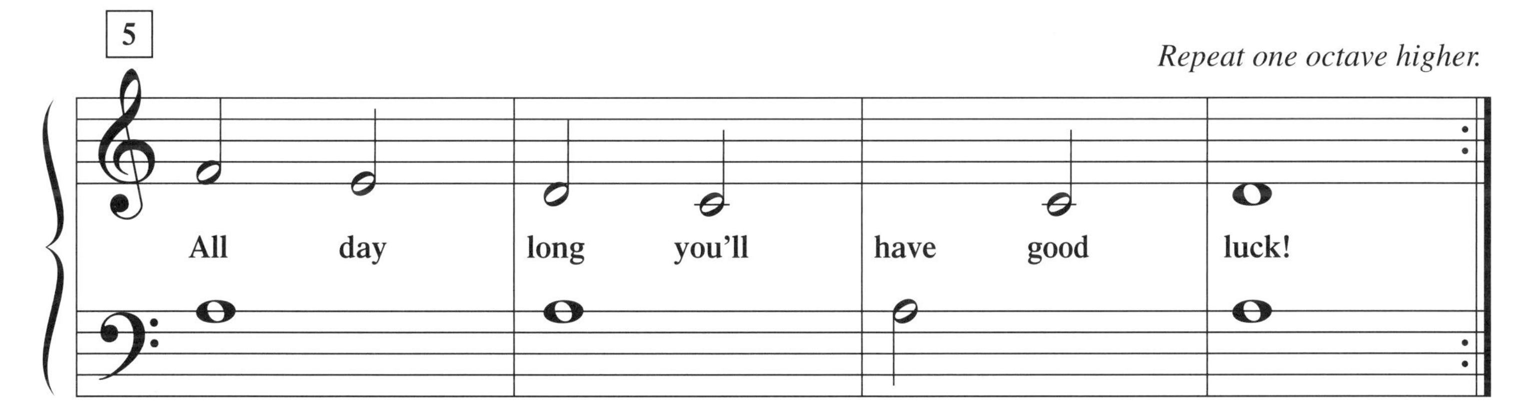
5
Repeat one octave higher.
All day long you'll have good luck!

After you are comfortable with this piece, try playing with **L.H.** finger **1** on **A.**

Teacher Duet: Student plays one octave higher.

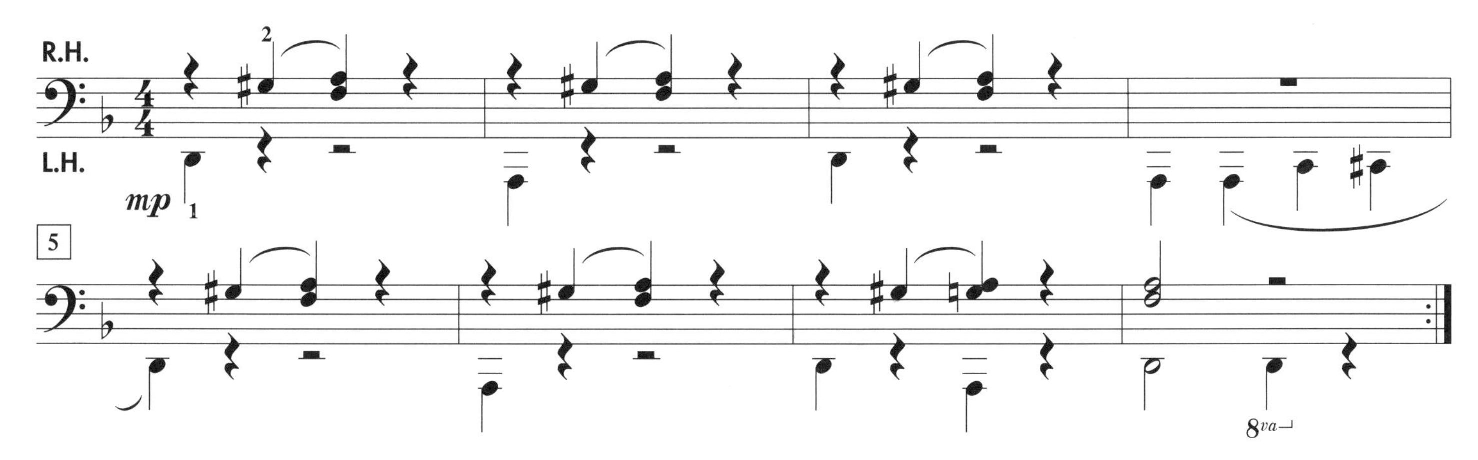
R.H.
L.H.
mp
5
8va

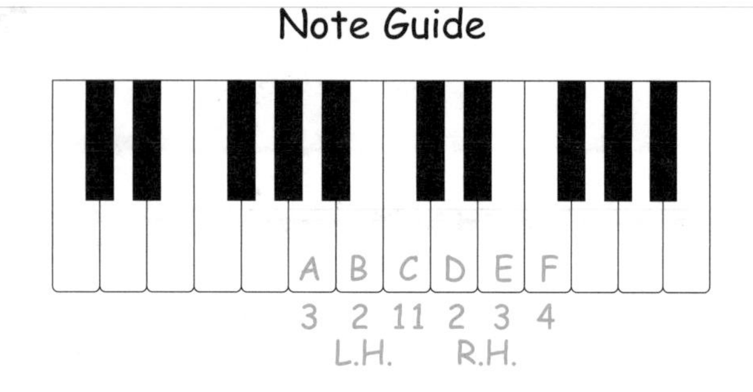
Note Guide
A B C D E F
3 2 1 1 2 3 4
L.H. R.H.

Corn on the Cob

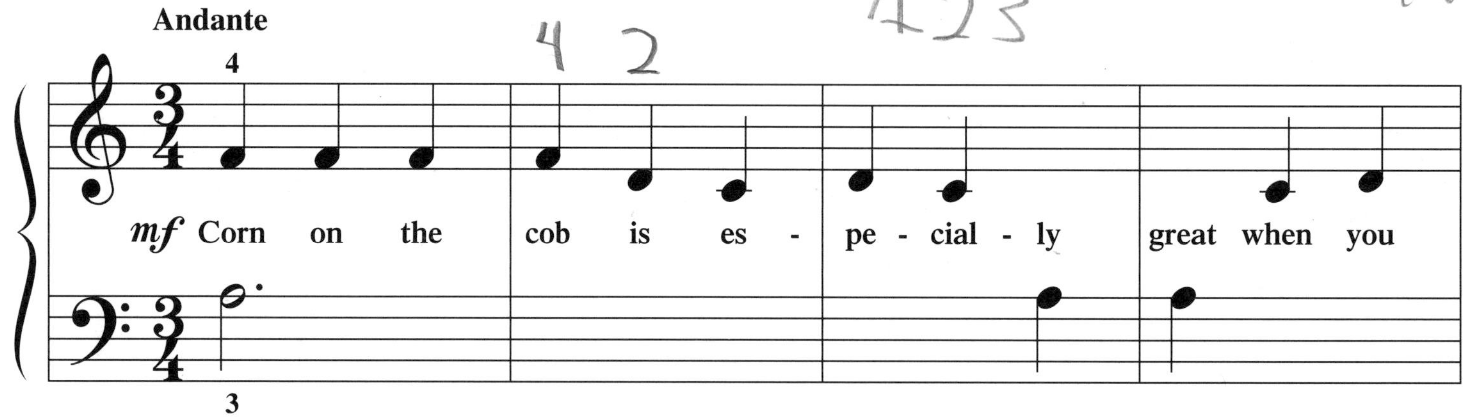
Andante
mf
Corn on the cob is es - pe - cial - ly great when you

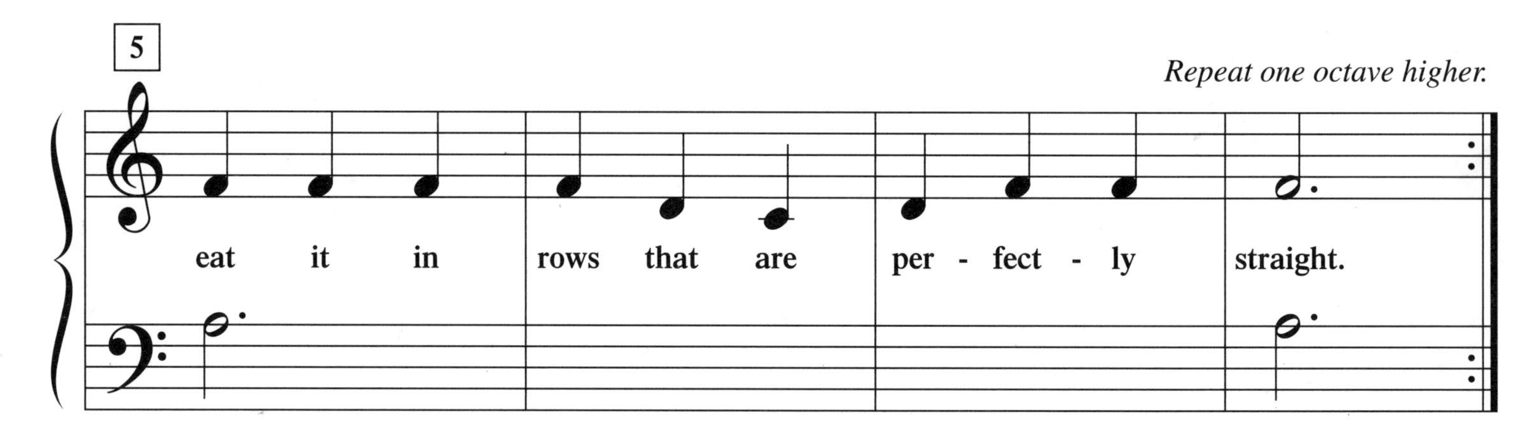
Repeat one octave higher.
eat it in rows that are per - fect - ly straight.

After you are comfortable with this piece, try playing with **L.H.** finger **1** on **A.**

Teacher Duet: Student plays one octave higher.

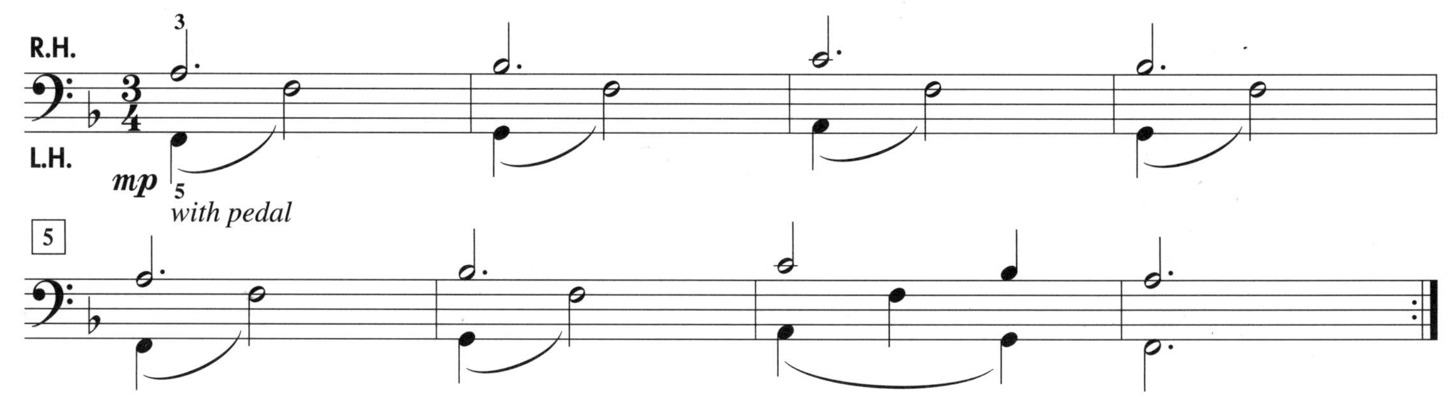
R.H.
L.H.
mp
with pedal

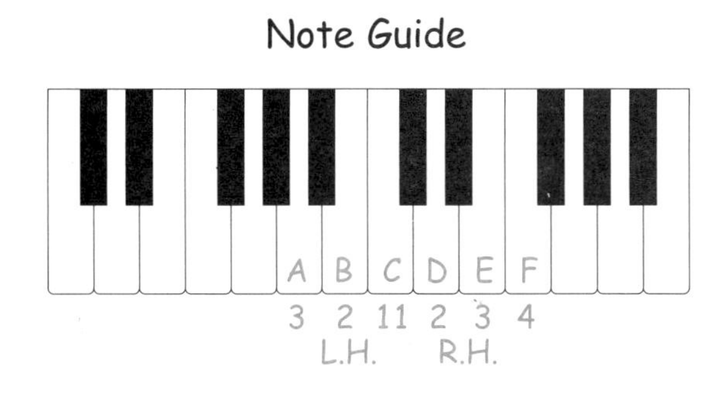
Note Guide
A B C D E F
3 2 1 1 2 3 4
L.H. R.H.

Full of Dishes

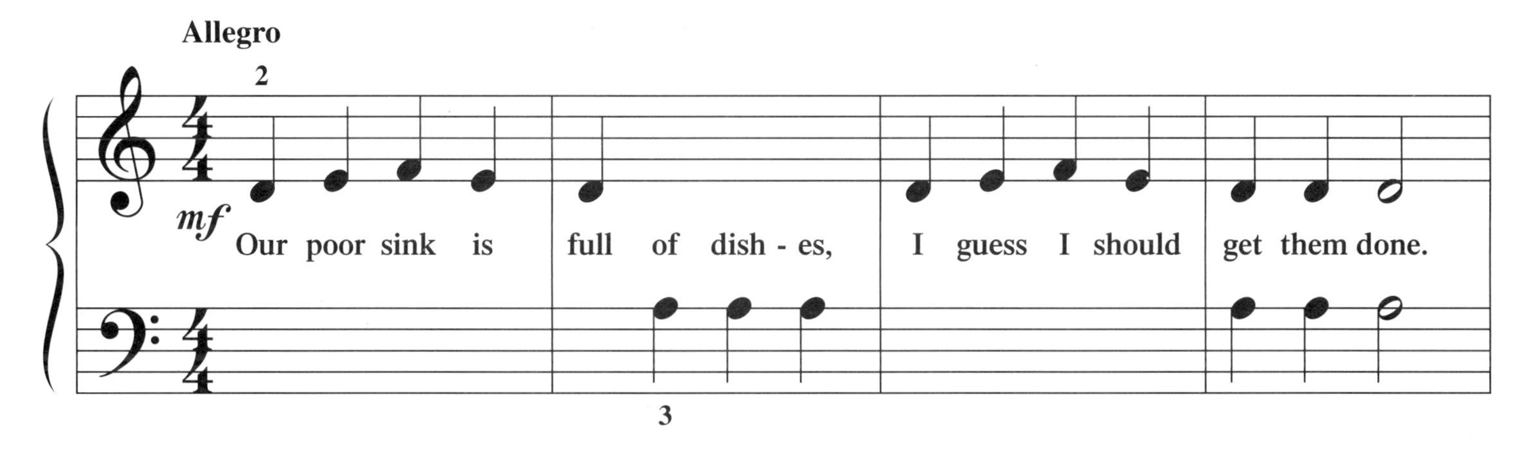
Allegro
2
mf
Our poor sink is full of dish - es, I guess I should get them done.
3

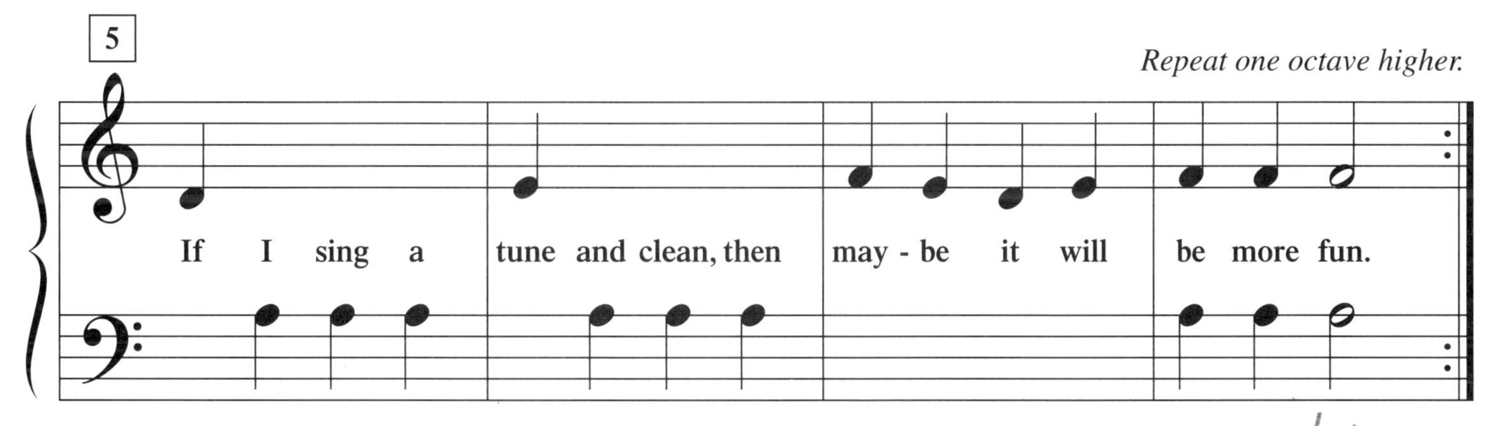
5
Repeat one octave higher.
If I sing a tune and clean, then may - be it will be more fun.

After you are comfortable with this piece, try playing with **L.H.** finger **2** on **A.**

Teacher Duet: Student plays as written.

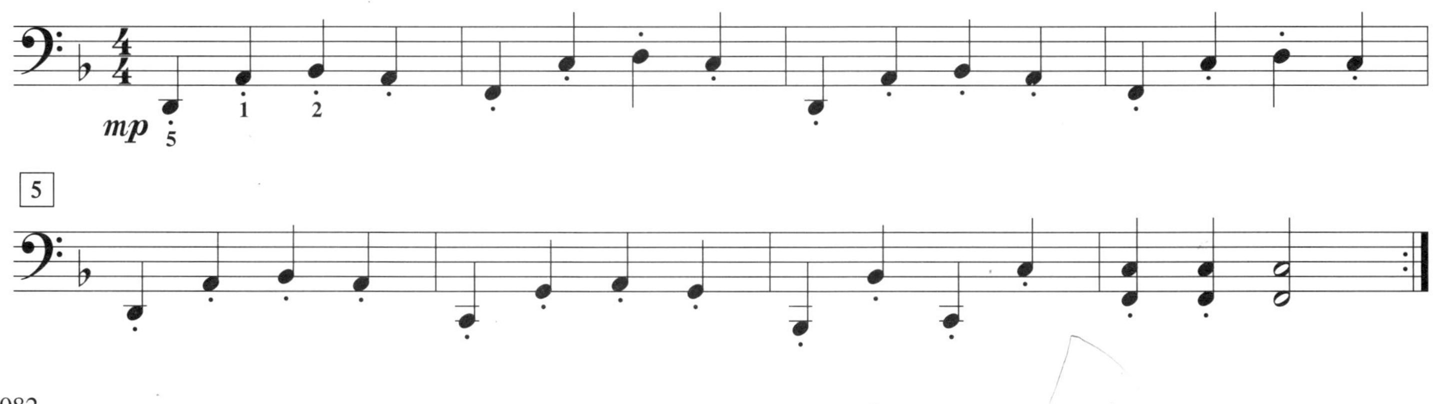
mp
5 1 2
5

Note Guide
A B C D E F
3 2 1 1 2 3 4
L.H. R.H.
Ghost Stories
28/10/21
Andante
Hold - ing a flash - light right up to my face, I
mp
When played as a solo, press the right (damper) pedal for the entire piece.
5
Repeat one octave higher.
tell spook - y sto - ries be - neath the stair - case!

After you are comfortable with this piece, try playing with **R.H.** finger **1** on **D.**

Teacher Duet: Student plays as written.

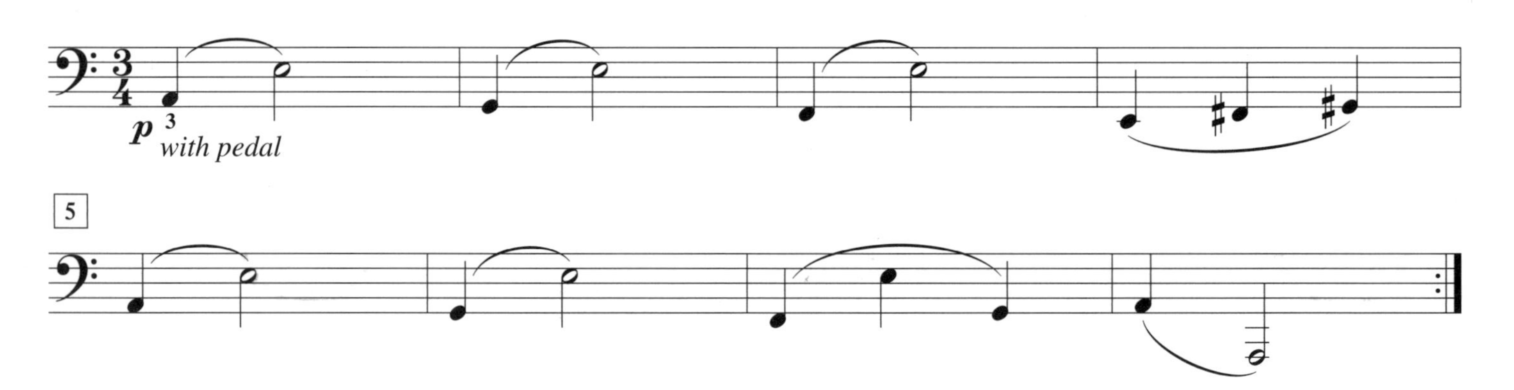
p
with pedal
5

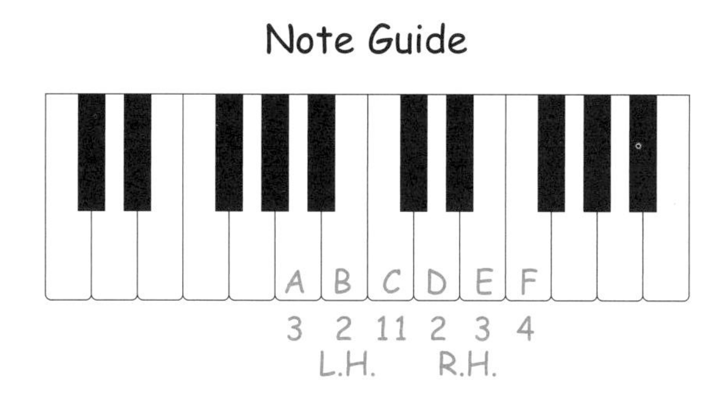
Note Guide
A B C D E F
3 2 1 1 2 3 4
L.H. R.H.

A Skunk for a Pet

28/10/21

TIE — A curved line connecting two identical notes called *tied* notes. Play and hold the first note for the combined value of the notes. 𝅗𝅥. ‿ 𝅗𝅥. = 6 beats.

Andante

f
You won't be - lieve me, I bet, that
2
3

When played as a solo, press the right (damper) pedal for the entire piece.

Repeat one octave higher.

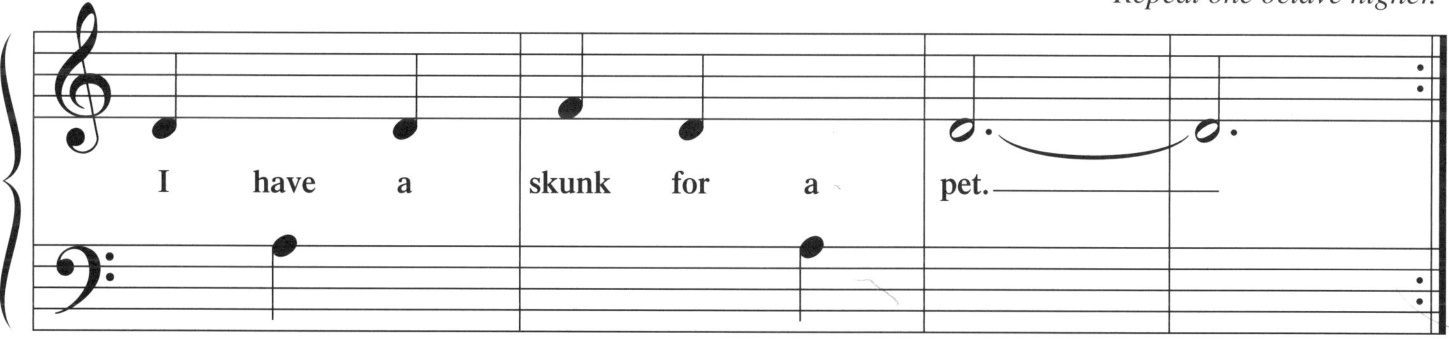
5
I have a skunk for a pet.

After you are comfortable with this piece, try playing with **L.H.** finger **1** on **A.**

Teacher Duet: Student plays as written.

R.H.
L.H.
mf
2
2
5

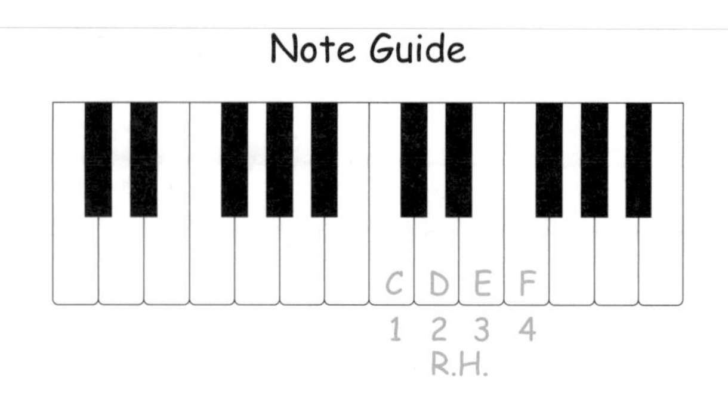
Note Guide
C D E F
1 2 3 4
R.H.

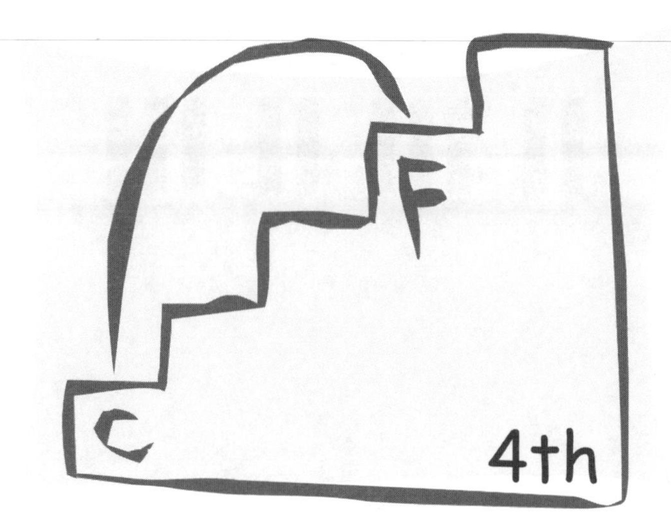
F
C
4th

Leap and Hop with C and F

28/10/21

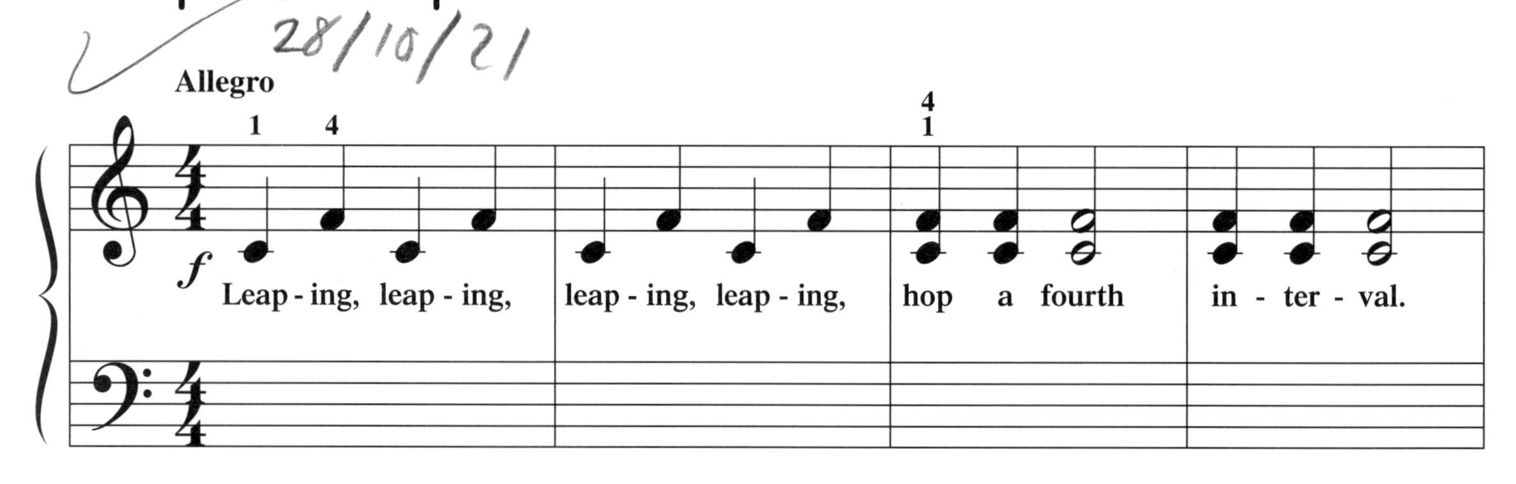
Allegro
1 4
4 1
f
Leap - ing, leap - ing, leap - ing, leap - ing, hop a fourth in - ter - val.

5
Repeat one octave higher.
Leap - ing, leap - ing, leap - ing, leap - ing, hop a fourth in - ter - val.

After you are comfortable with this piece, try playing with **R.H.** finger **2** on **C.**

Teacher Duet: Student plays as written.

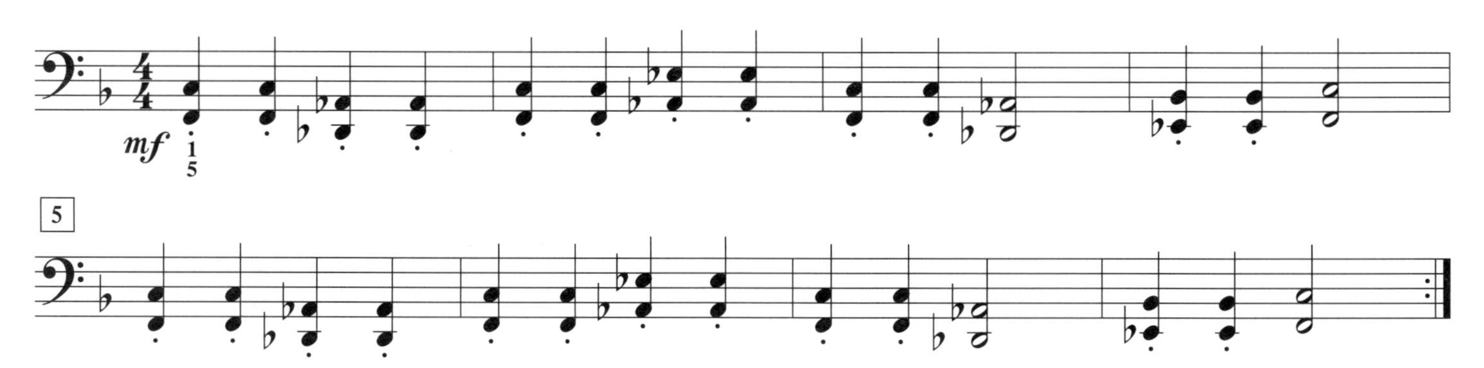
mf
1
5
5

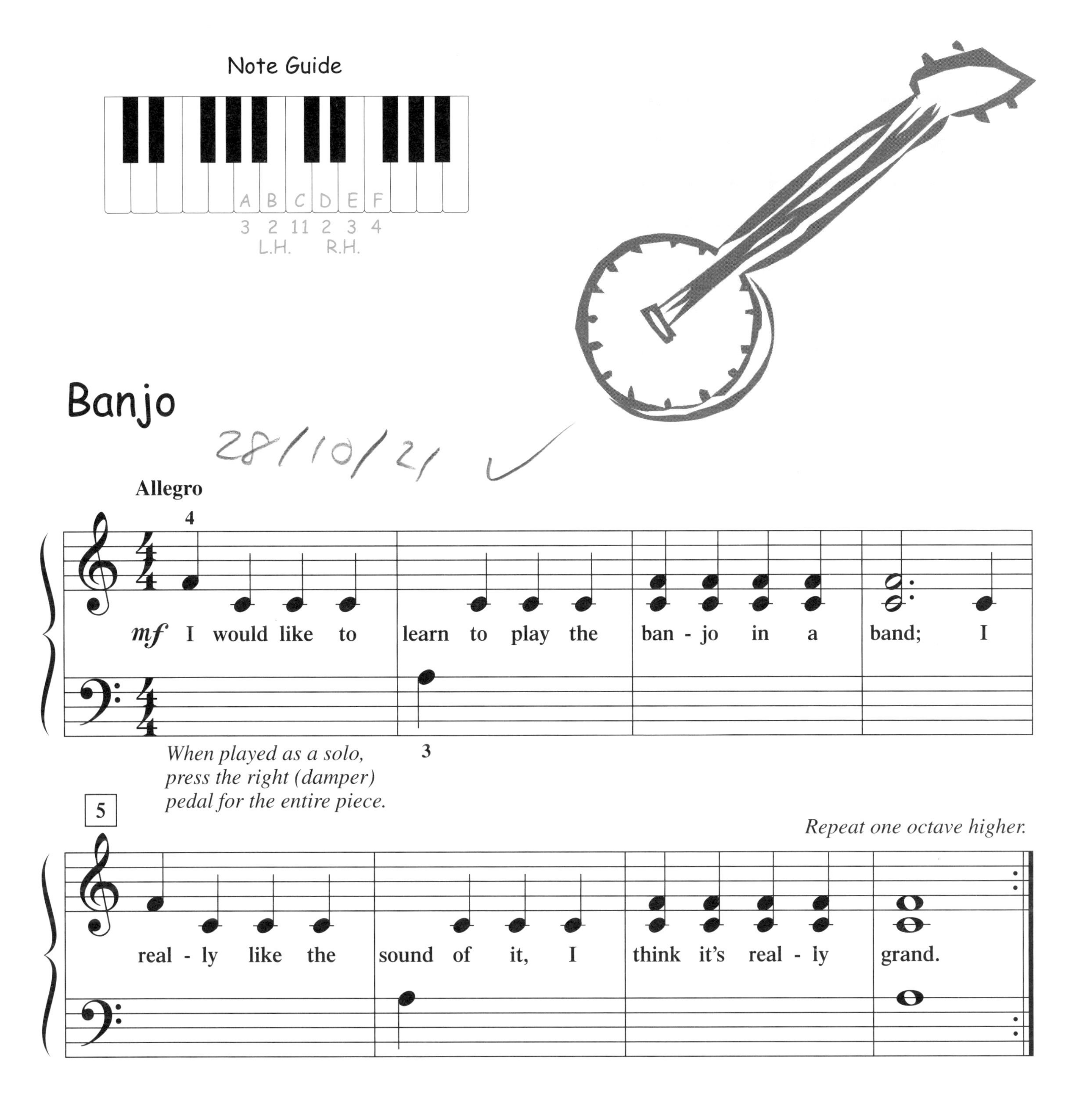
Note Guide
A B C D E F
3 2 1 1 2 3 4
L.H. R.H.
Banjo
Allegro
mf I would like to learn to play the ban - jo in a band; I
When played as a solo, press the right (damper) pedal for the entire piece.
Repeat one octave higher.
real - ly like the sound of it, I think it's real - ly grand.

After you are comfortable with this piece, try playing with **L.H.** finger **1** on **A.**

Teacher Duet: Student plays one octave higher.
R.H.
L.H.
mp
8va

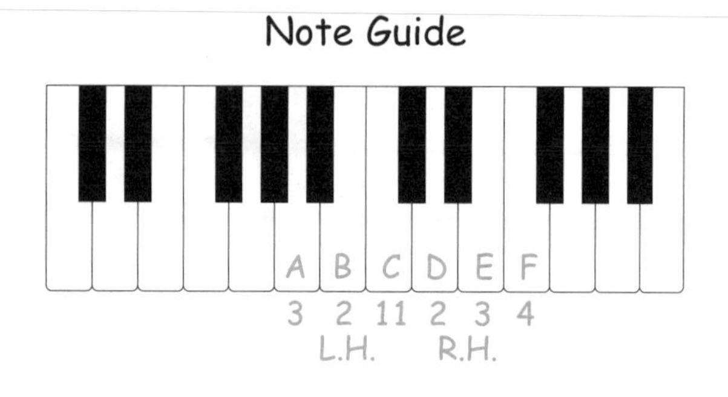
Note Guide
A B C D E F
3 2 1 1 2 3 4
L.H. R.H.

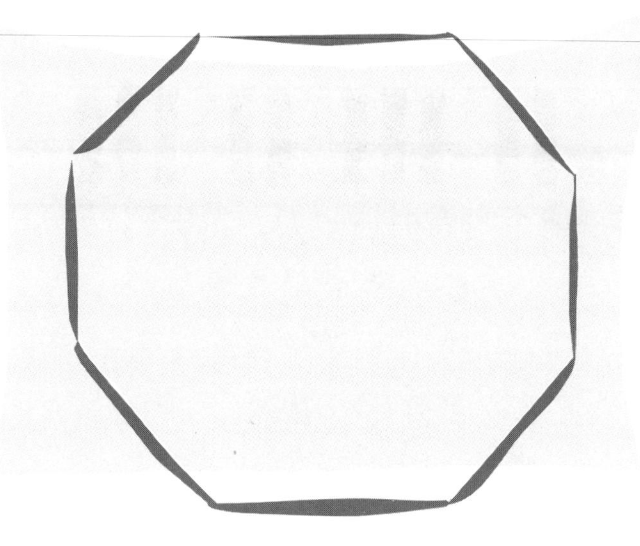

Eight Sides on an Octagon

Andante

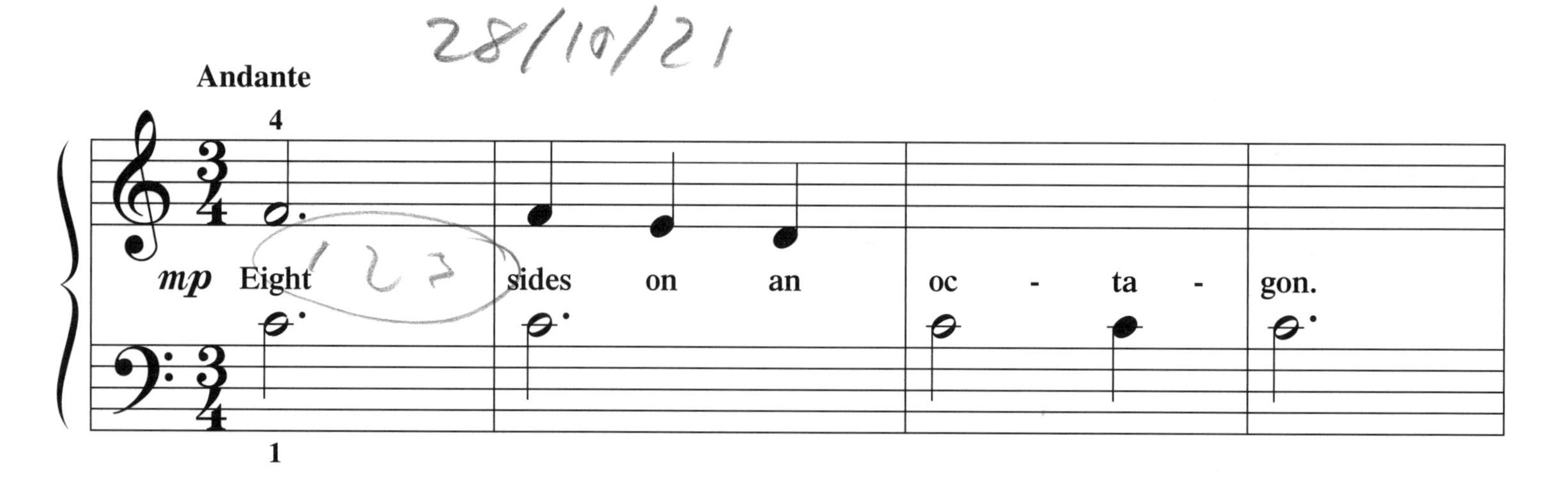
mp
Eight sides on an oc - ta - gon.

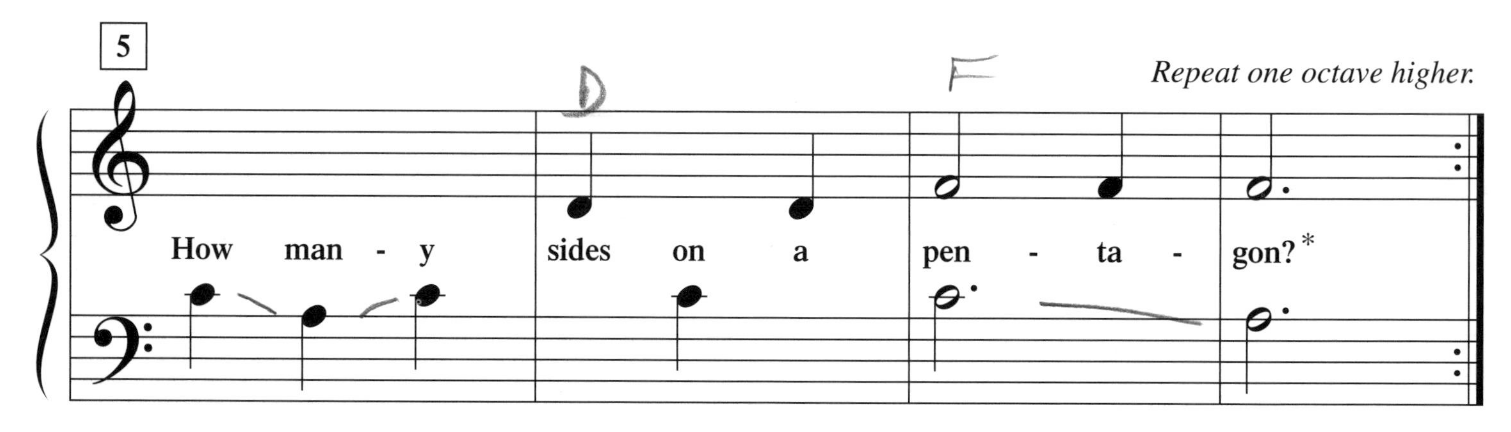
Repeat one octave higher.
How man - y sides on a pen - ta - gon?*

After you are comfortable with this piece, try playing with **R.H.** finger **3** on **F.**

Teacher Duet: Student plays one octave higher.

R.H.
L.H.
p
with pedal
8va

* *The answer is five.*

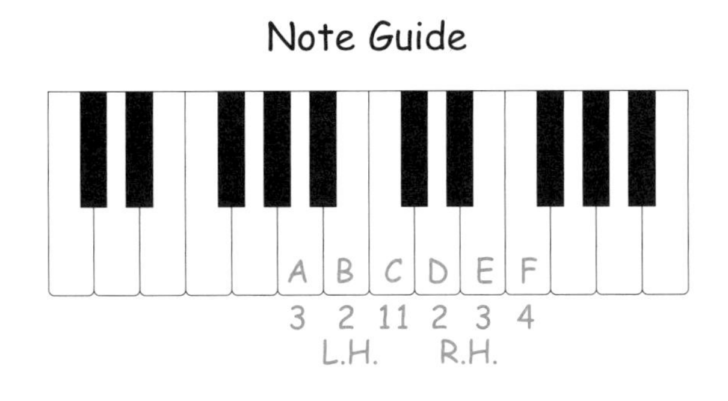
Note Guide
A B C D E F
3 2 1 1 2 3 4
L.H. R.H.

EVERY ONE IS A WINNER

Sports

Allegro

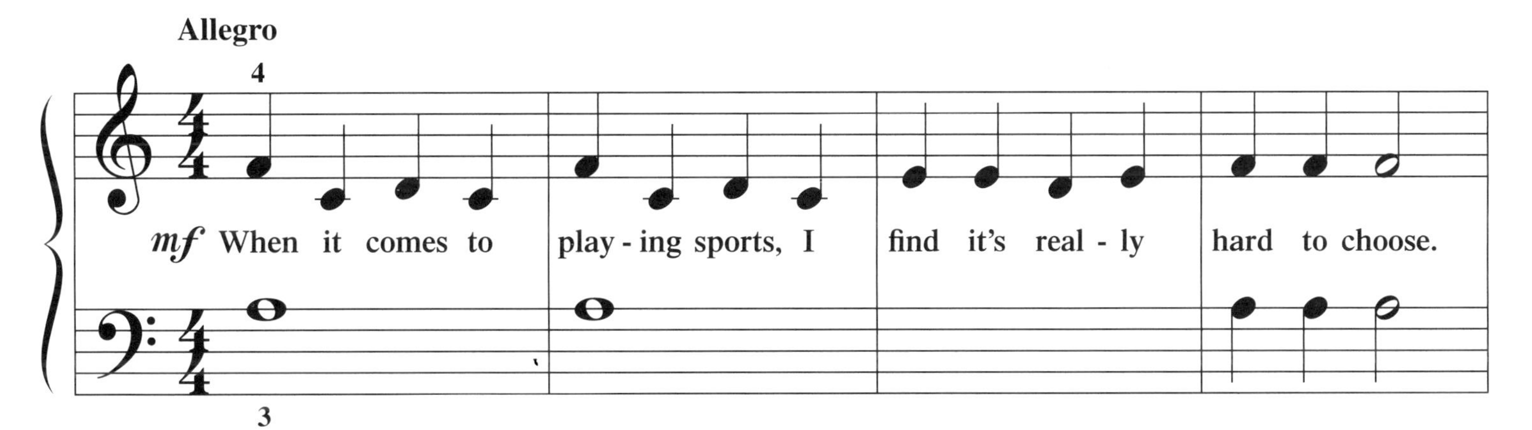
4
mf When it comes to play - ing sports, I find it's real - ly hard to choose.
3

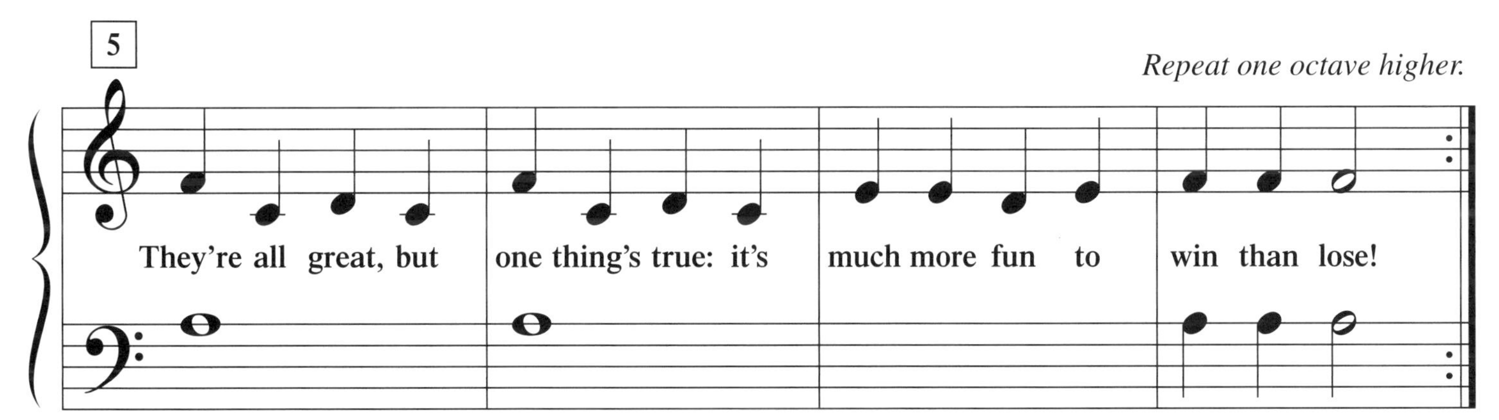
5
Repeat one octave higher.
They're all great, but one thing's true: it's much more fun to win than lose!

After you are comfortable with this piece, try playing with **L.H.** finger **1** on **A.**

Teacher Duet: Student plays one octave higher.

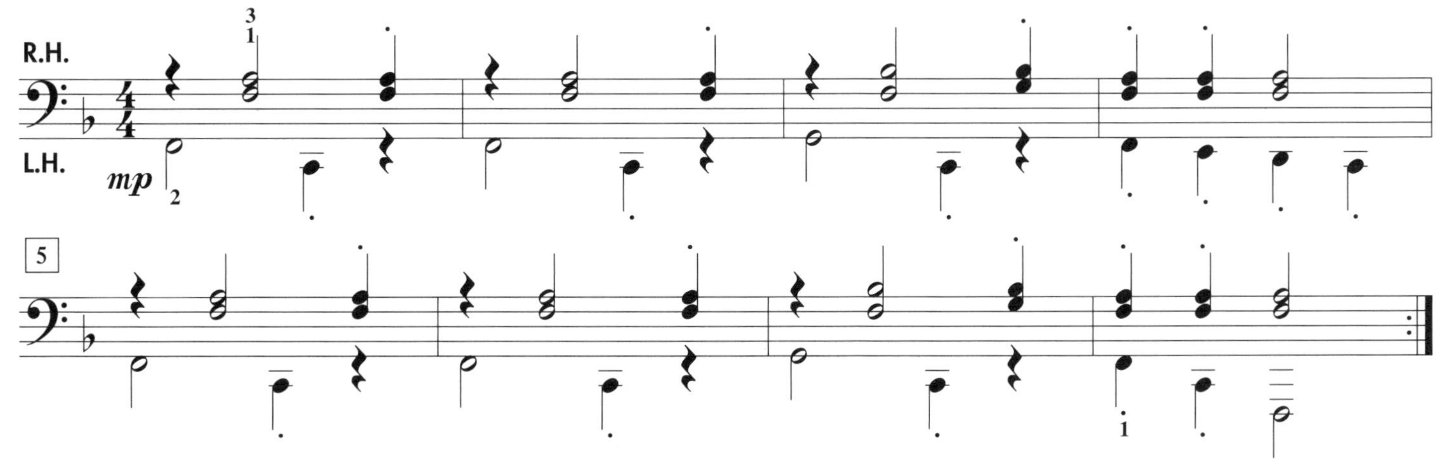
R.H.
L.H.
mp
5

G on the Keyboard

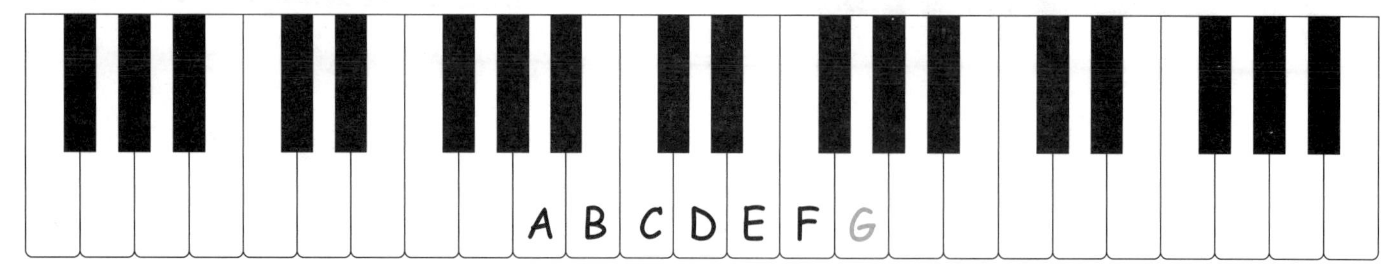
A B C D E F G
3 2 1 1 2 3 4 5
Left Hand Right Hand

Remember that hand positions are just guides. When you are comfortable with the pieces in this unit, explore using different fingers.

G on the Treble Staff

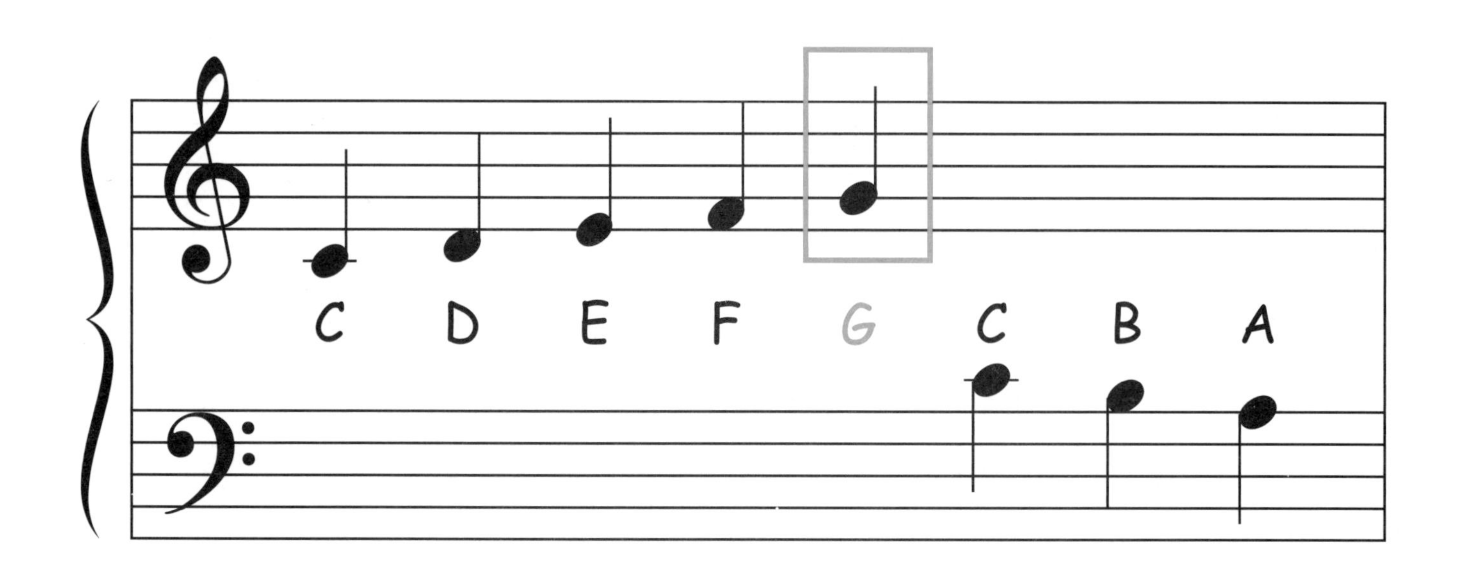
C D E F G C B A

Play the example below, keeping your eyes on the music.

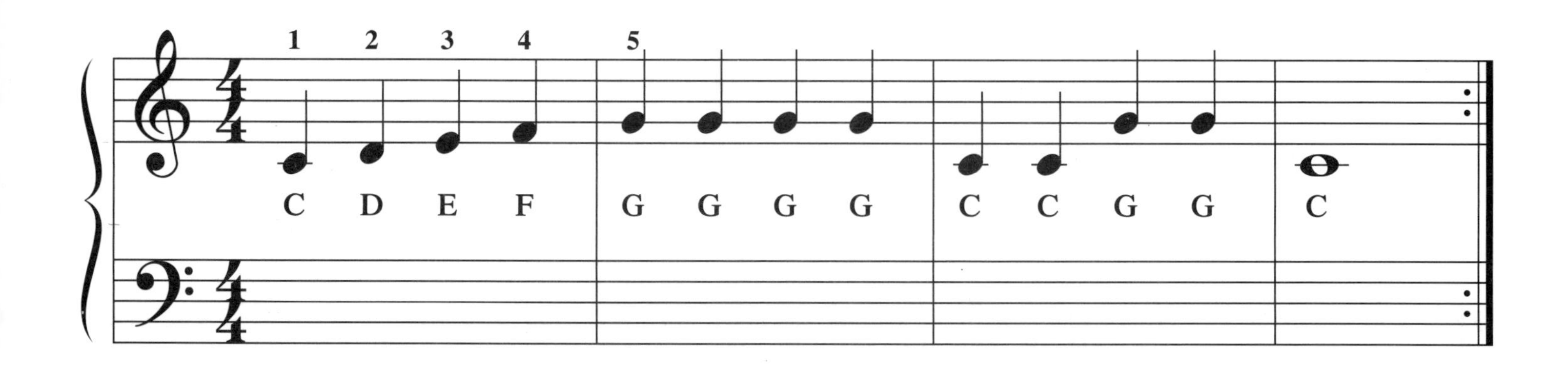
1 2 3 4 5
C D E F G G G G C C G G C

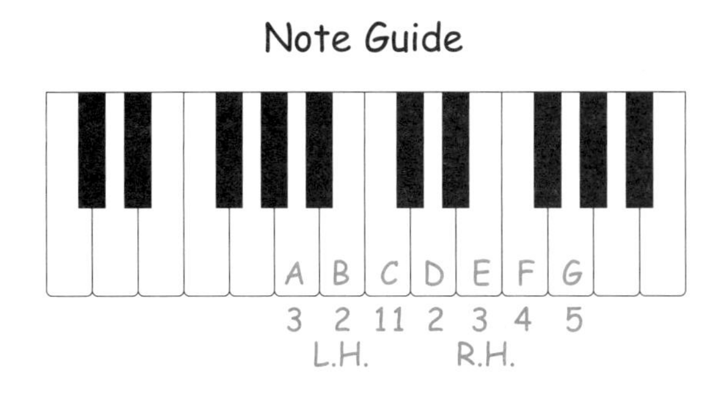
Note Guide
A B C D E F G
3 2 1 1 2 3 4 5
L.H. R.H.

Reading Books

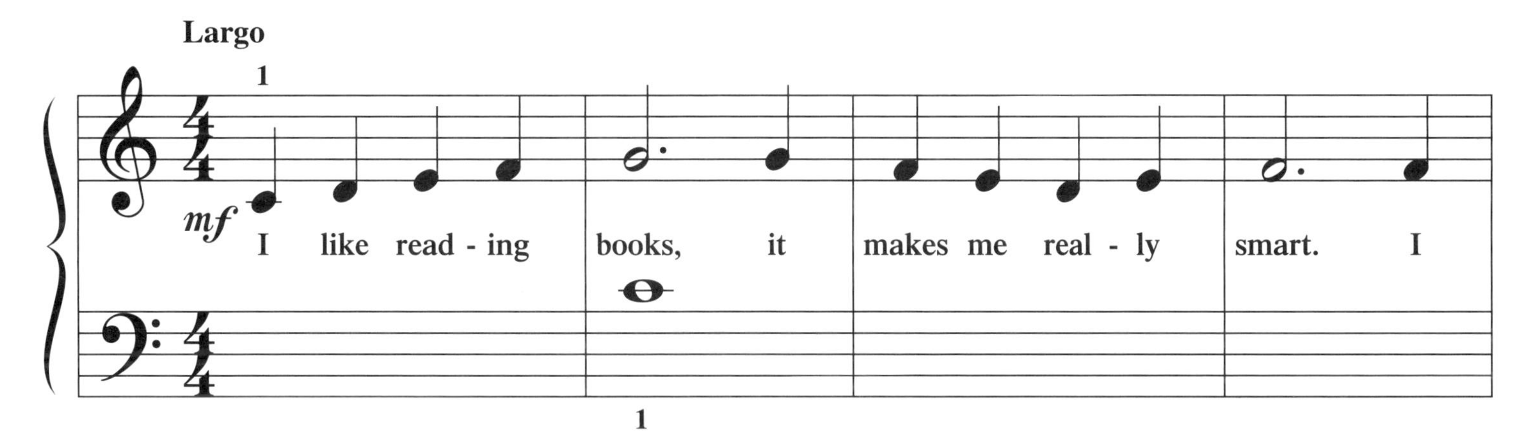
Largo
mf
I like read - ing books, it makes me real - ly smart. I

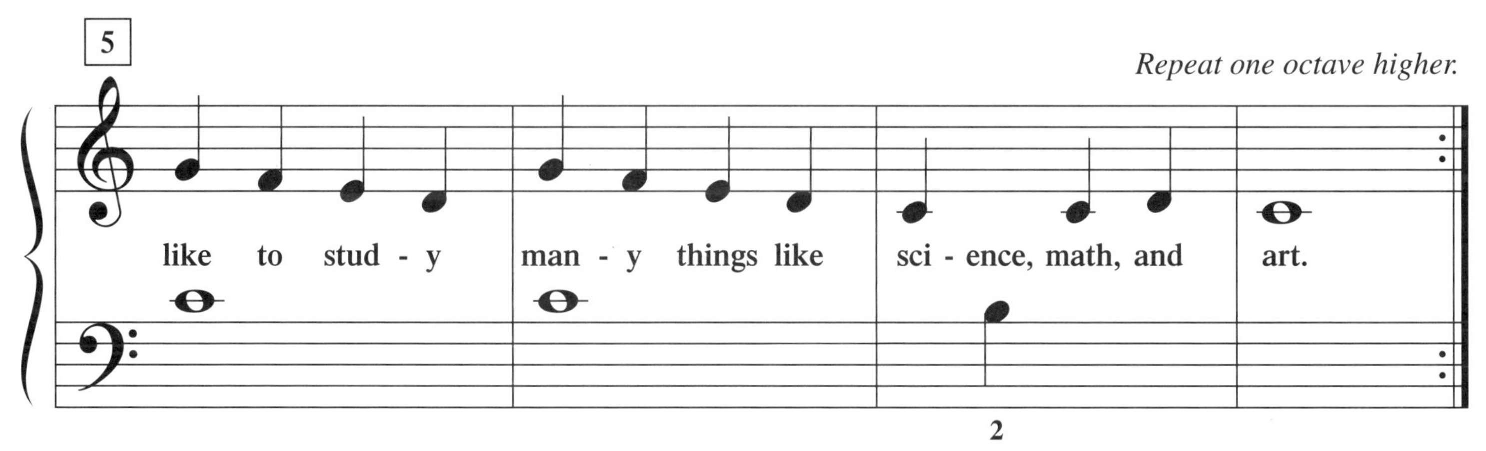
5
Repeat one octave higher.
like to stud - y man - y things like sci - ence, math, and art.

Teacher Duet: Student plays one octave higher.

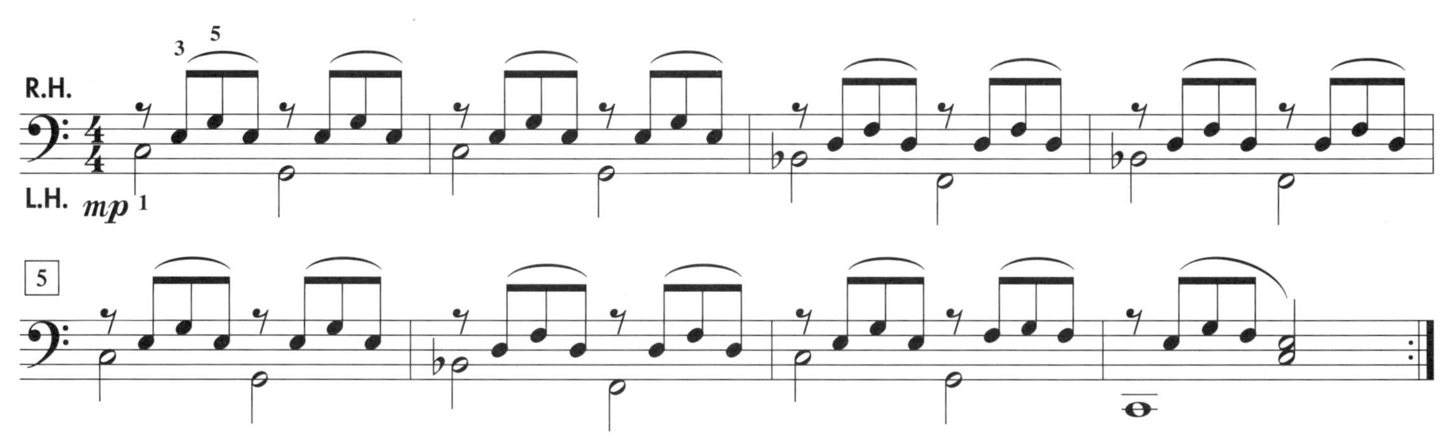
R.H.
L.H.
mp
5

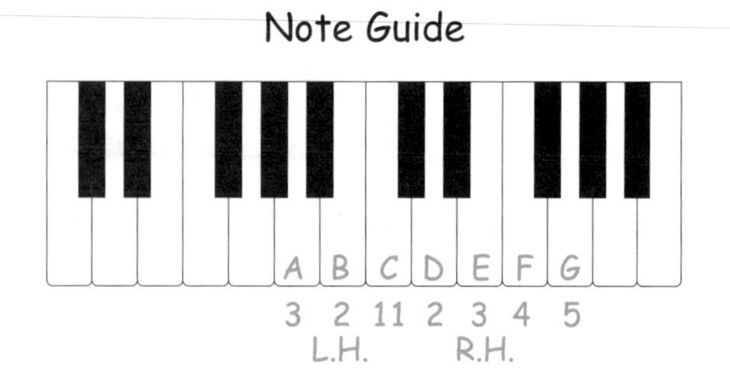
Note Guide
A B C D E F G
3 2 1 1 2 3 4 5
L.H. R.H.

Skipping Rocks

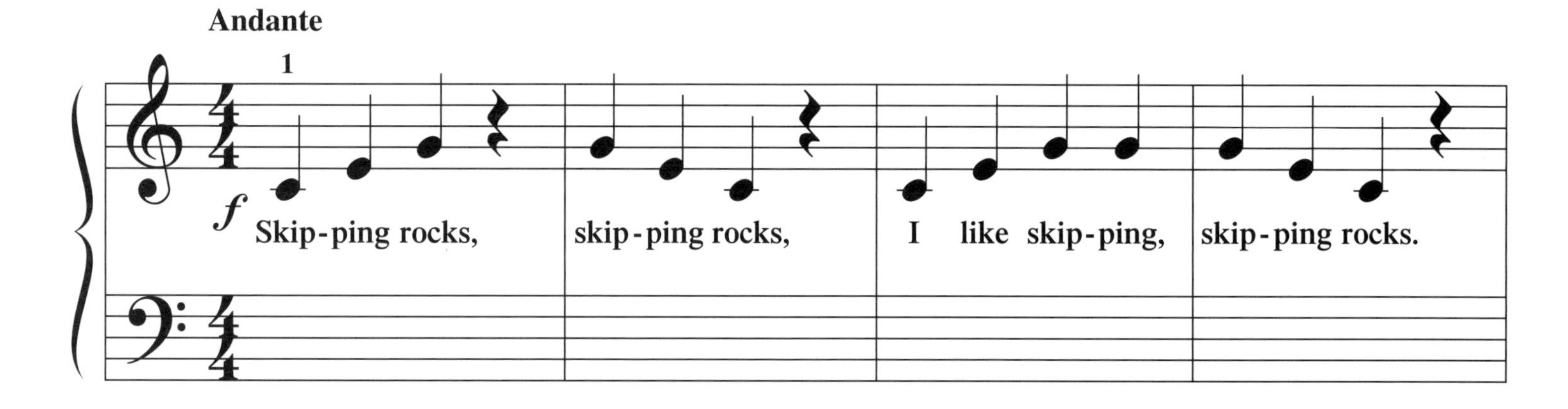
Andante
1
f
Skip-ping rocks, skip-ping rocks, I like skip-ping, skip-ping rocks.

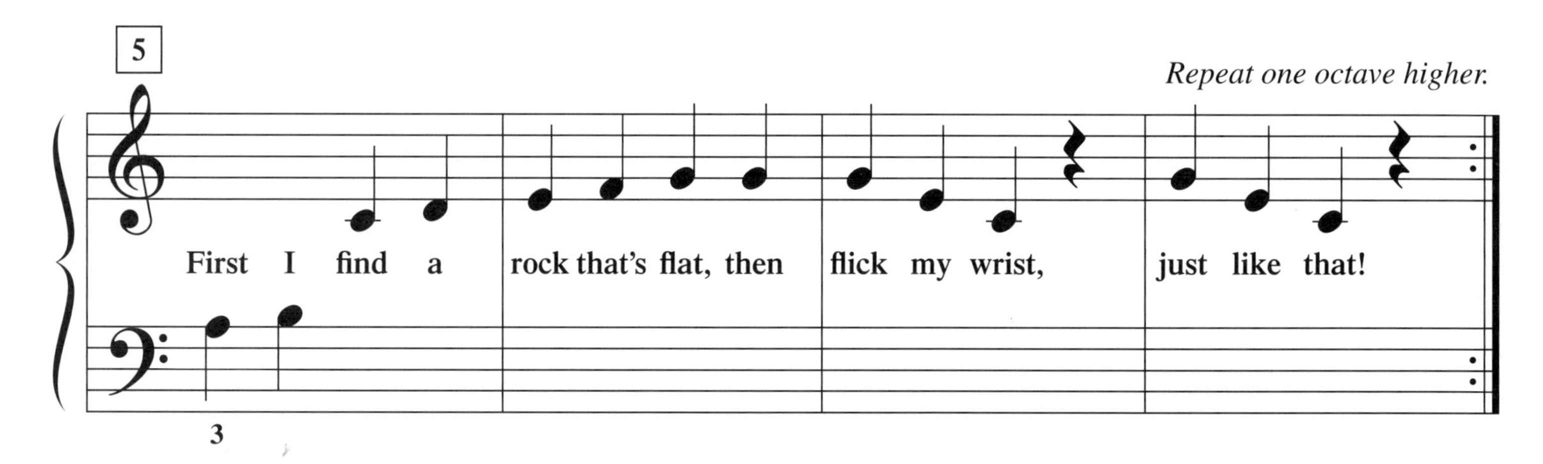
5
Repeat one octave higher.
First I find a rock that's flat, then flick my wrist, just like that!
3

After you are comfortable with this piece, try playing with **L.H.** finger **2** on **A.**

Teacher Duet: Student plays as written.

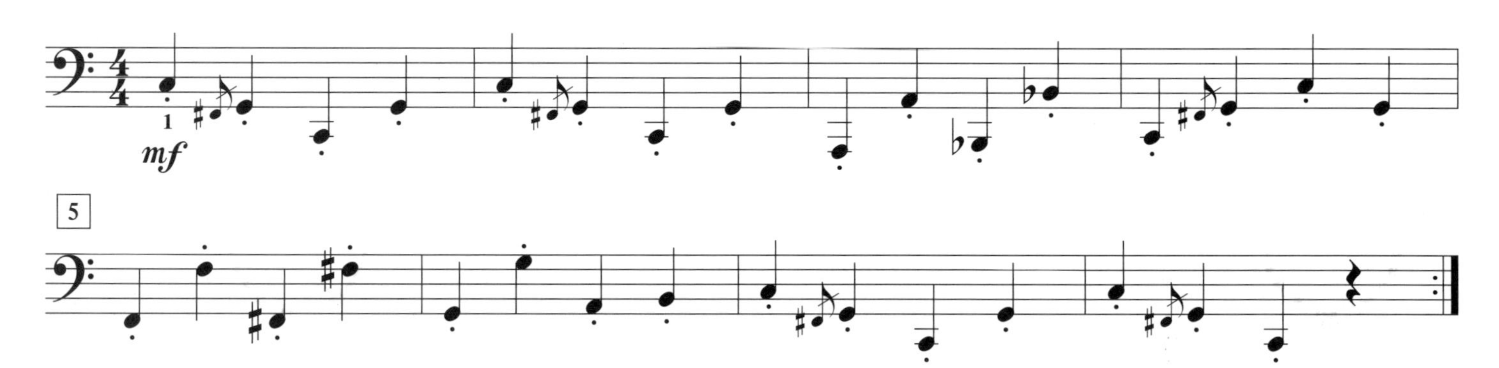
1
mf
5

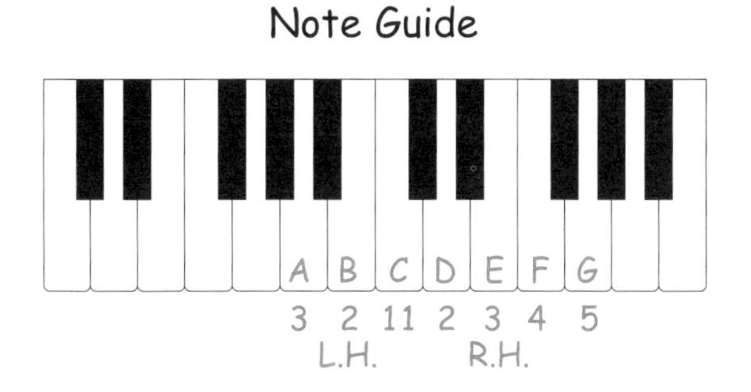
Note Guide
A B C D E F G
3 2 1 1 2 3 4 5
L.H. R.H.

SCHOOL BUS

Missing the Bus

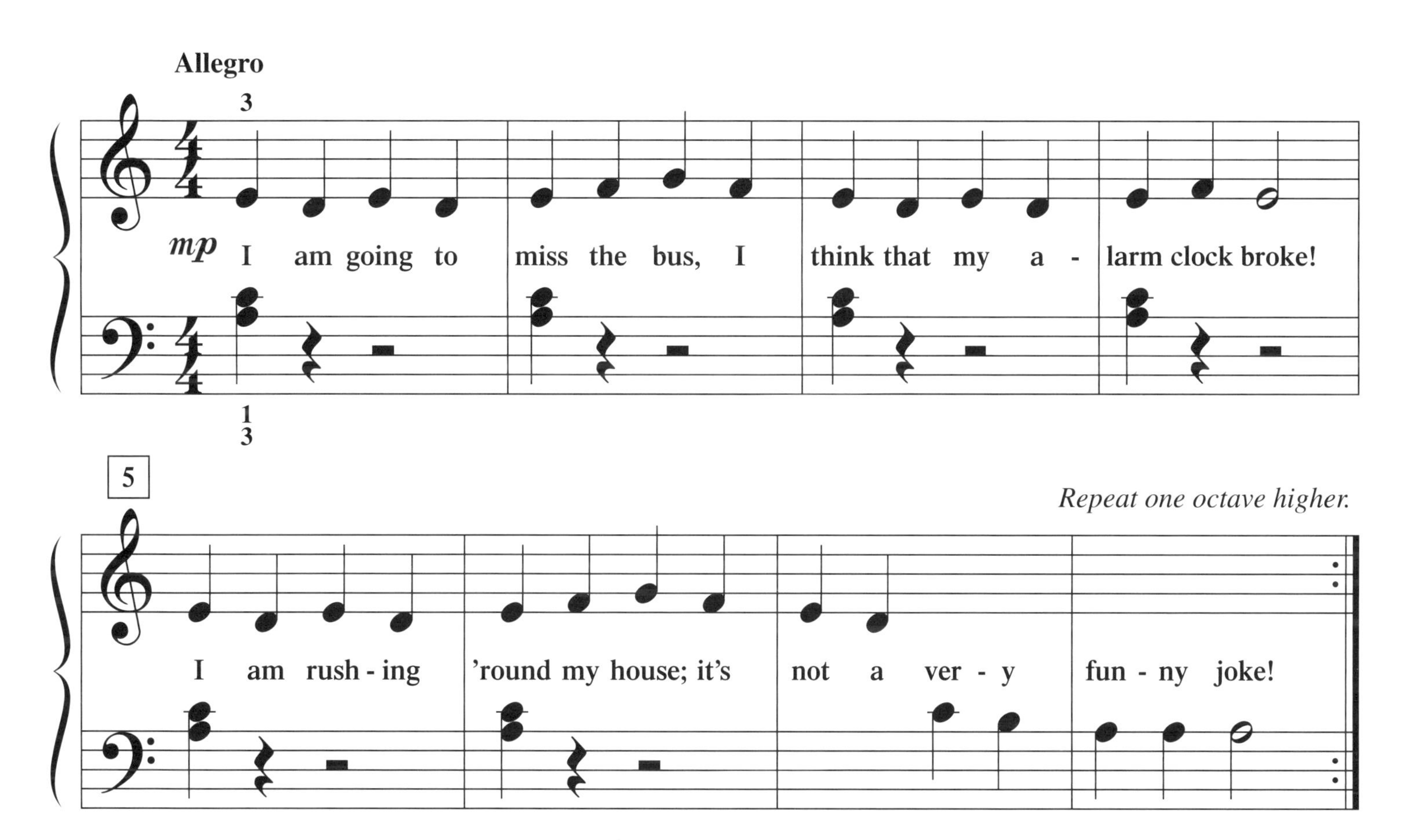
Allegro
mp
I am going to miss the bus, I think that my a - larm clock broke!
I am rush - ing 'round my house; it's not a ver - y fun - ny joke!
Repeat one octave higher.

After you are comfortable with this piece, try playing with **R.H.** finger **2** on **E.**

Teacher Duet: Student plays one octave higher.

R.H.
L.H.
p

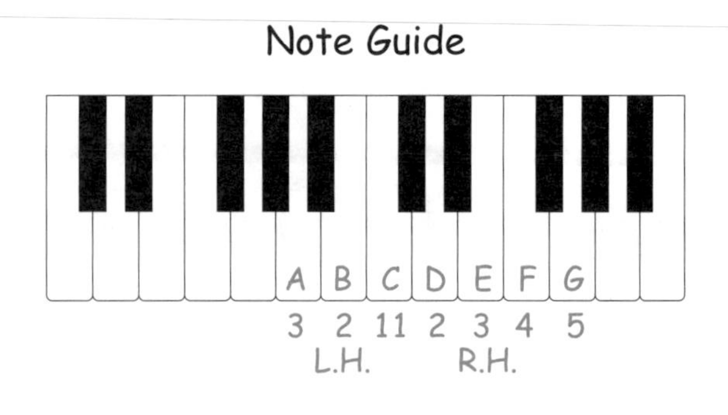
Note Guide
A B C D E F G
3 2 1 1 2 3 4 5
L.H. R.H.

Pillow Fight

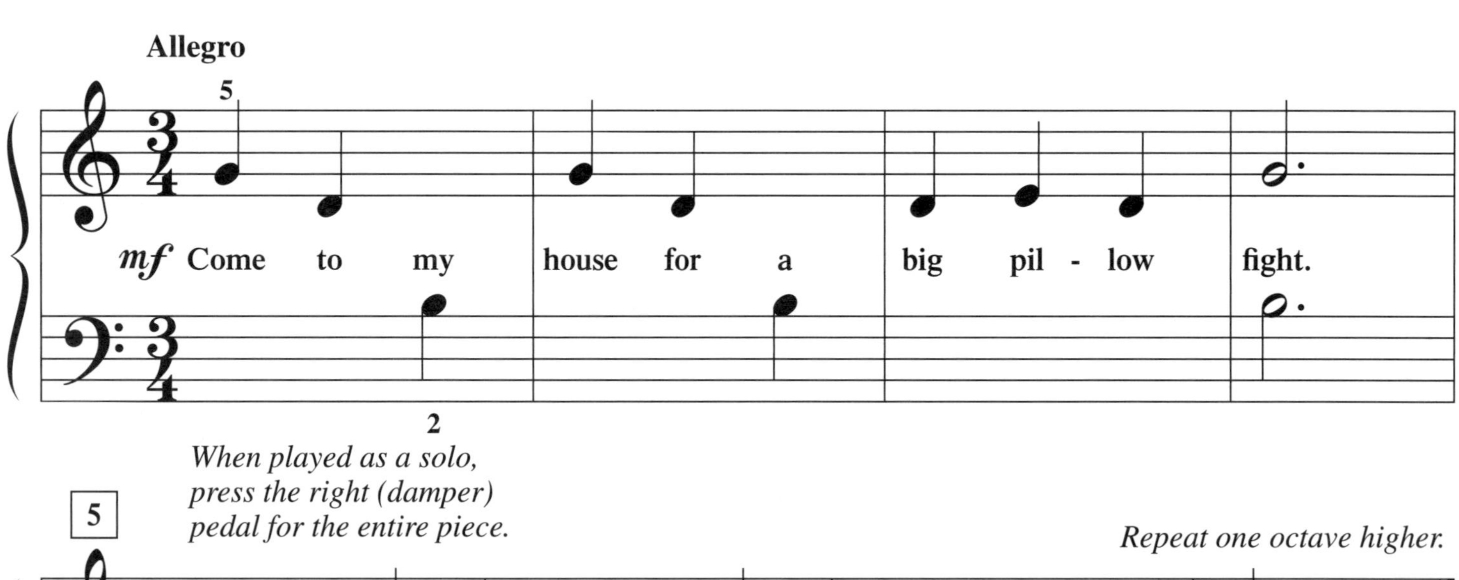
Allegro
mf
Come to my house for a big pil - low fight.

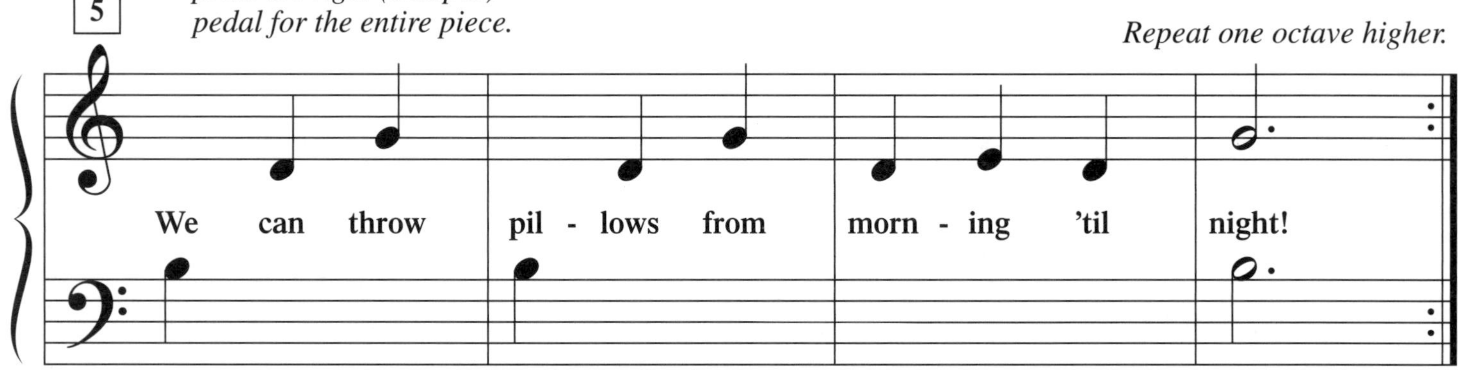
When played as a solo, press the right (damper) pedal for the entire piece.
Repeat one octave higher.
We can throw pil - lows from morn - ing 'til night!

After you are comfortable with this piece, try playing with **L.H.** finger **1** on **B.**

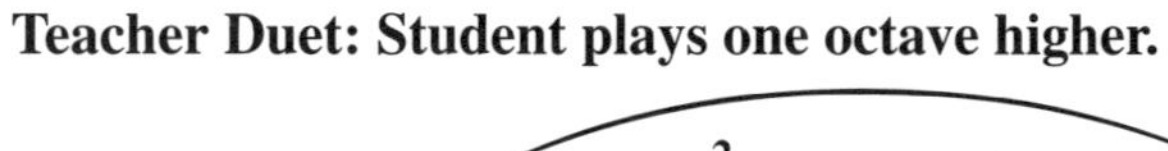
Teacher Duet: Student plays one octave higher.

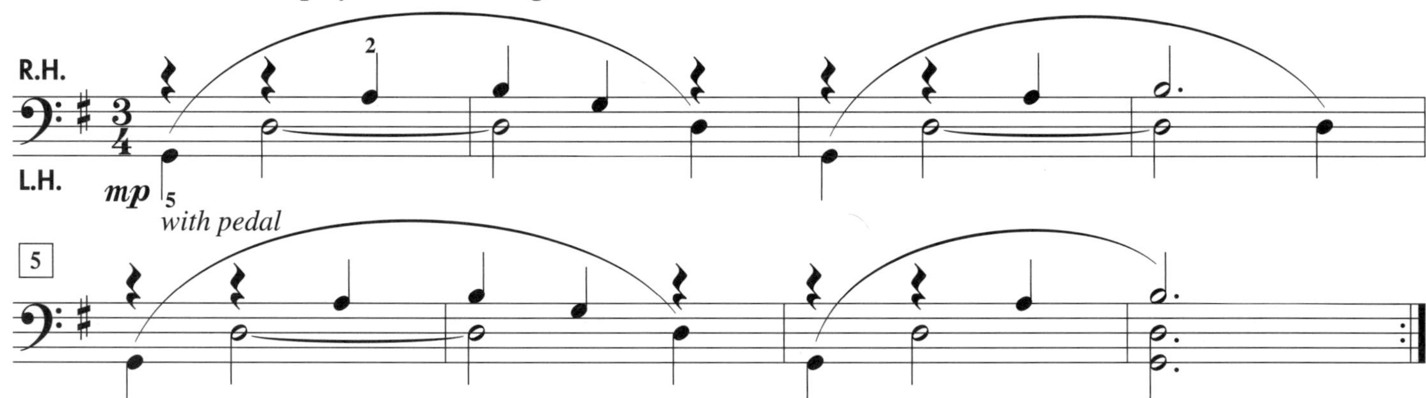
R.H.
L.H.
mp
with pedal

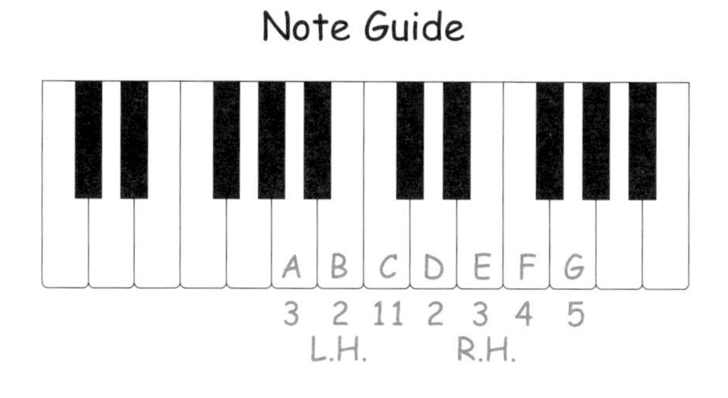
Note Guide
A B C D E F G
3 2 1 1 2 3 4 5
L.H. R.H.

Getting Dizzy

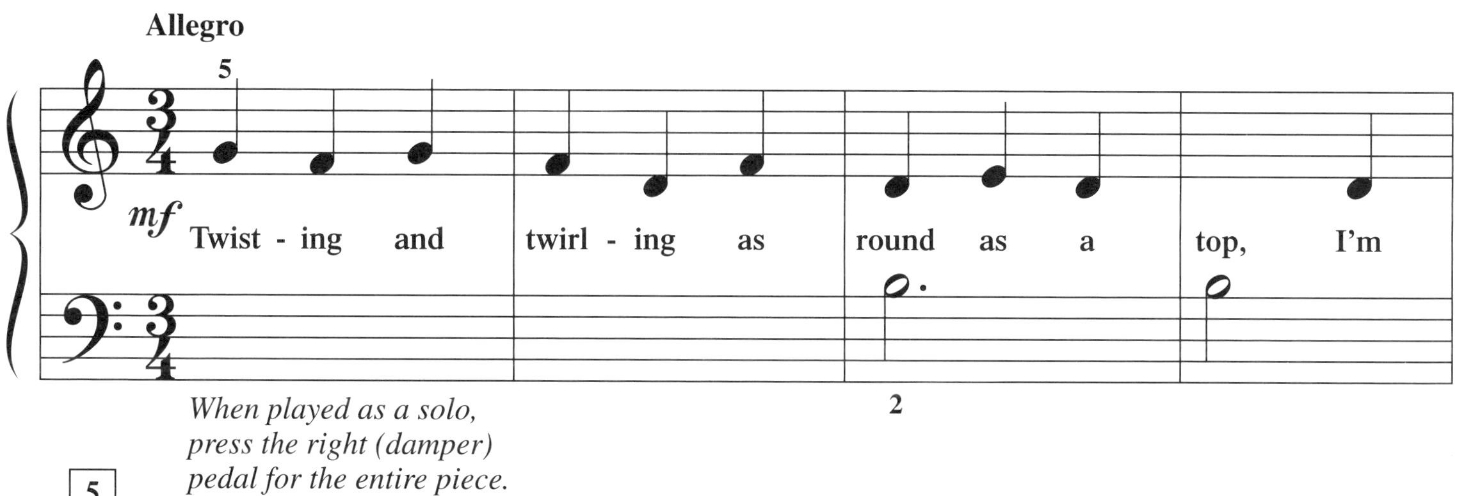
Allegro
mf
Twist - ing and twirl - ing as round as a top, I'm
When played as a solo, press the right (damper) pedal for the entire piece.

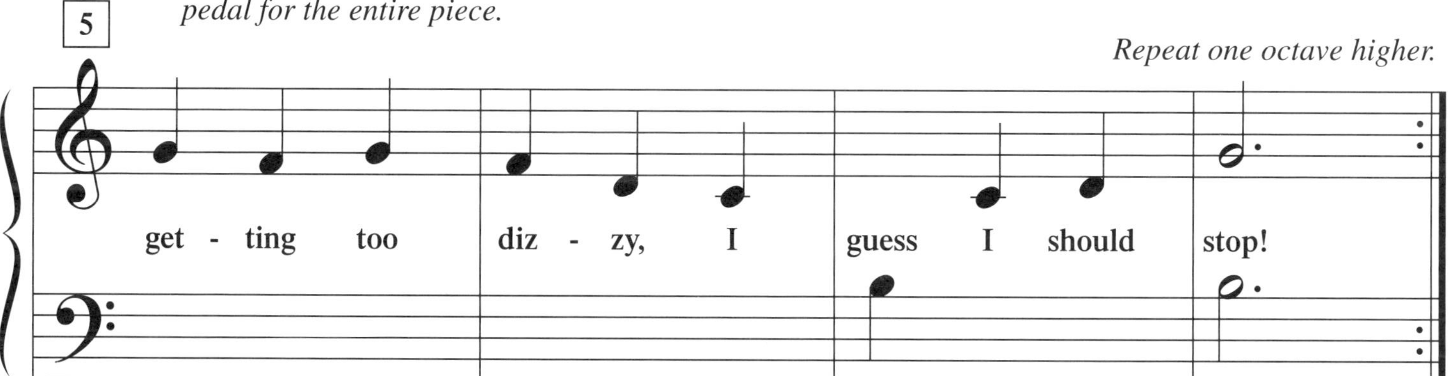
Repeat one octave higher.
get - ting too diz - zy, I guess I should stop!

After you are comfortable with this piece, try playing with **L.H.** finger **1** on **B.**

Teacher Duet: Student plays one octave higher.

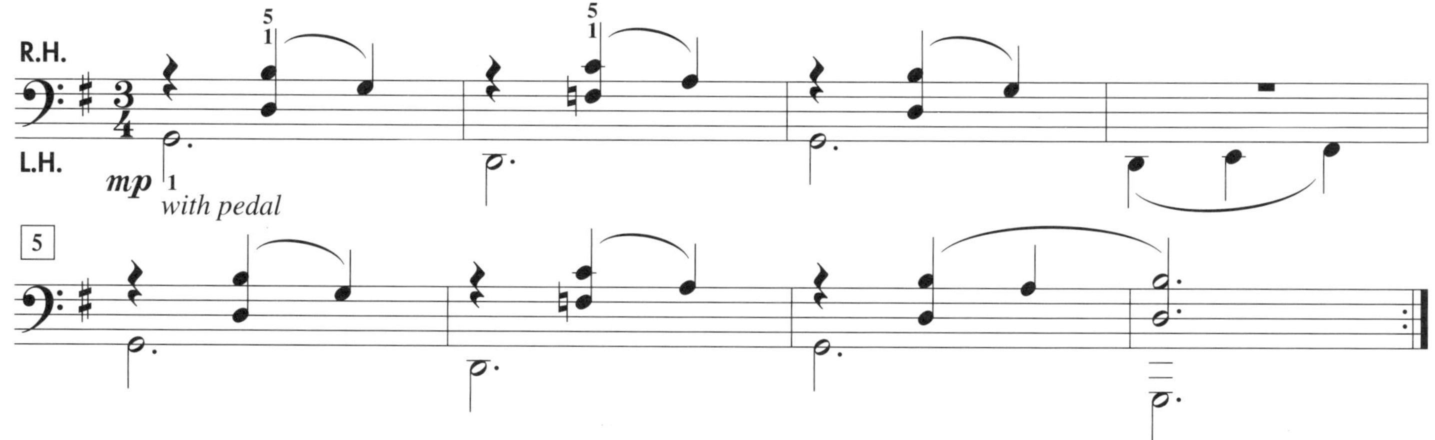
R.H.
L.H.
mp
with pedal

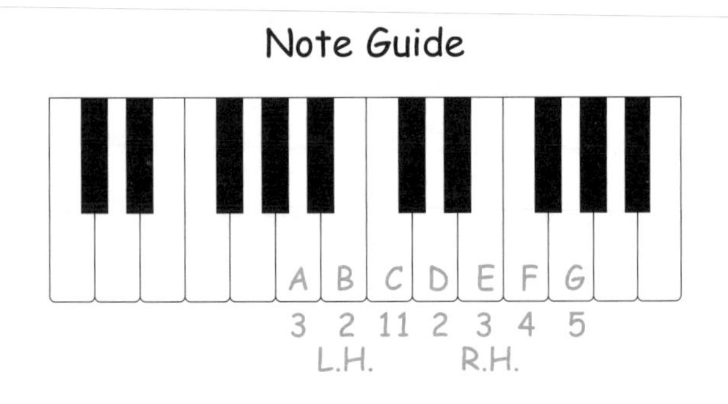
Note Guide
A B C D E F G
3 2 1 1 2 3 4 5
L.H. R.H.

Red Cabbage

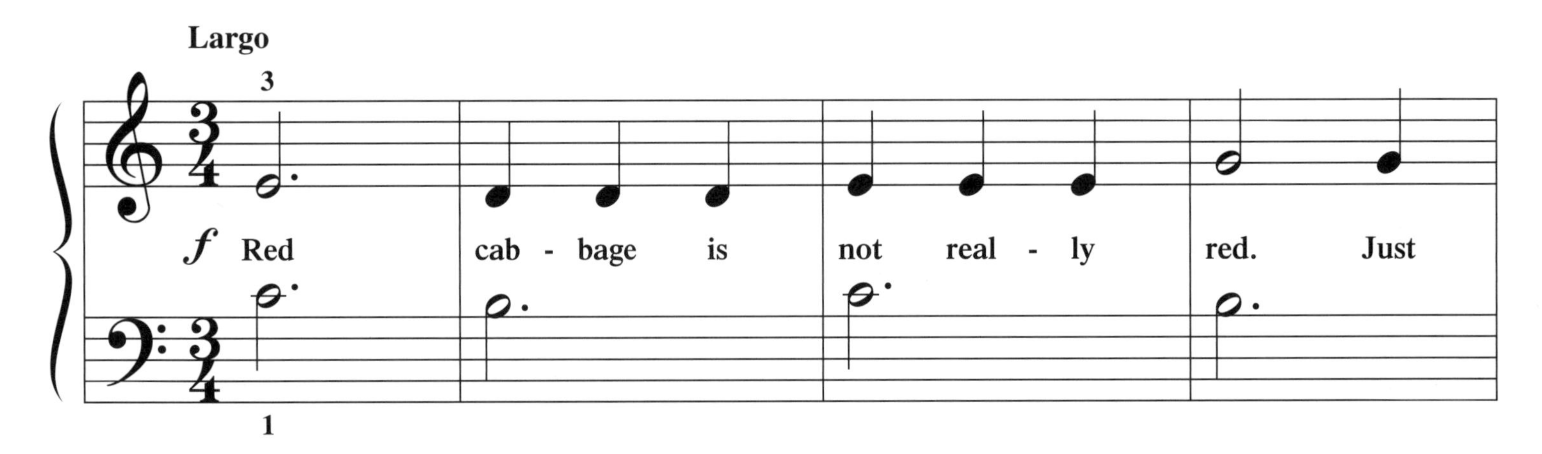
Largo
3
f Red cab - bage is not real - ly red. Just
1

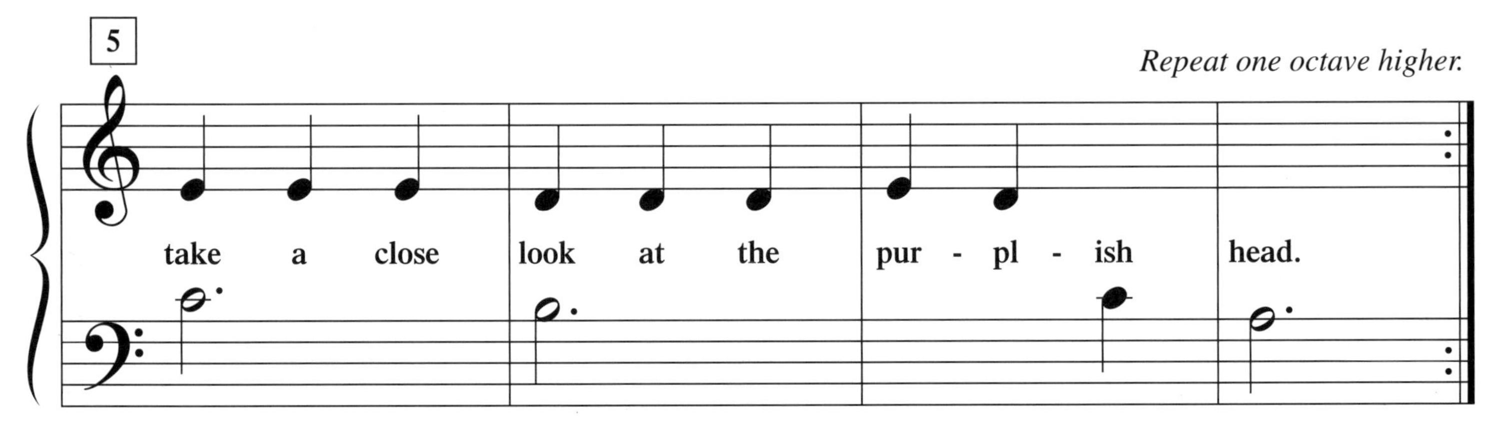
5
Repeat one octave higher.
take a close look at the pur - pl - ish head.

After you are comfortable with this piece, try playing with **R.H.** finger **2** on **E.**

Teacher Duet: Student plays one octave higher.

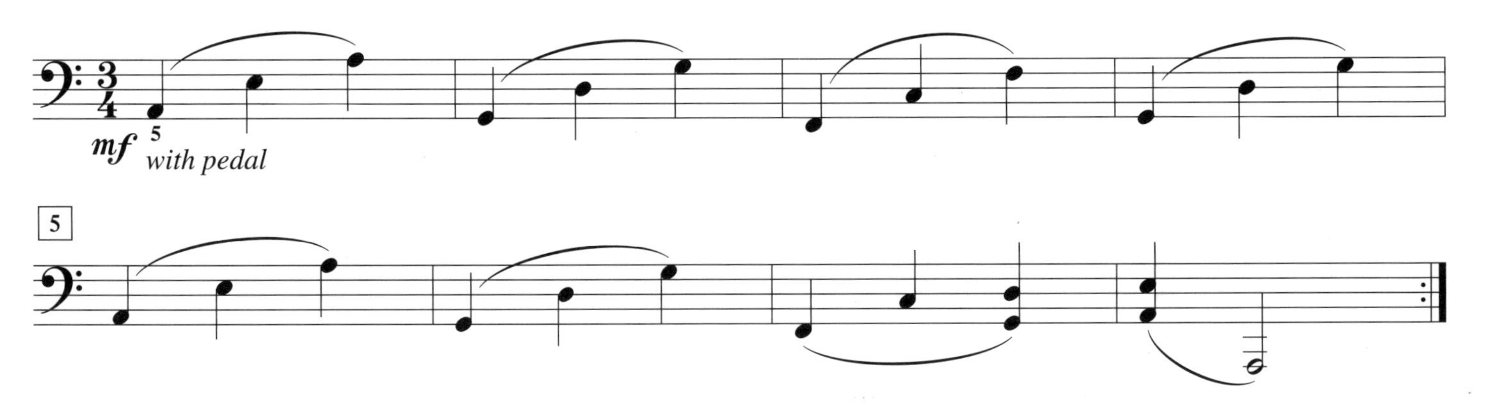
mf
5
with pedal
5

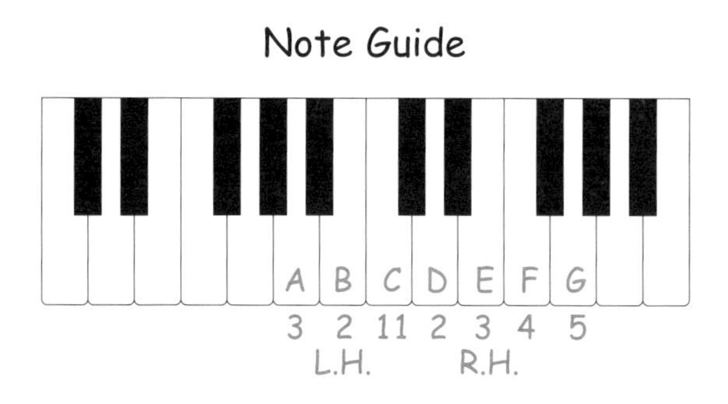
Note Guide
A B C D E F G
3 2 1 1 2 3 4 5
L.H. R.H.

Video Games

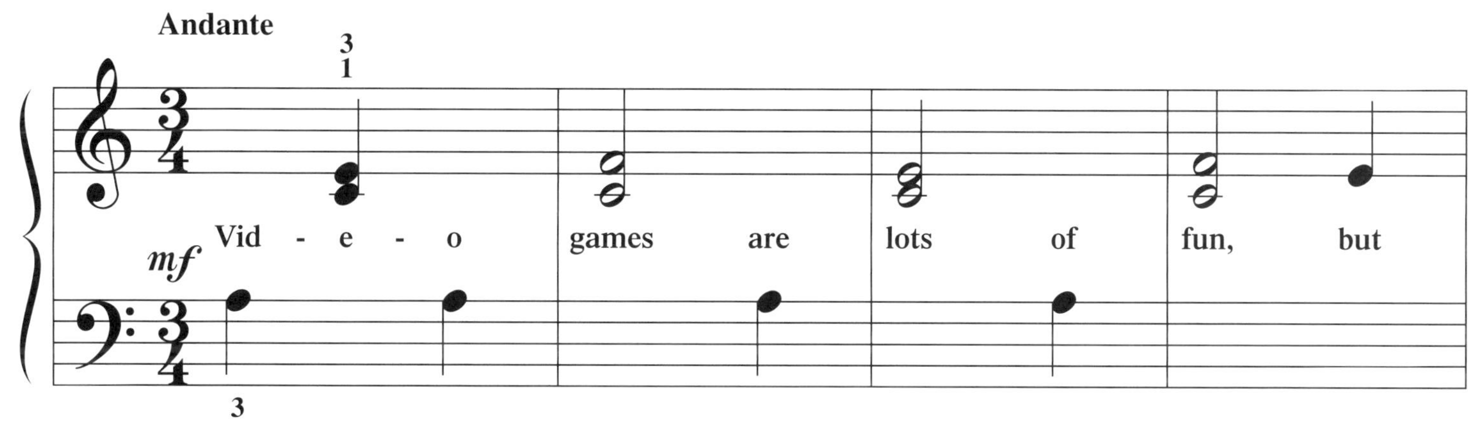
Andante
mf
Vid - e - o games are lots of fun, but

5
Repeat one octave higher.
I can - not play them 'til my chores are done.

After you are comfortable with this piece, try playing with **L.H.** finger **1** on **A.**

Teacher Duet: Student plays as written.

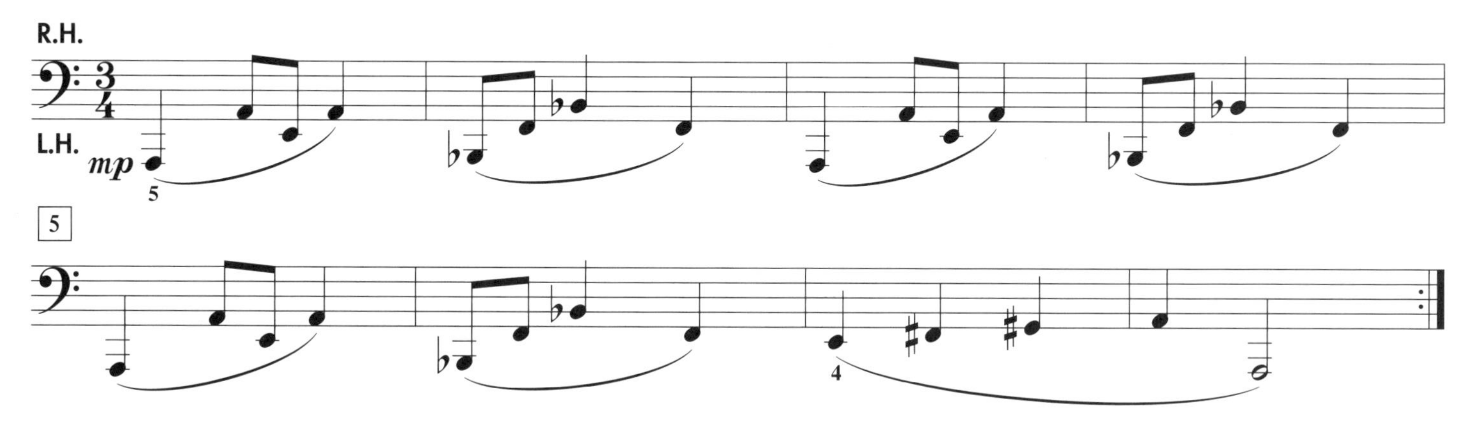
R.H.
L.H.
mp
5

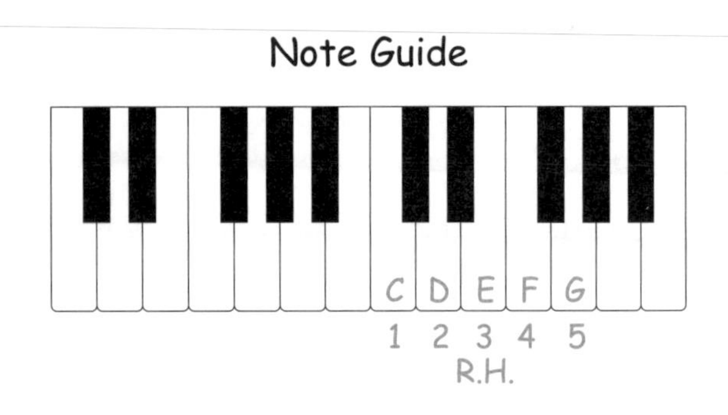
Note Guide
C D E F G
1 2 3 4 5
R.H.

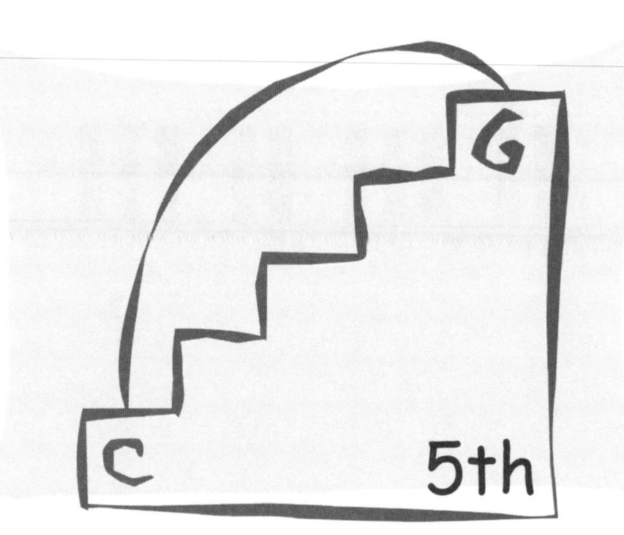
G
C
5th

Leap and Hop with C and G

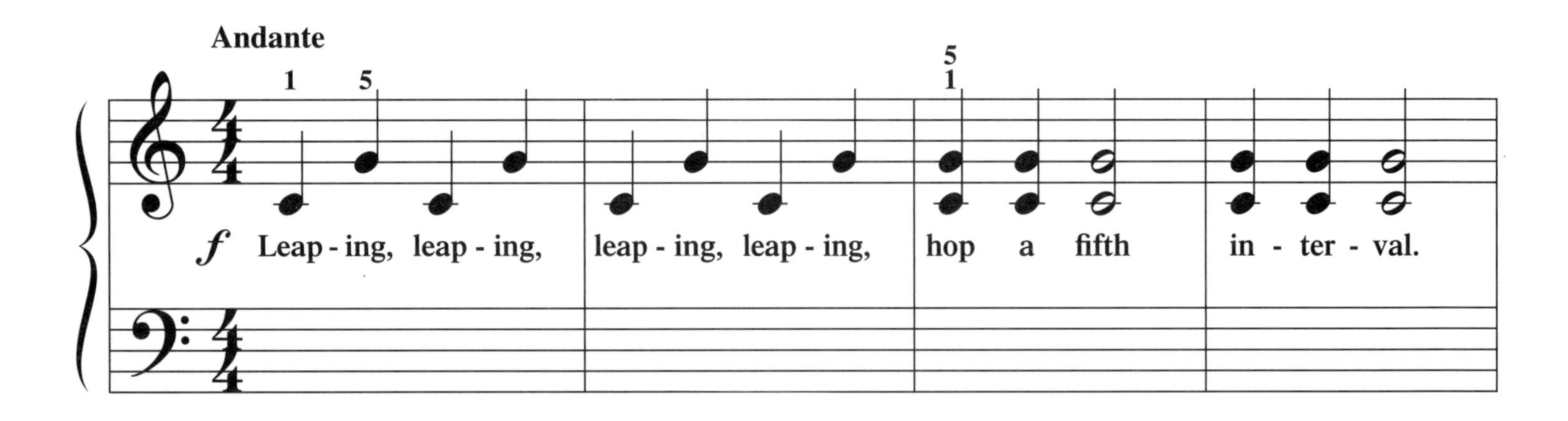
Andante
1 5
5
1
f Leap - ing, leap - ing, leap - ing, leap - ing, hop a fifth in - ter - val.

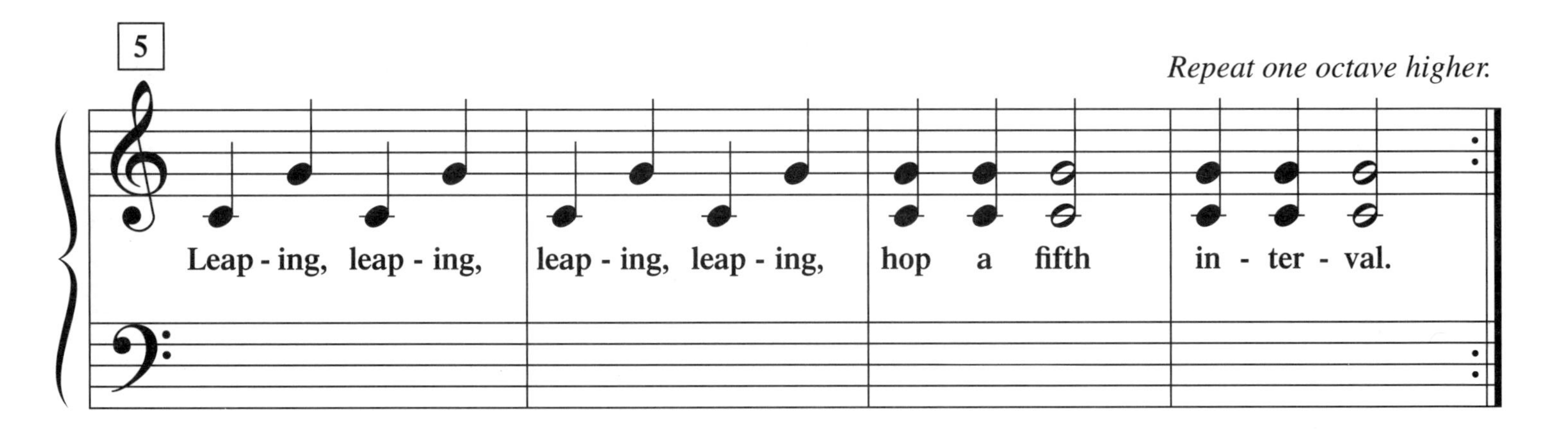
5
Repeat one octave higher.
Leap - ing, leap - ing, leap - ing, leap - ing, hop a fifth in - ter - val.

Teacher Duet: Student plays as written.

mf
1
5
5

Note Guide
A B C D E F G
3 2 1 1 2 3 4 5
L.H. R.H.

Pianos in a Marching Band

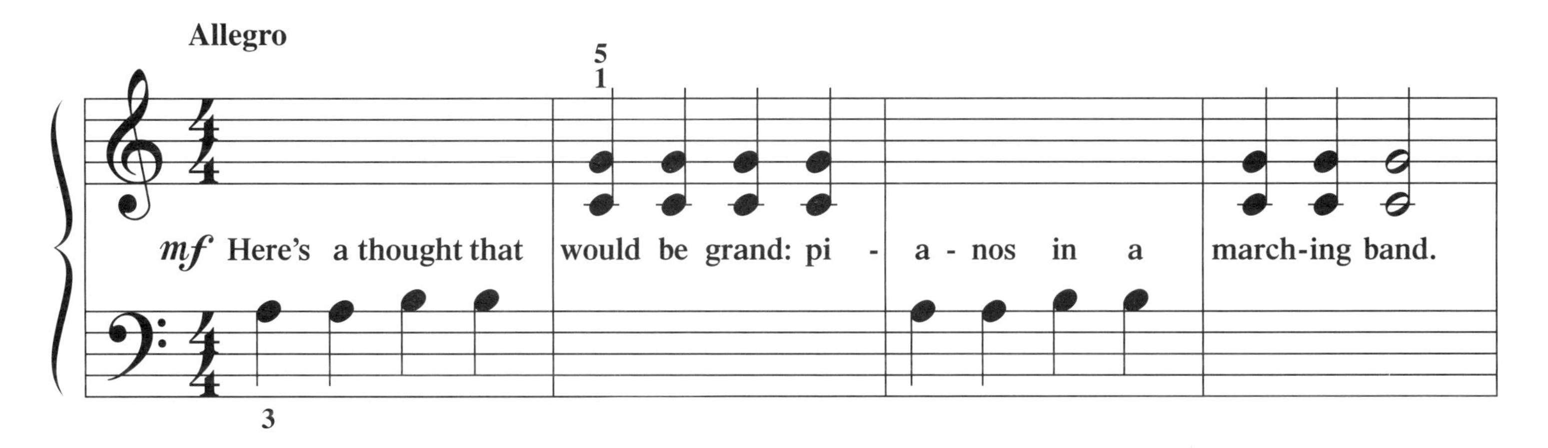
Allegro
mf Here's a thought that would be grand: pi - a - nos in a march-ing band.

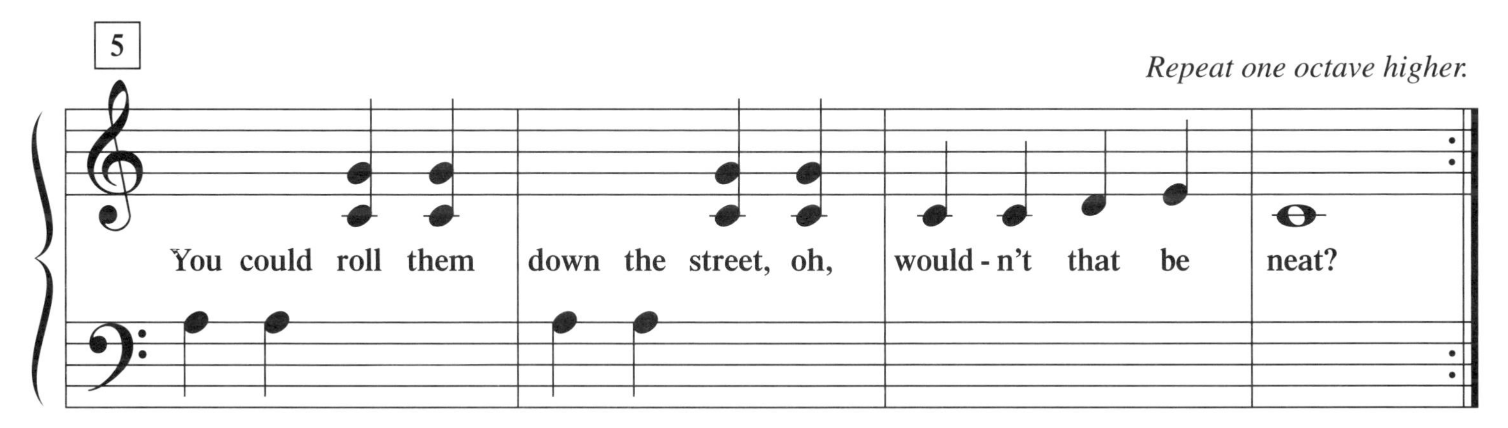
Repeat one octave higher.
You could roll them down the street, oh, would - n't that be neat?

After you are comfortable with this piece, try playing with **L.H.** finger **2** on **A.**

Teacher Duet: Student plays as written.

mp

Unit 7 Another G on the Keyboard

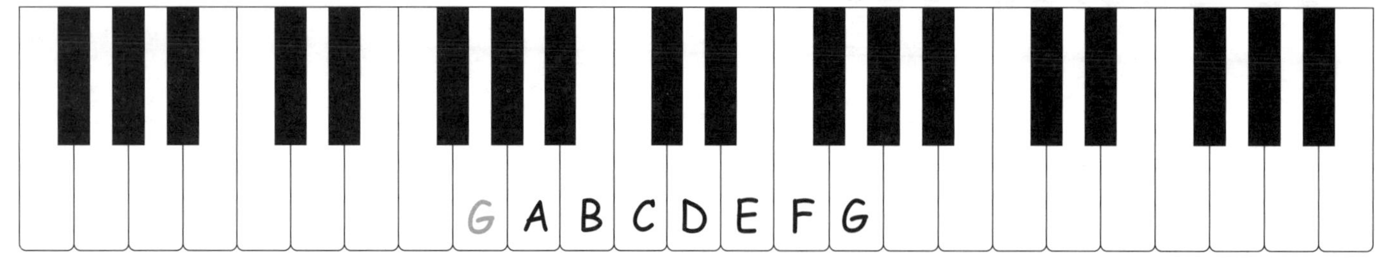
G A B C D E F G

4 3 2 1 1 2 3 4 5

Left Hand Right Hand

Remember that hand positions are just guides. When you are comfortable with your pieces in this unit, explore using different fingers.

G on the Bass Staff

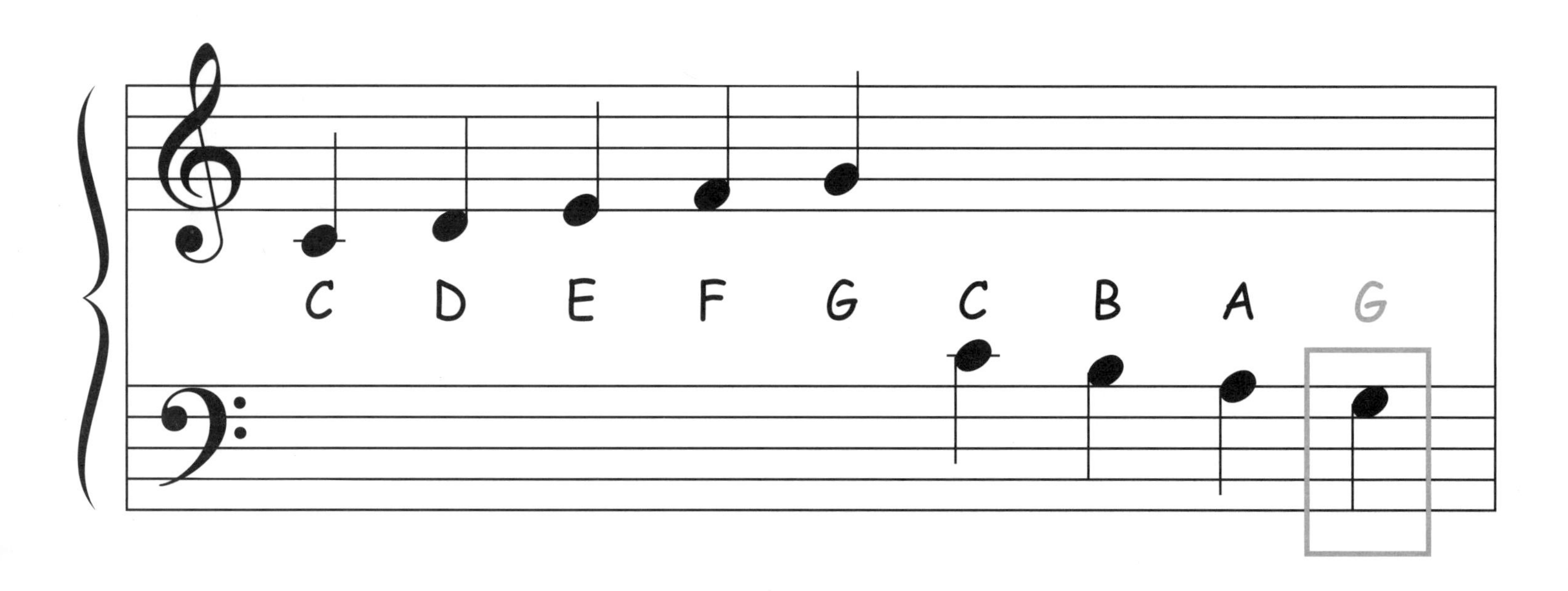
C D E F G C B A G

Play the example below, keeping your eyes on the music.

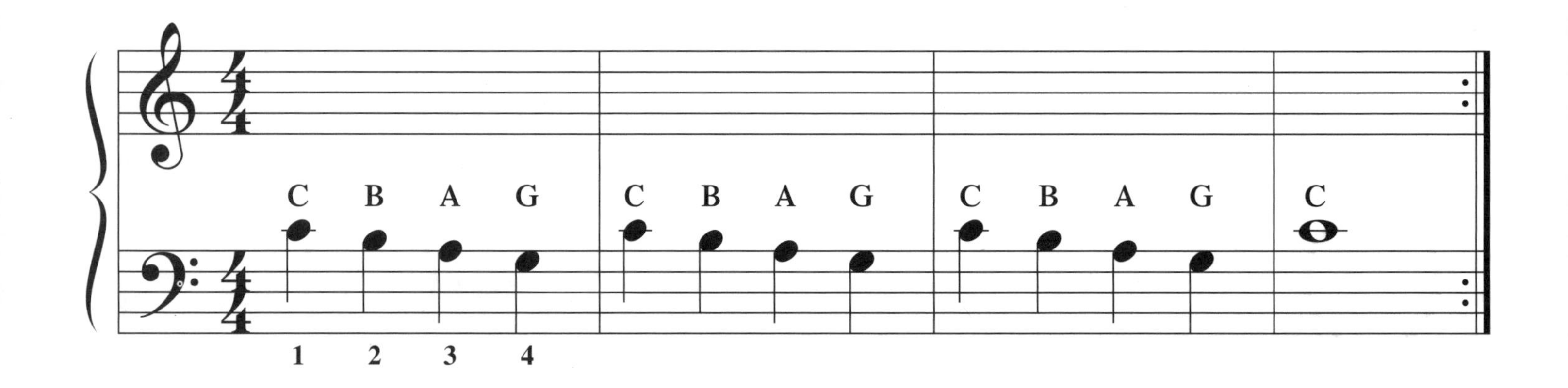
C B A G C B A G C B A G C
1 2 3 4

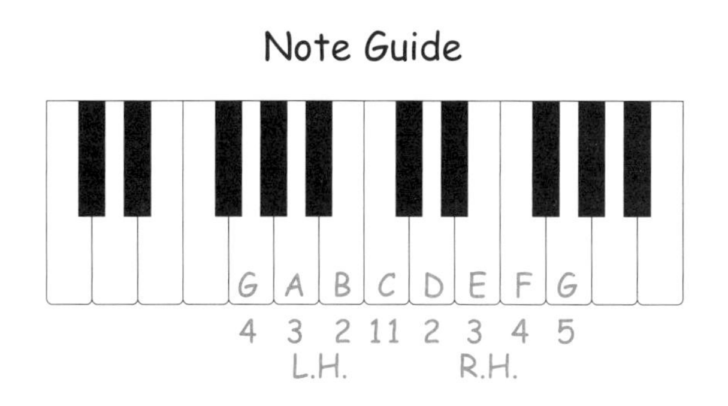
Note Guide
G A B C D E F G
4 3 2 1 1 2 3 4 5
L.H.
R.H.

PEANUT
BUTTER
Yuck!

Peanut Butter and Banana Sandwich

3/2/22

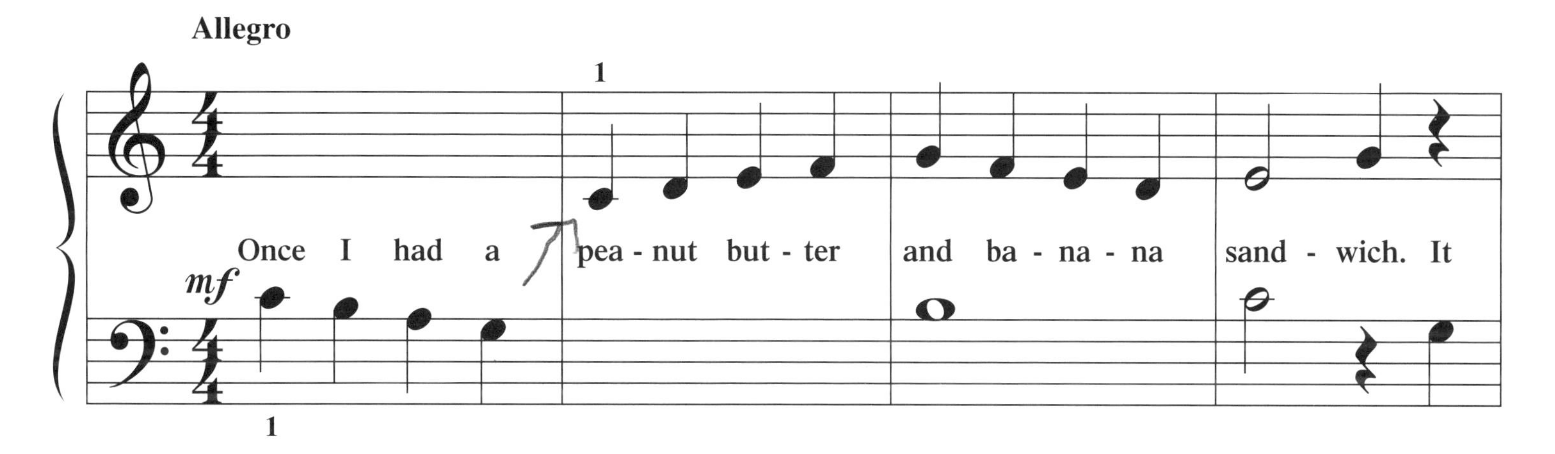
Allegro
1
Once I had a pea - nut but - ter and ba - na - na sand - wich. It
mf
1

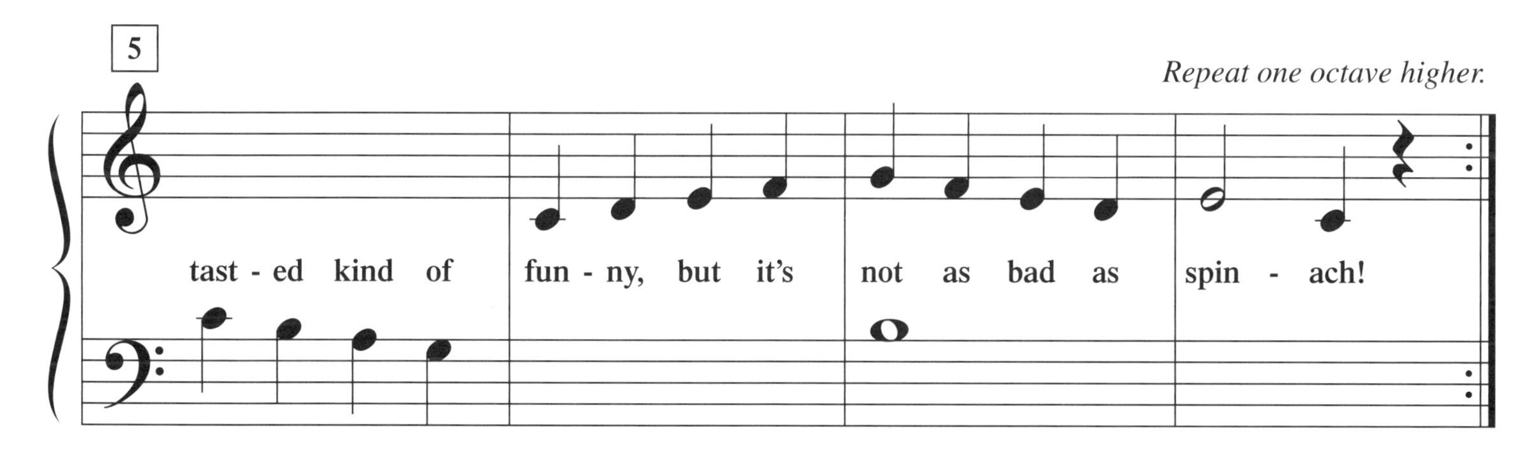
5
Repeat one octave higher.
tast - ed kind of fun - ny, but it's not as bad as spin - ach!

Teacher Duet: Student plays as written.

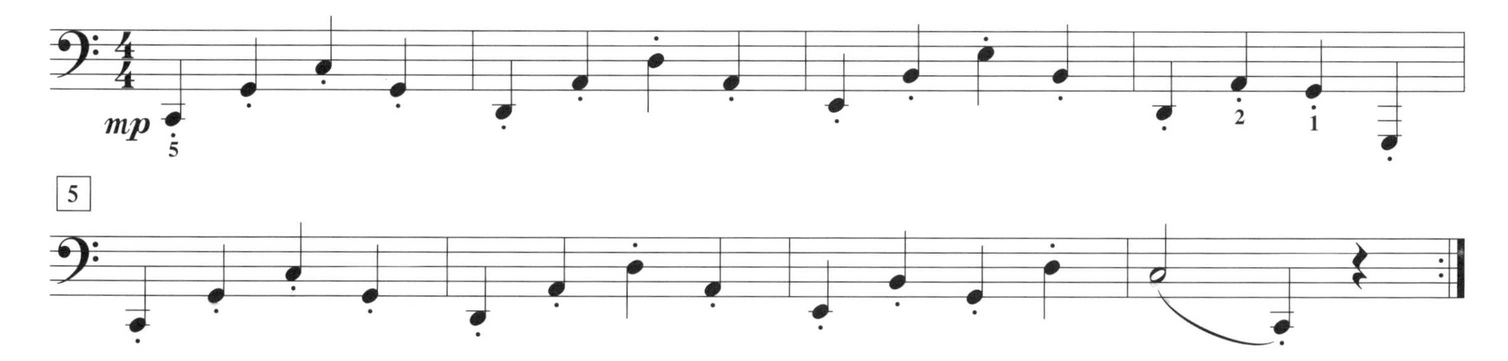
mp
5
2
1
5

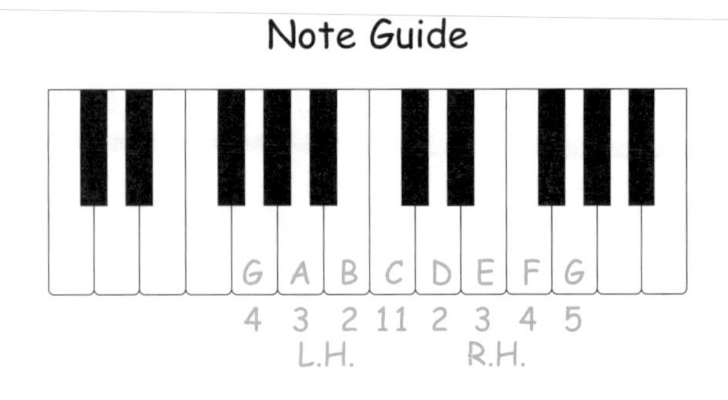
Note Guide
G A B C D E F G
4 3 2 1 1 2 3 4 5
L.H.
R.H.

Different Dogs

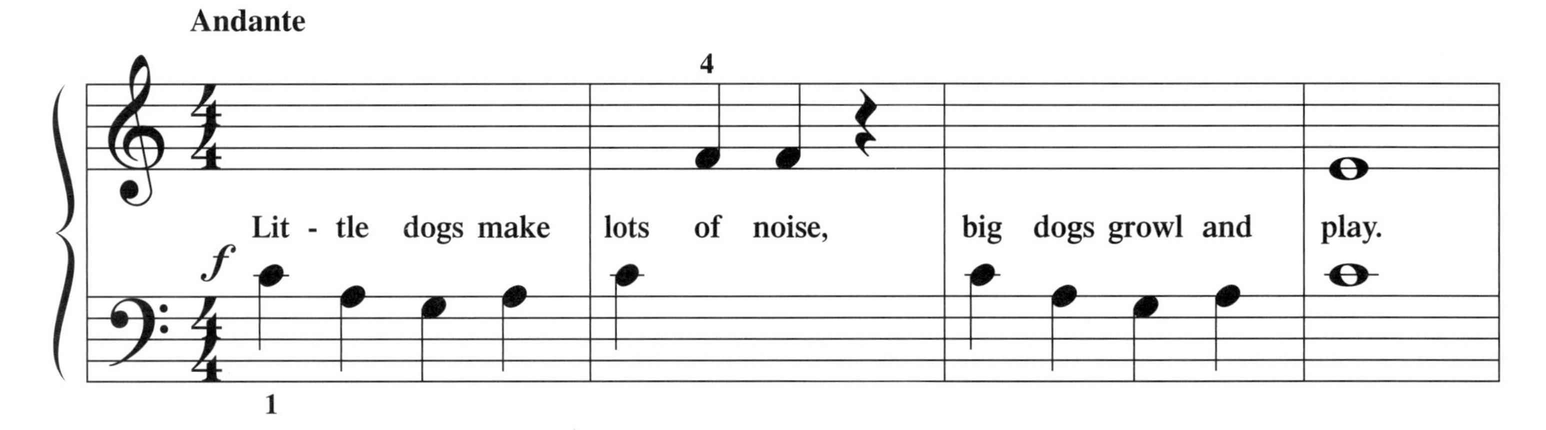
Andante
4
Lit - tle dogs make
lots of noise,
big dogs growl and
play.
f
1

5
Repeat one octave higher.
My dog is - n't
like the rest,
he just sleeps all
day!

After you are comfortable with this piece, try playing with **R.H.** finger **3** on **F.**

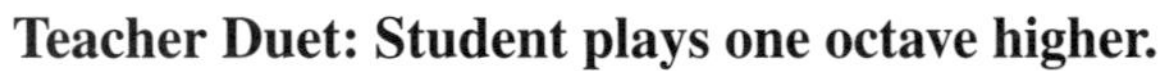
Teacher Duet: Student plays one octave higher.

R.H.
L.H.
mf
5
1
2
3
1
2
5

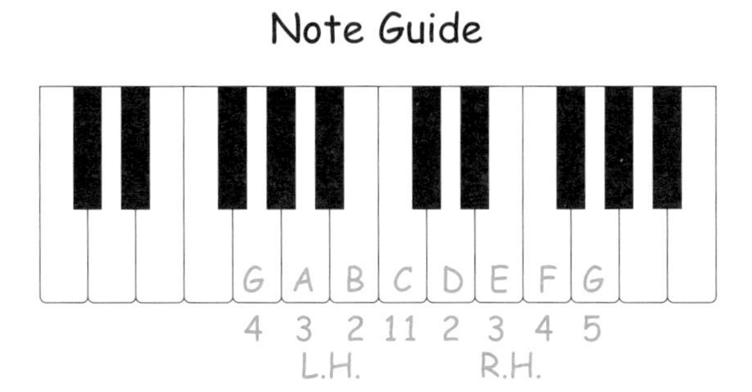
Note Guide
G A B C D E F G
4 3 2 1 1 2 3 4 5
L.H.
R.H.

Taking Your Photograph

Allegro
mf
Take a seat and sit real still, I'd like to take your pho - to - graph.

5
Repeat one octave higher.
Smile big and do not blink, and please, oh please, try not to laugh!

After you are comfortable with this piece, try playing with **R.H.** finger **1** on **D.**

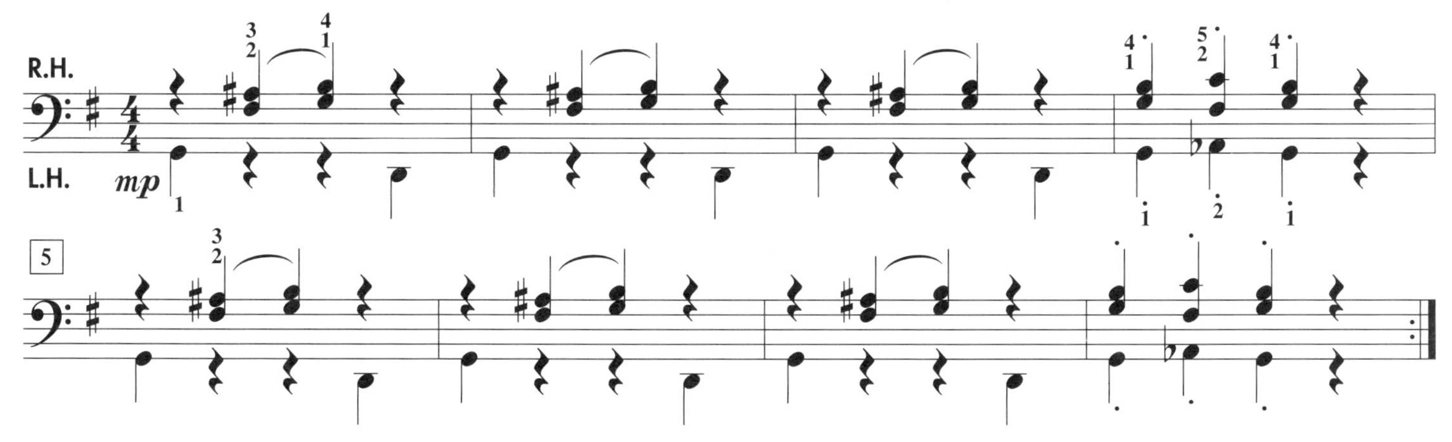
Teacher Duet: Student plays one octave higher.
R.H.
L.H.
mp
5

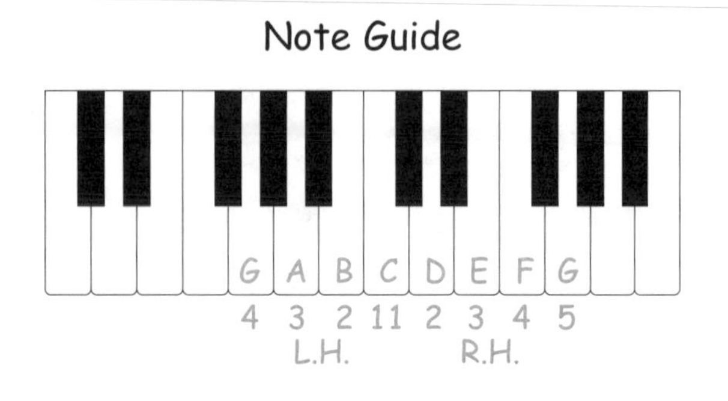
Note Guide
G A B C D E F G
4 3 2 1 1 2 3 4 5
L.H. R.H.

Beach Dreams

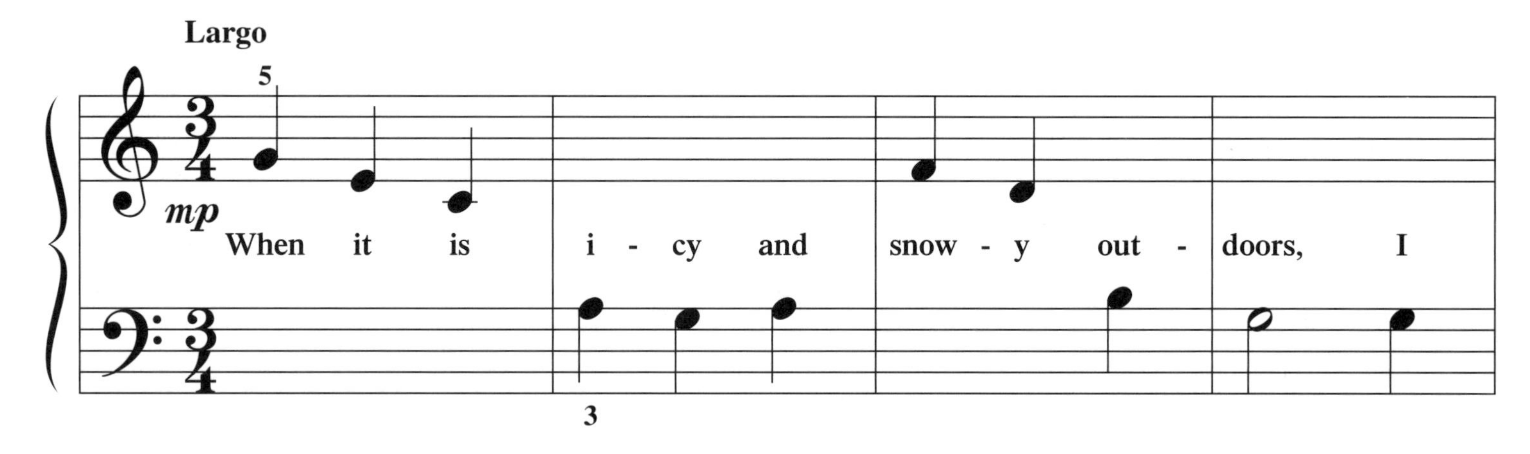
Largo
mp
When it is i - cy and snow - y out - doors, I

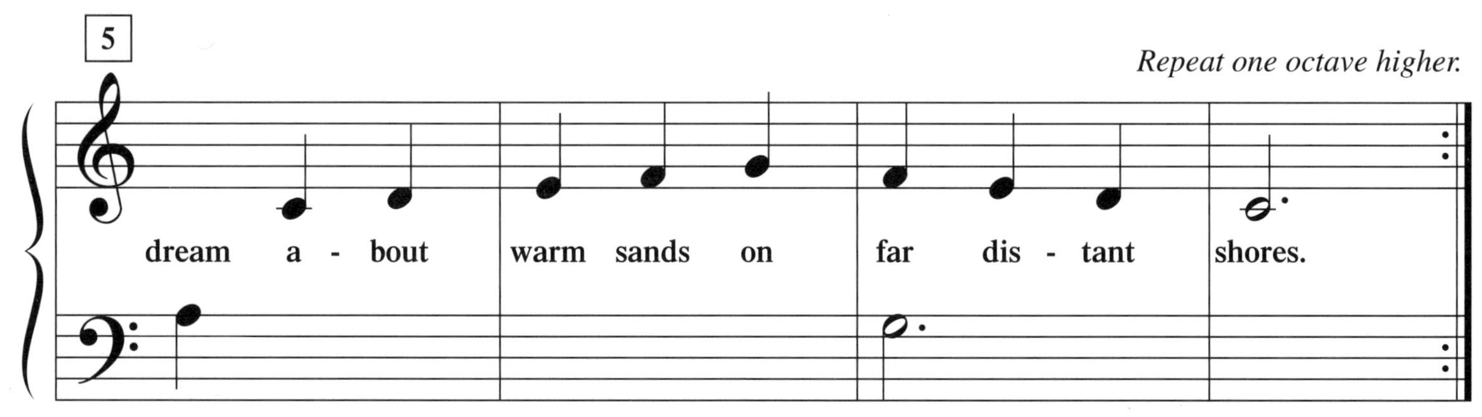
Repeat one octave higher.
dream a - bout warm sands on far dis - tant shores.

After you are comfortable with this piece, try playing with **L.H.** finger **2** on **A.**

Teacher Duet: Student plays one octave higher.

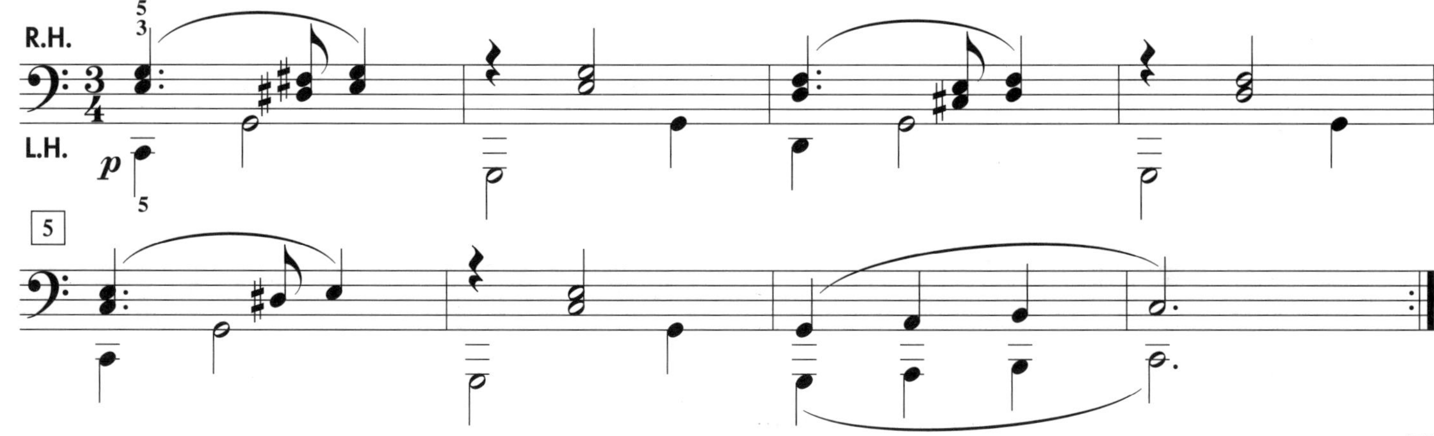
R.H.
L.H.
p

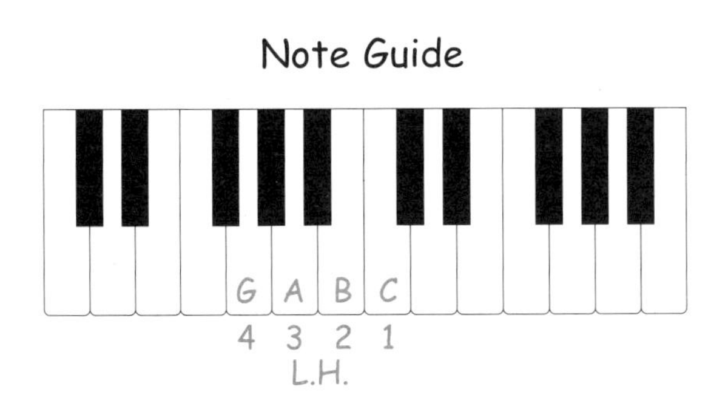
Note Guide
G A B C
4 3 2 1
L.H.

C
G
4th

Leap and Hop with C and G

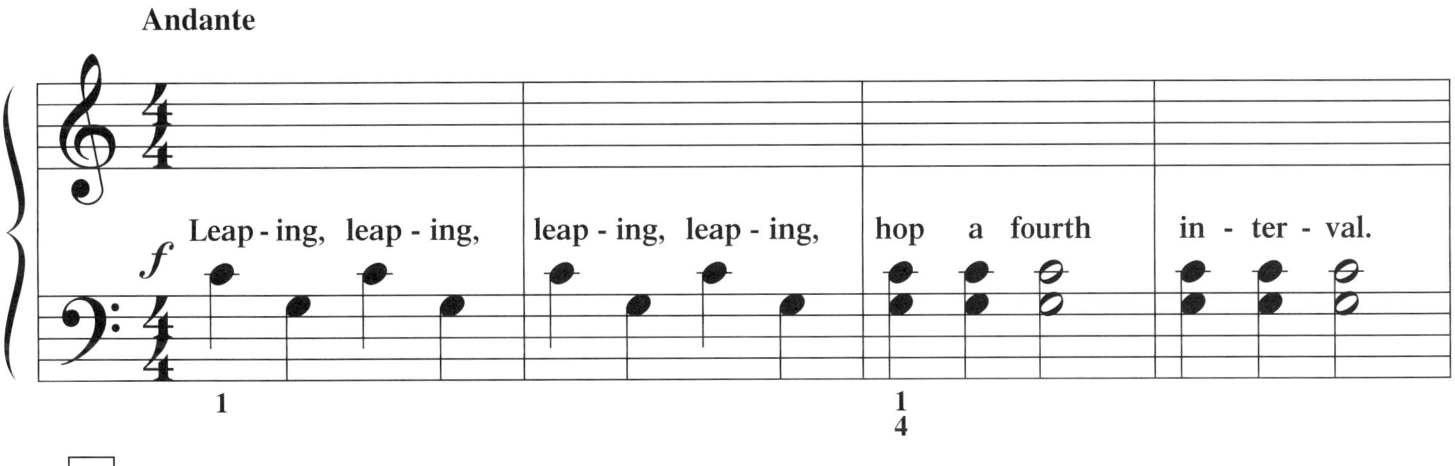
Andante
Leap - ing, leap - ing, leap - ing, leap - ing, hop a fourth in - ter - val.
f
1
1
4

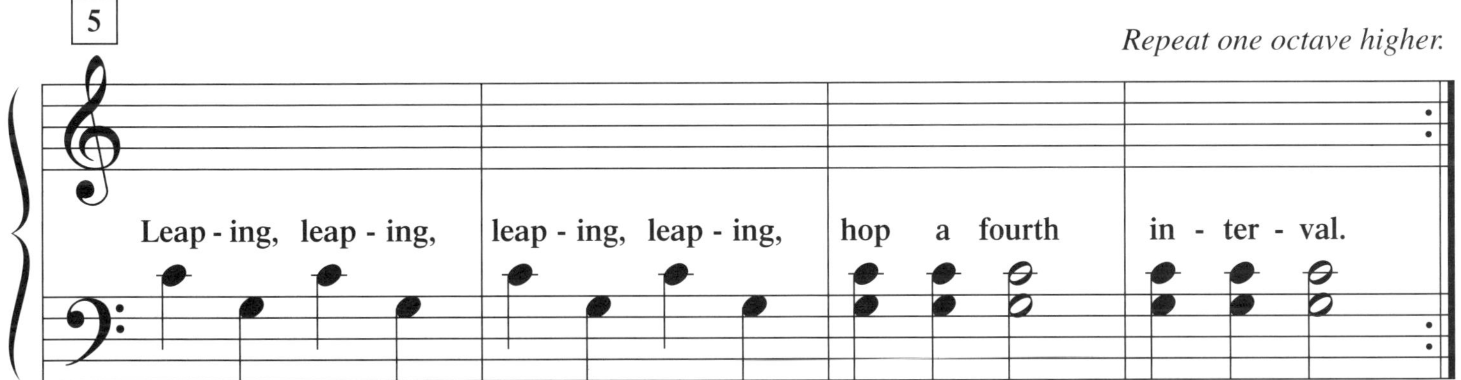
5
Repeat one octave higher.
Leap - ing, leap - ing, leap - ing, leap - ing, hop a fourth in - ter - val.

After you are comfortable with this piece, try playing with **L.H.** finger **2** on **C.**

Teacher Duet: Student plays as written.

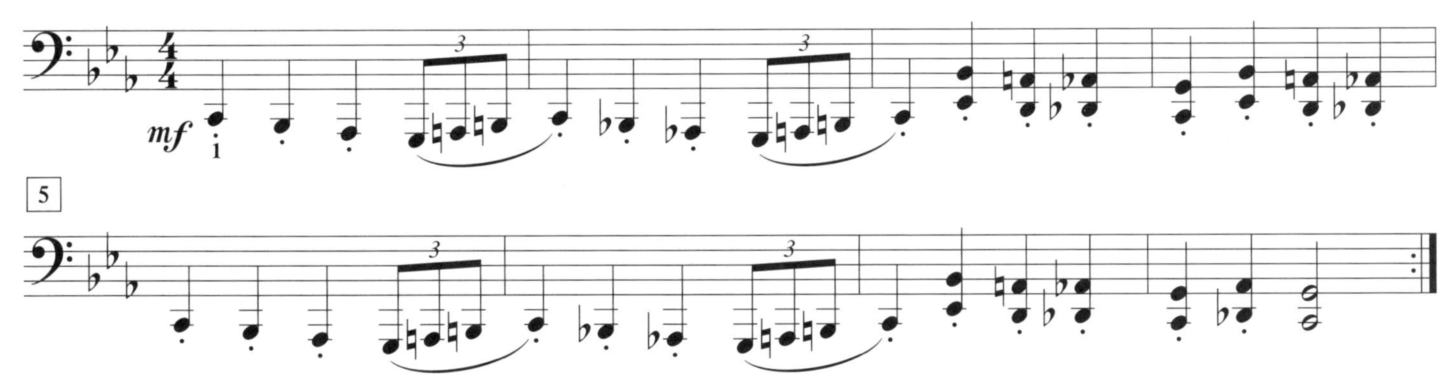
mf
1
3
5

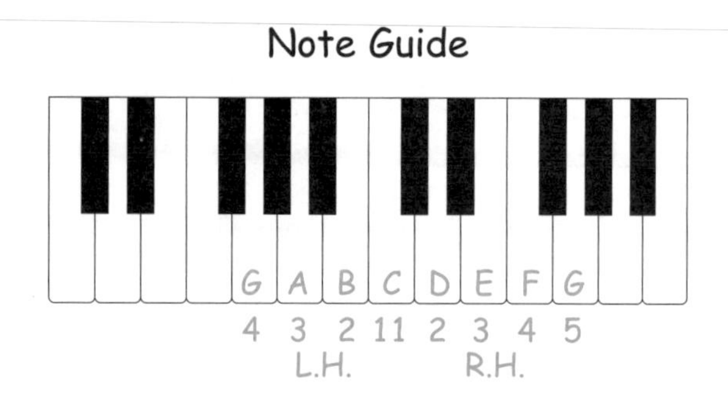
Note Guide
G A B C D E F G
4 3 2 1 1 2 3 4 5
L.H. R.H.

Walking Backwards

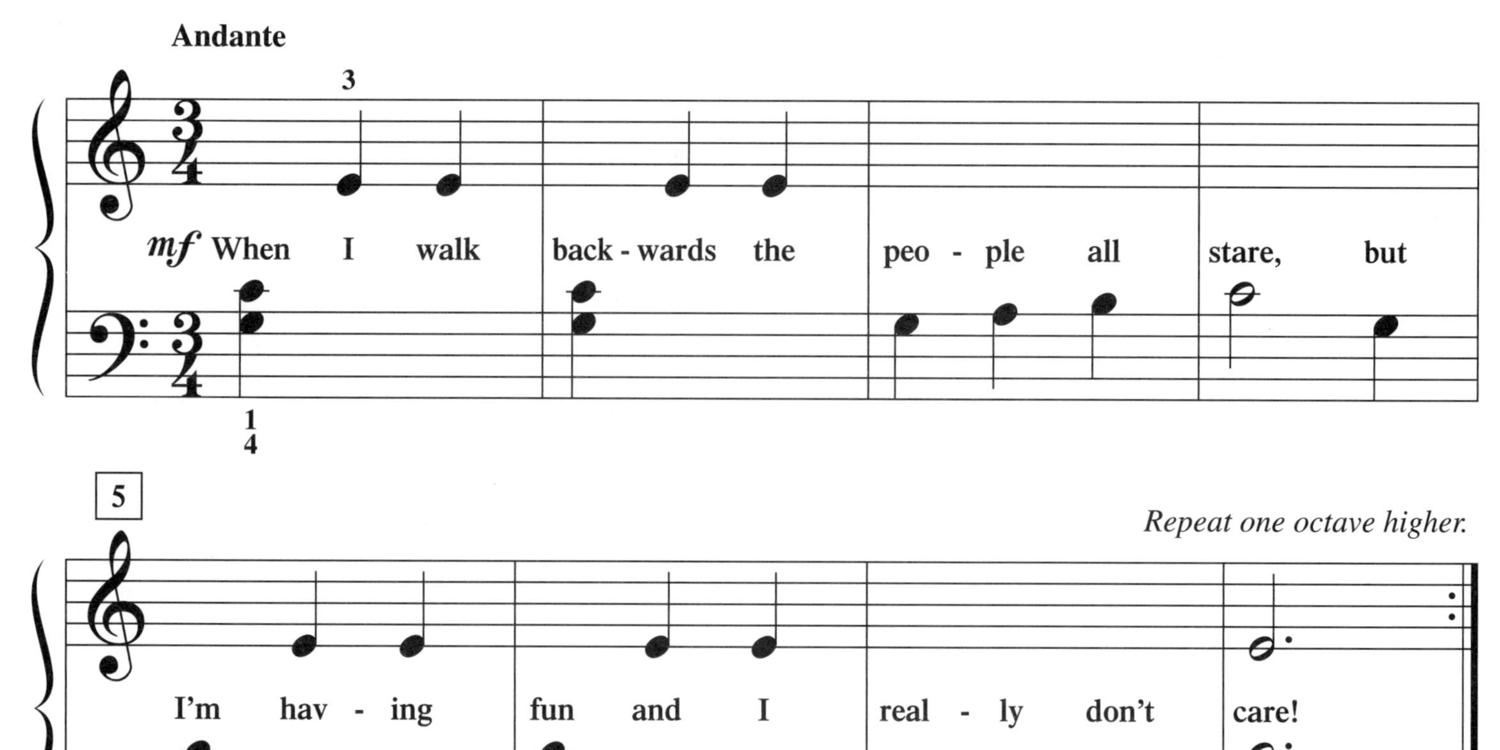
Andante
mf When I walk back - wards the peo - ple all stare, but
I'm hav - ing fun and I real - ly don't care!
Repeat one octave higher.

After you are comfortable with this piece, try playing with **R.H.** finger **2** on **E.**

Teacher Duet: Student plays one octave higher.

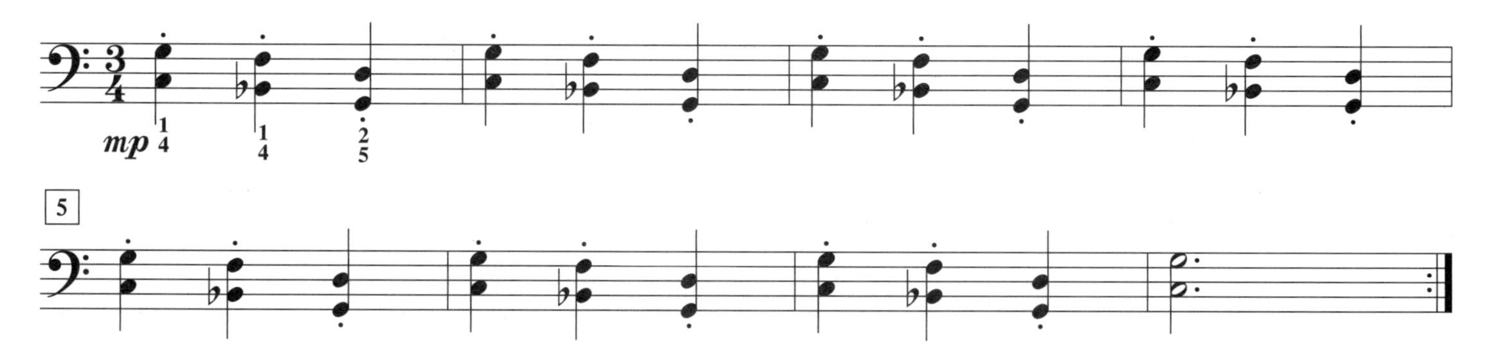
mp

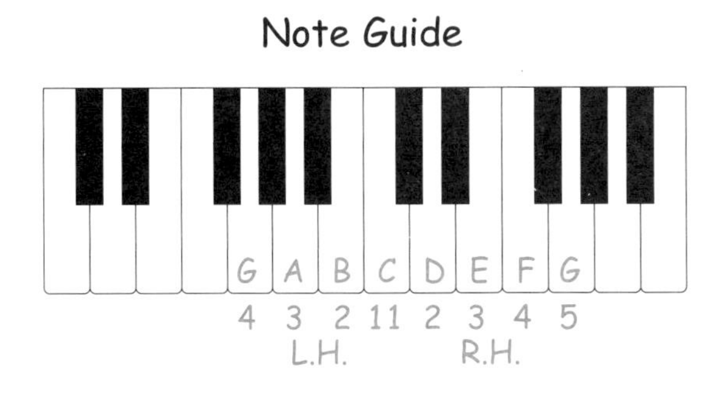
Note Guide
G A B C D E F G
4 3 2 1 1 2 3 4 5
L.H. R.H.

Standing on My Tiptoes

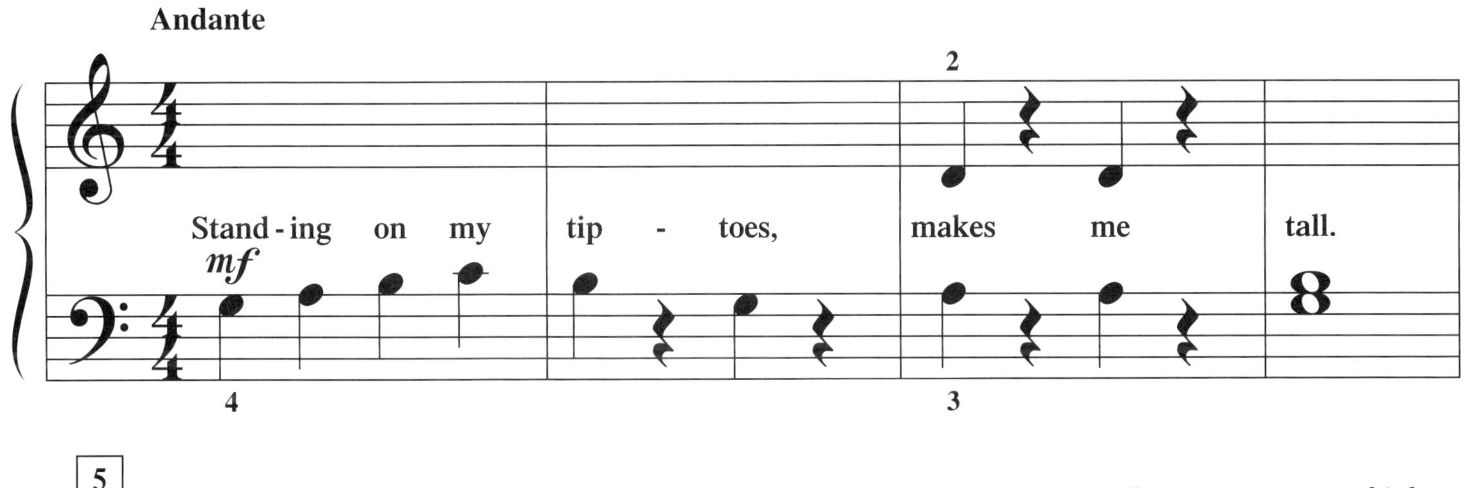
Andante
Stand - ing on my tip - toes, makes me tall.
mf

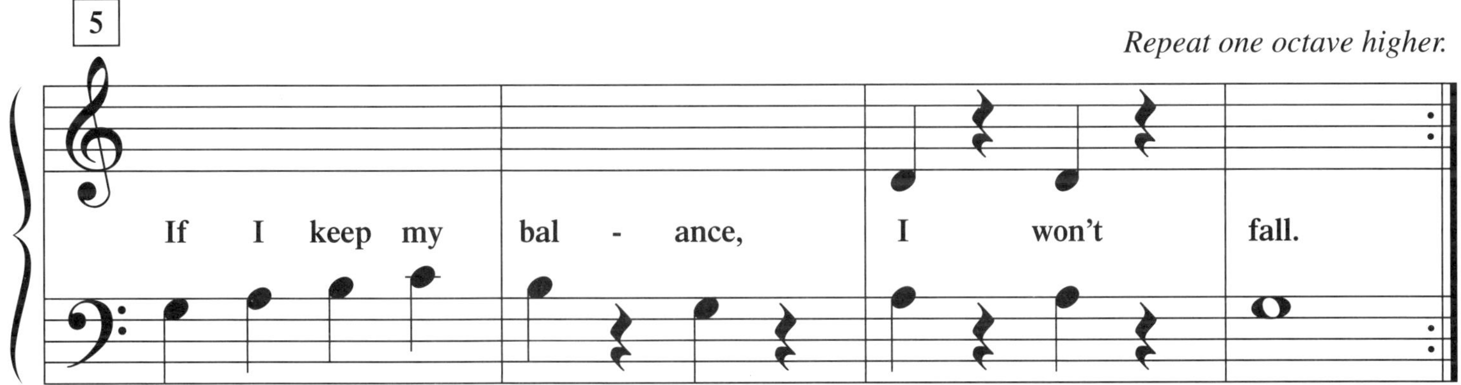
5
Repeat one octave higher.
If I keep my bal - ance, I won't fall.

After you are comfortable with this piece, try playing with **R.H.** finger **1** on **D.**

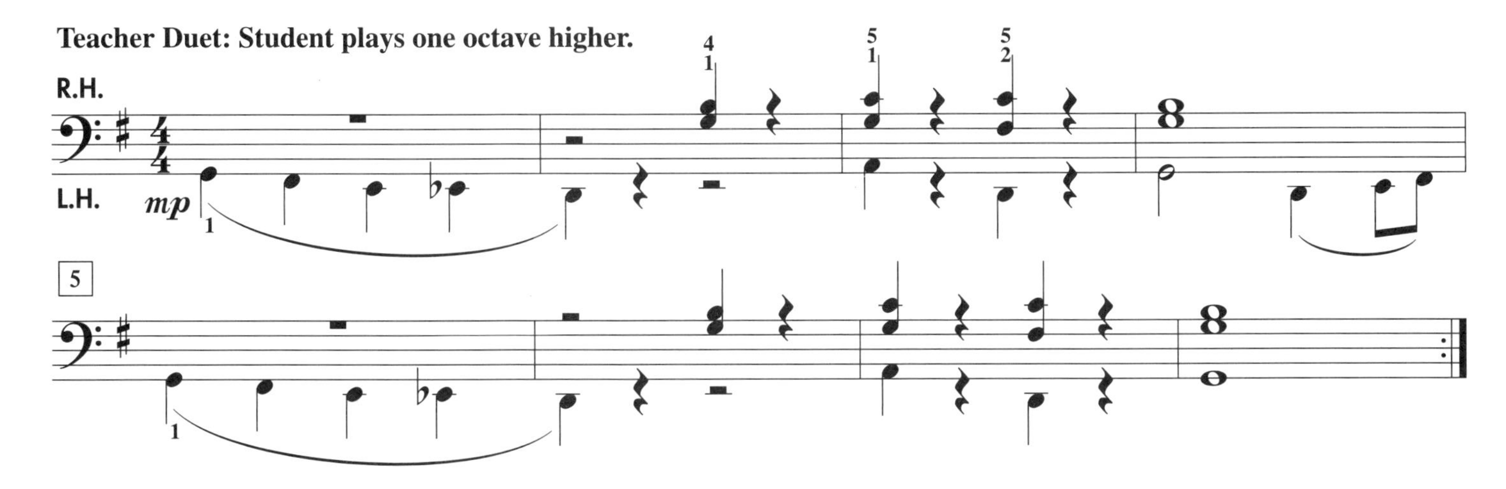
Teacher Duet: Student plays one octave higher.
R.H.
L.H.
mp
5

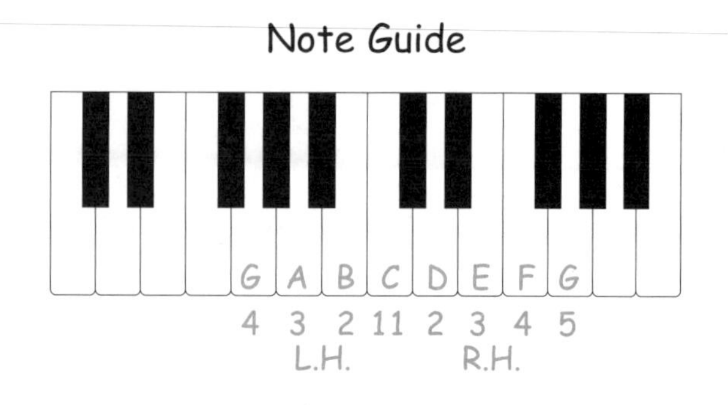
Note Guide
G A B C D E F G
4 3 2 1 1 2 3 4 5
L.H. R.H.

KETCHUP

Empty Ketchup Bottle

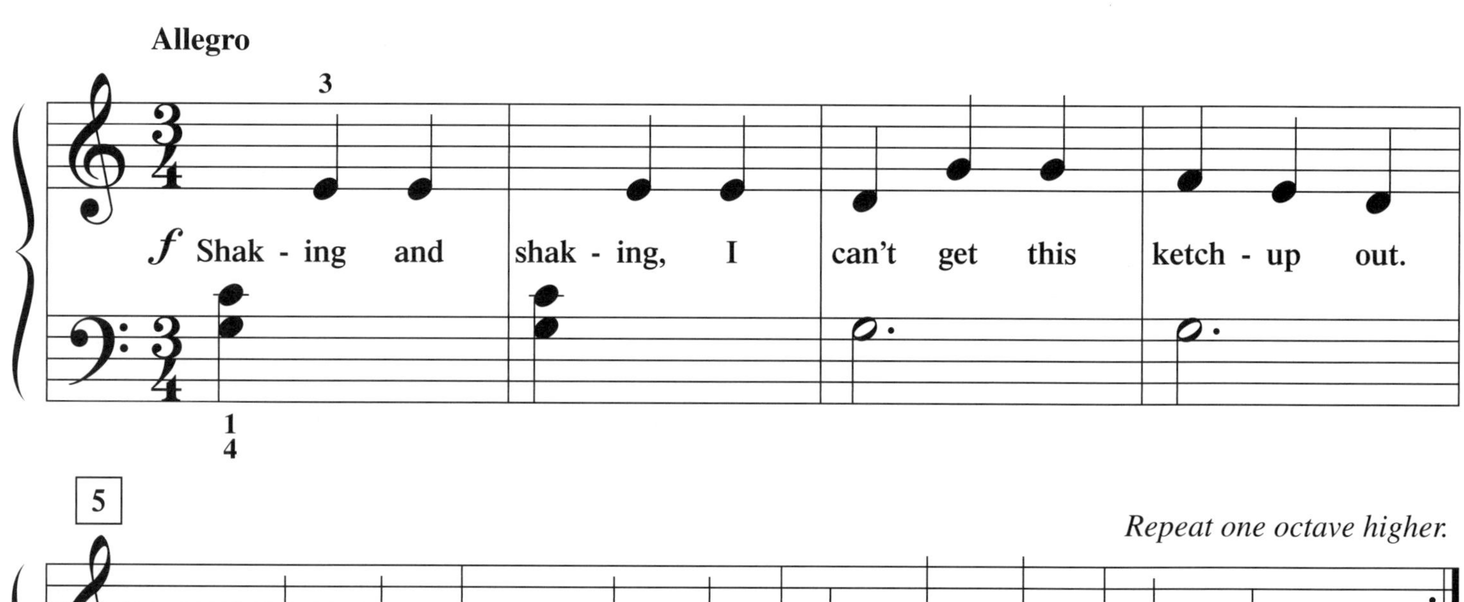
Allegro
3
f Shak - ing and shak - ing, I can't get this ketch - up out.
1
4

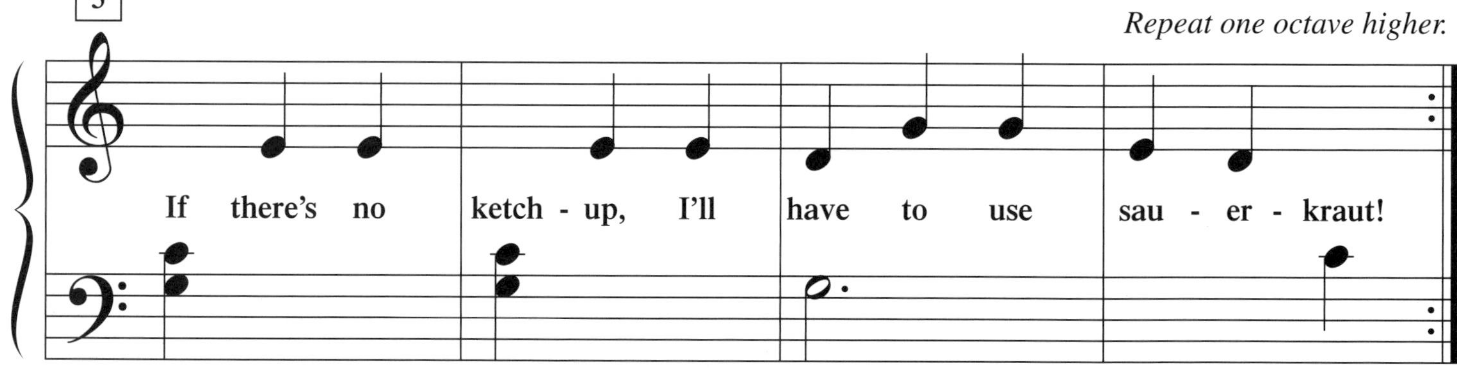
5
Repeat one octave higher.
If there's no ketch - up, I'll have to use sau - er - kraut!

After you are comfortable with this piece, try playing with **R.H.** finger **2** on **E.**

Teacher Duet: Student plays one octave higher.

4
1
R.H.
L.H.
mf
5
5
8va

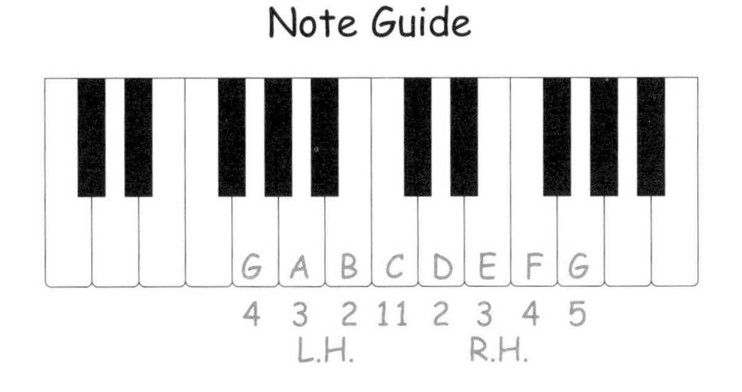
Note Guide
G A B C D E F G
4 3 2 1 1 2 3 4 5
L.H. R.H.

Boats

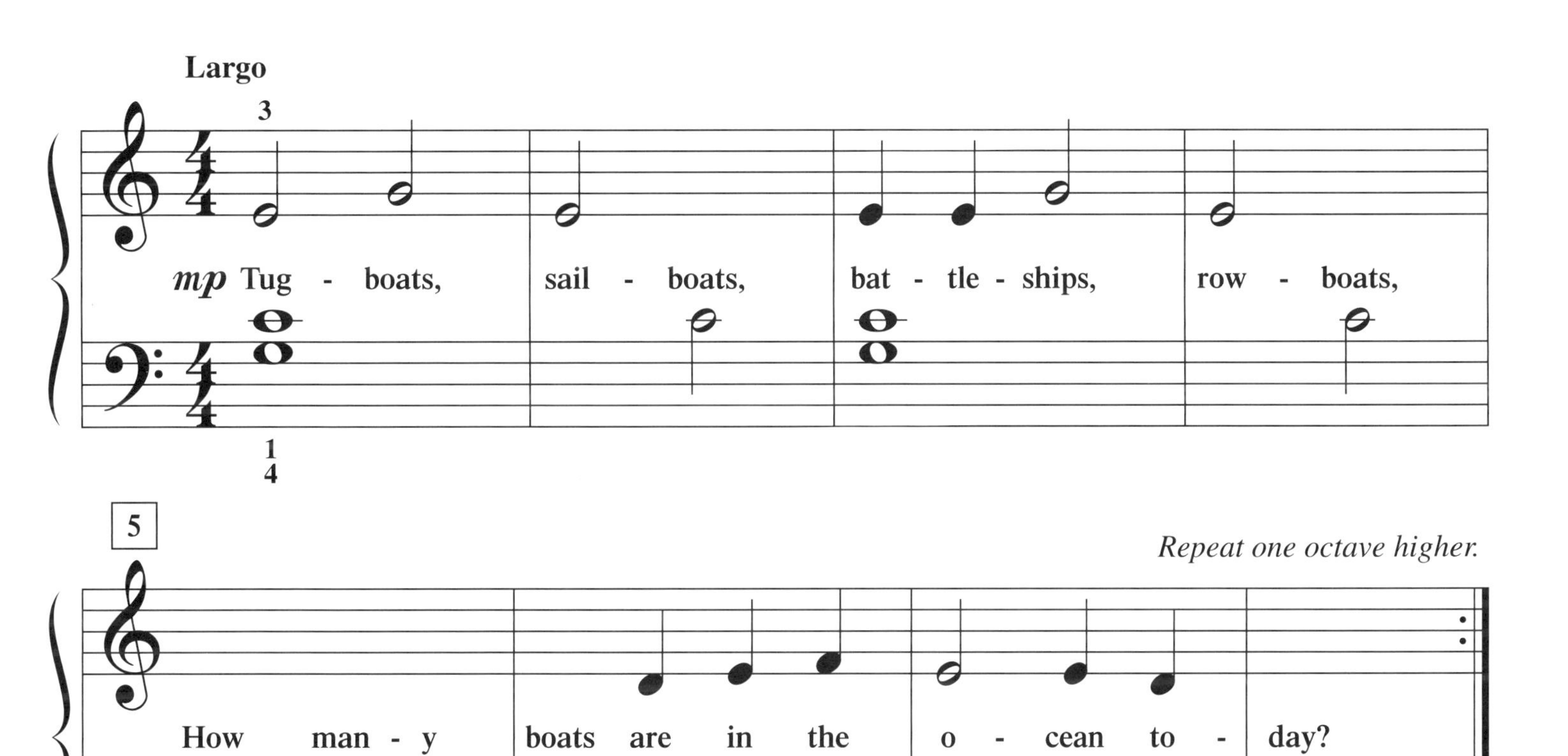
Largo
3
mp Tug - boats, sail - boats, bat - tle - ships, row - boats,
1
4
5
Repeat one octave higher.
How man - y boats are in the o - cean to - day?

After you are comfortable with this piece, try playing with **R.H.** finger **2** on **E.**

Teacher Duet: Student plays one octave higher.

R.H.
3
1
L.H.
p
5
with pedal
5

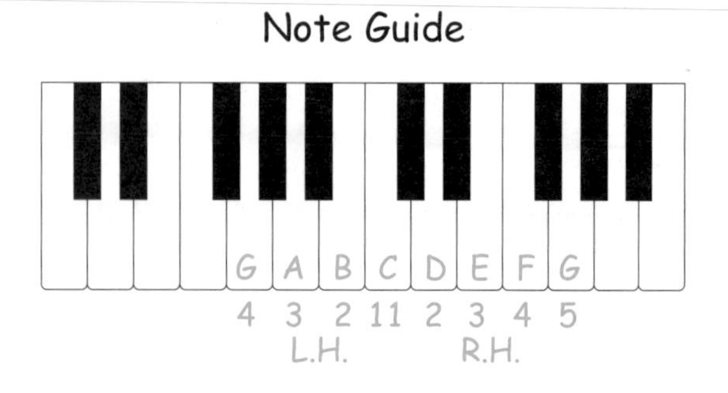
Note Guide
G A B C D E F G
4 3 2 1 1 2 3 4 5
L.H. R.H.

Juggling

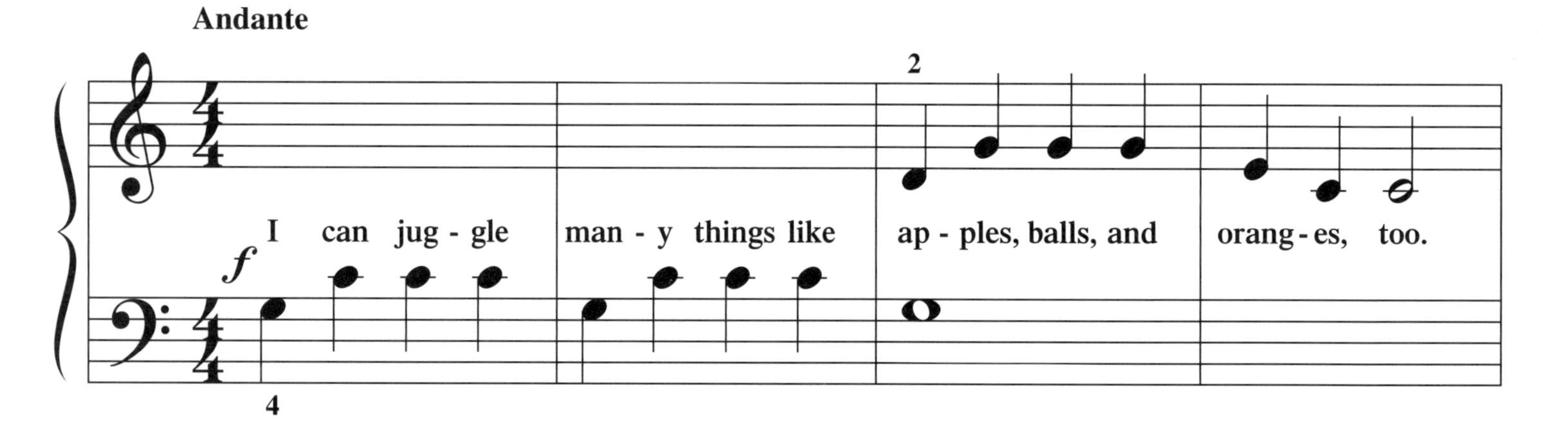
Andante
2
I can jug - gle man - y things like ap - ples, balls, and orang - es, too.
f
4

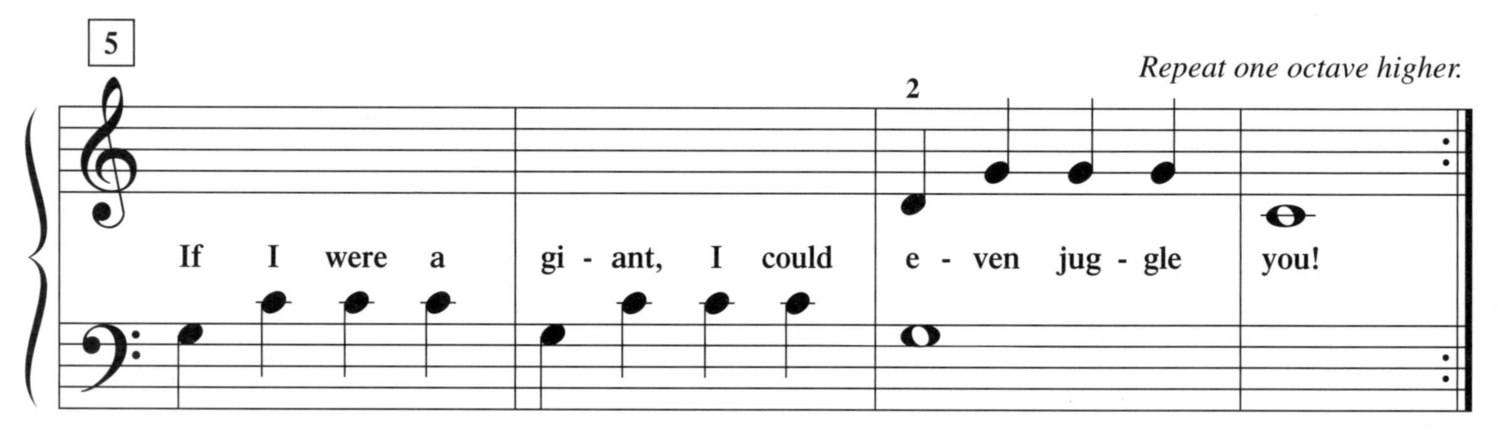
5
Repeat one octave higher.
2
If I were a gi - ant, I could e - ven jug - gle you!

Teacher Duet: Student plays as written.

mf
5
5
5

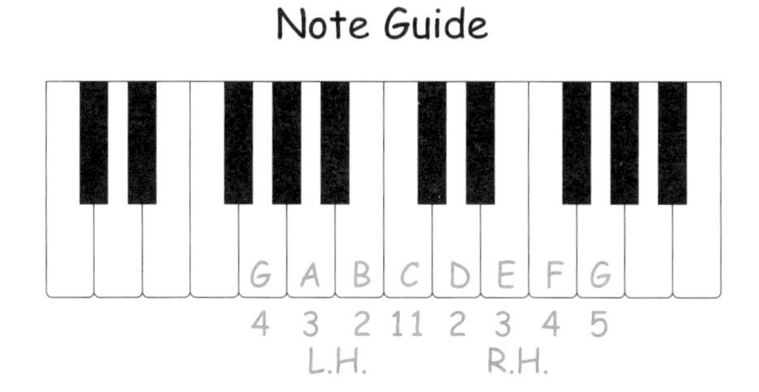
Note Guide
G A B C D E F G
4 3 2 1 1 2 3 4 5
L.H. R.H.

CAR WASH

Going Through the Car Wash

Andante
3
mf Go - ing through the car wash is my fa - v'rite thing to do.
1

5
Repeat one octave higher.
If the car gets dirt - y, I can go a - gain with you!

After you are comfortable with this piece, try playing with **R.H.** finger **2** on **E.**

Teacher Duet: Student plays one octave higher.
R.H.
L.H.
mp
5

Unit 8 Another F on the Keyboard

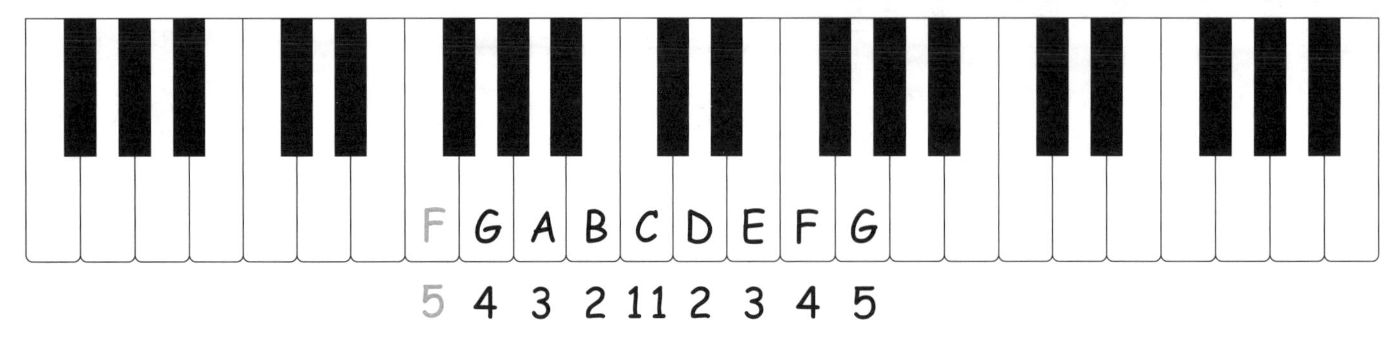
F G A B C D E F G
5 4 3 2 1 1 2 3 4 5
Left Hand Right Hand

Remember that hand positions are just guides. When you are comfortable with the pieces in this unit, explore using different fingers.

F on the Bass Staff

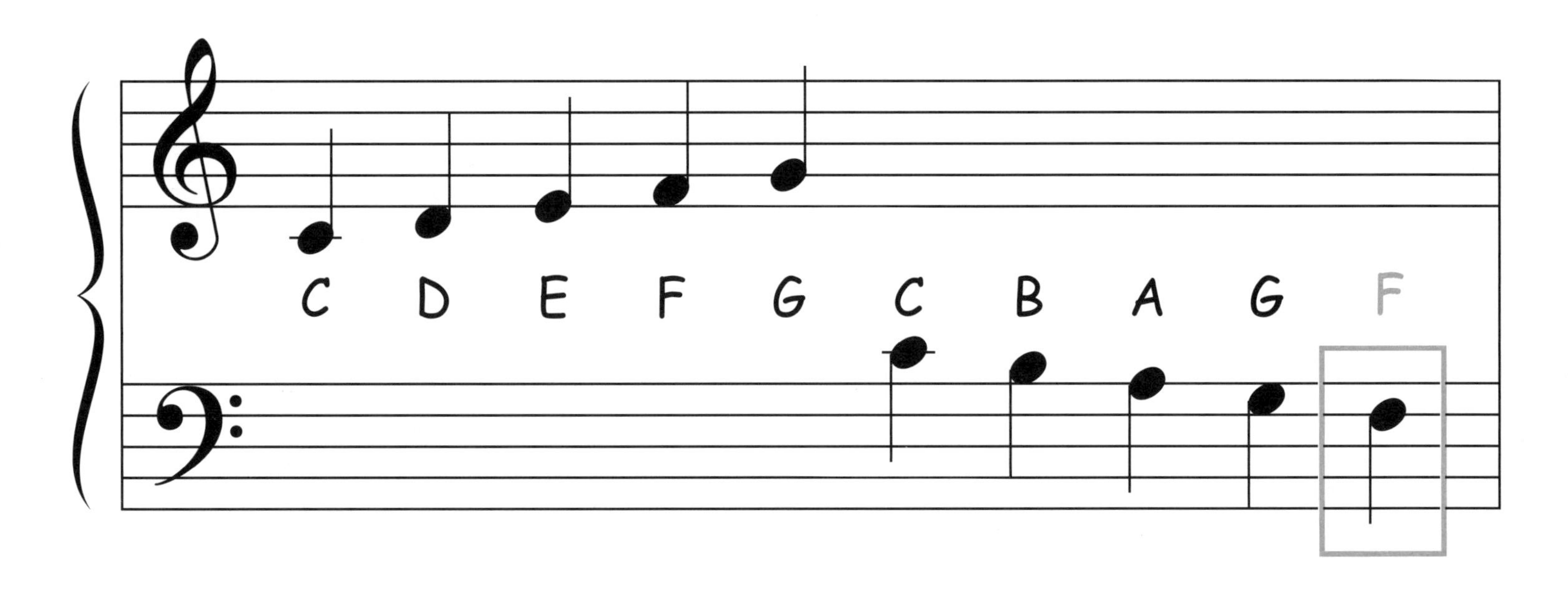
C D E F G C B A G F

Play the example below, keeping your eyes on the music.

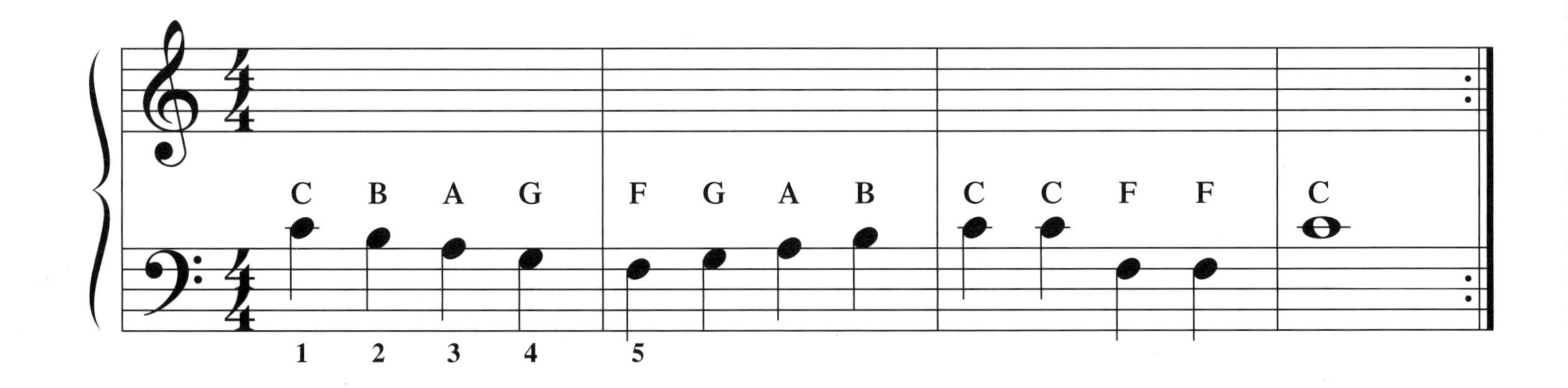
C B A G F G A B C C F F C
1 2 3 4 5

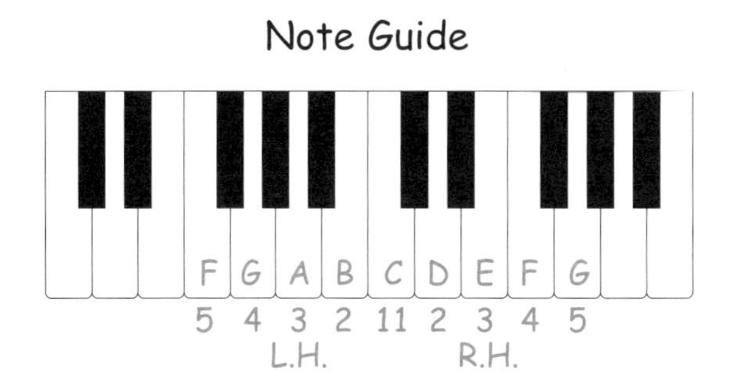
Note Guide
F G A B C D E F G
5 4 3 2 1 1 2 3 4 5
L.H.
R.H.

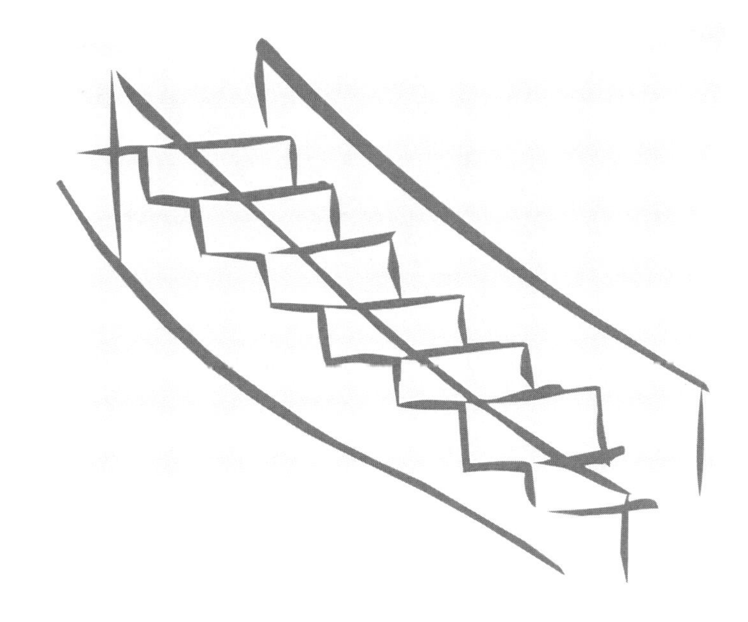

Escalators

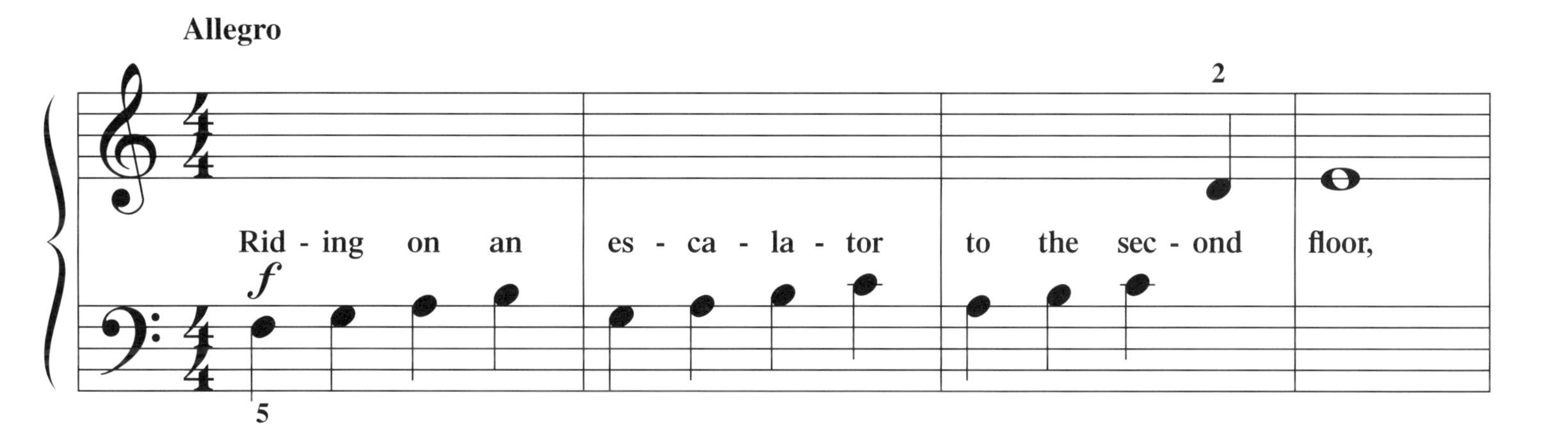
Allegro
Rid - ing on an es - ca - la - tor to the sec - ond floor,

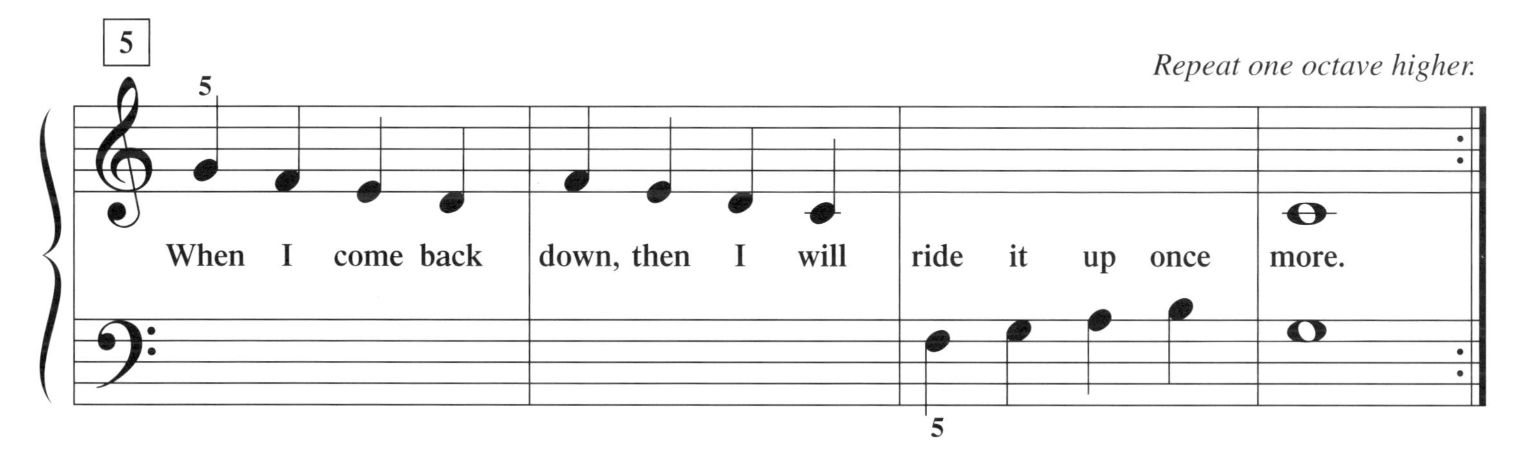
5
Repeat one octave higher.
When I come back down, then I will ride it up once more.

Teacher Duet: Student plays one octave higher.

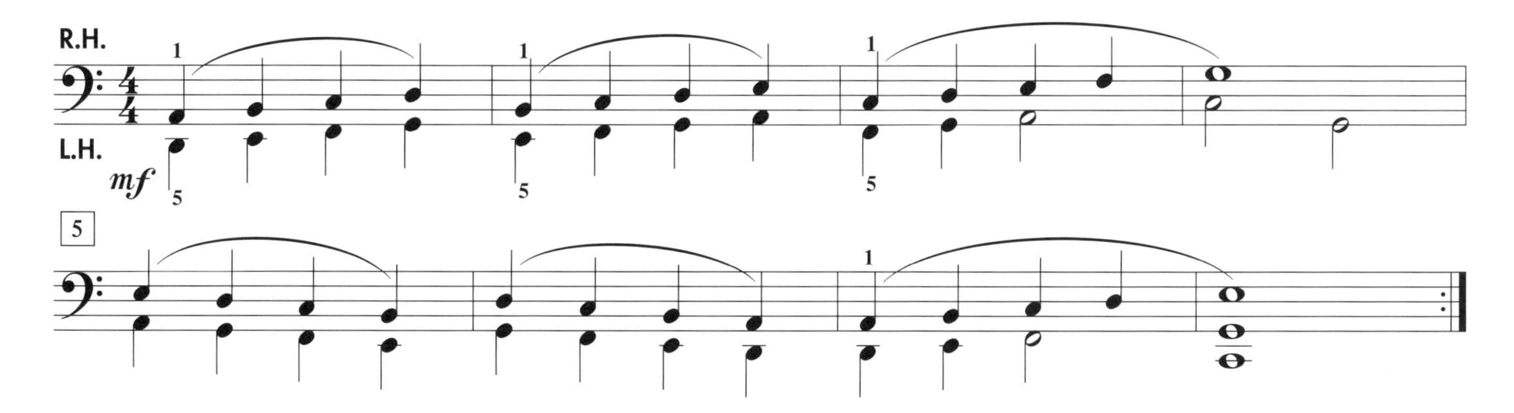
R.H.
L.H.
mf
5

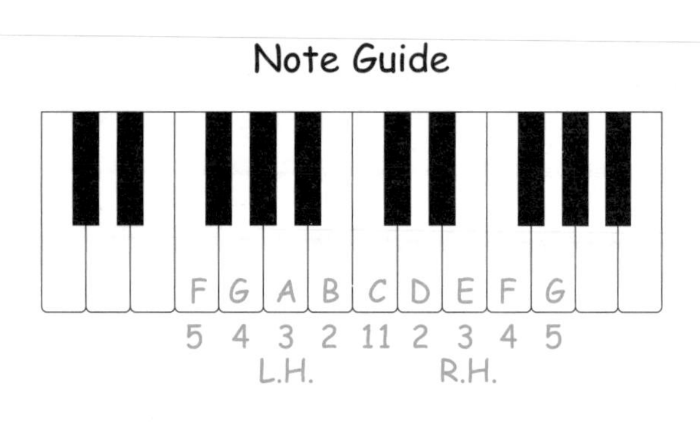
Note Guide
F G A B C D E F G
5 4 3 2 1 1 2 3 4 5
L.H.
R.H.

Hurry Scurry

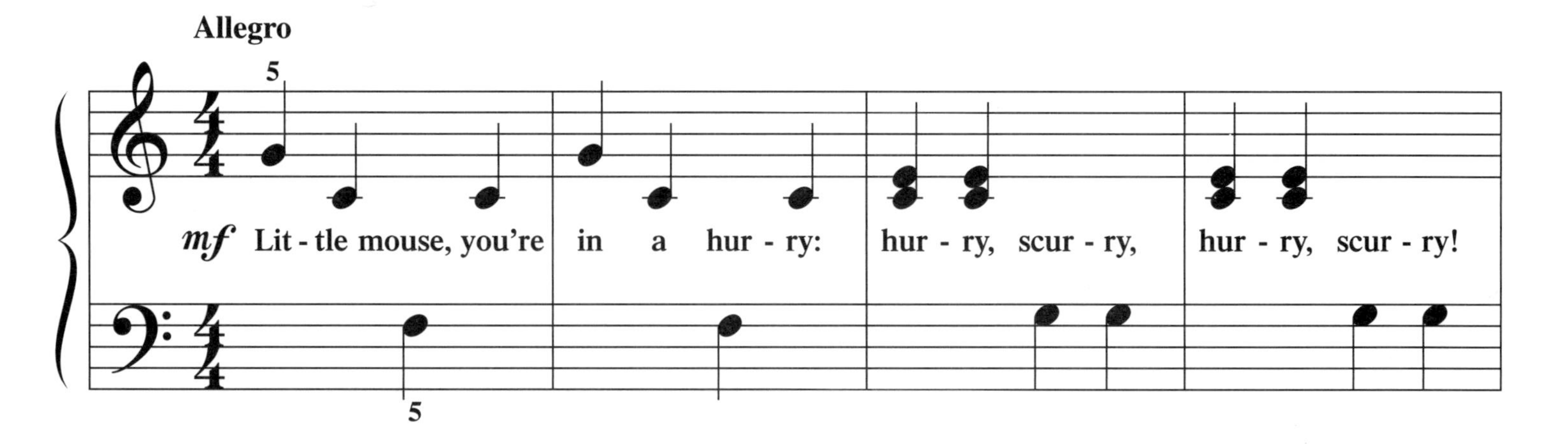
Allegro
5
mf Lit - tle mouse, you're in a hur - ry: hur - ry, scur - ry, hur - ry, scur - ry!
5

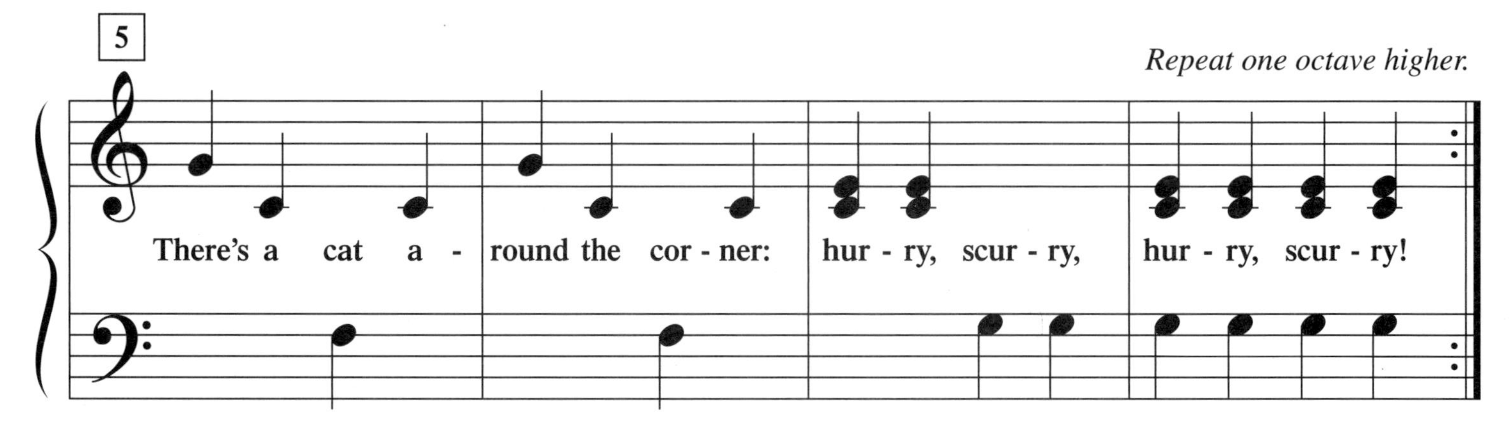
5
Repeat one octave higher.
There's a cat a - round the cor - ner: hur - ry, scur - ry, hur - ry, scur - ry!

After you are comfortable with this piece, try playing with **L.H.** finger **3** on **F.**

Teacher Duet: Student plays one octave higher.

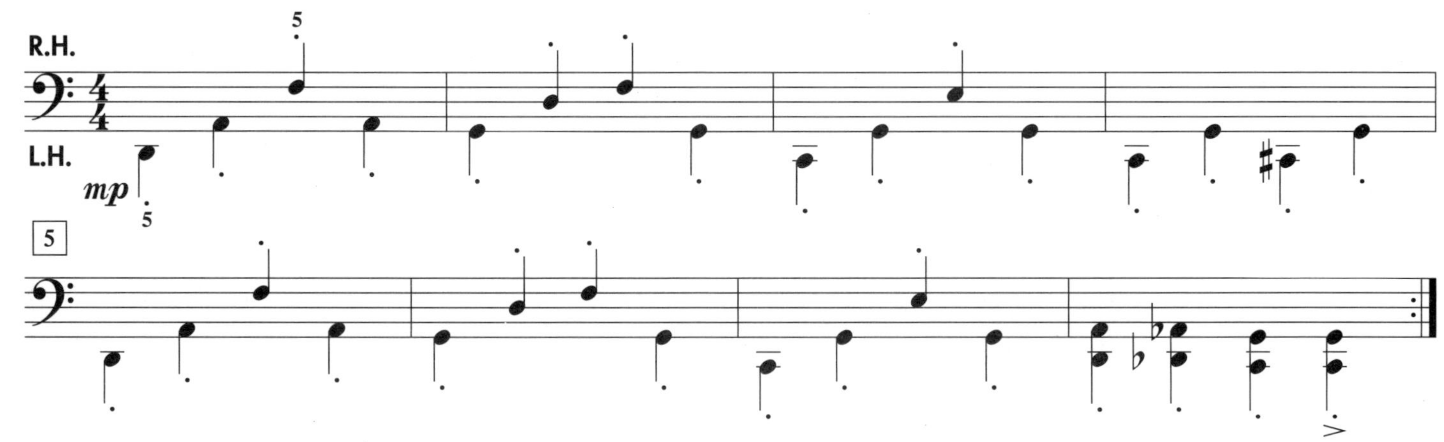
R.H.
L.H.
mp
5
5
5

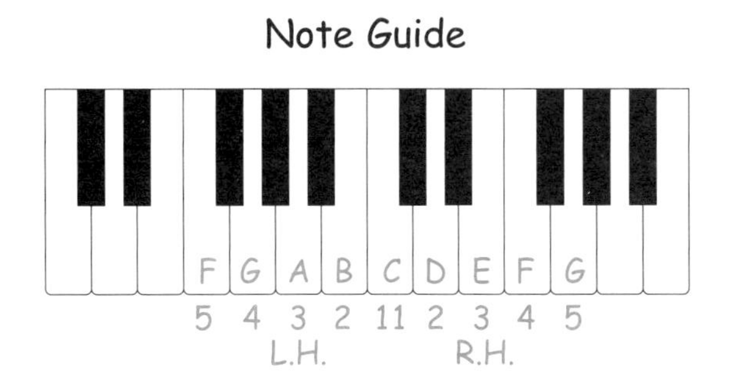
Note Guide
F G A B C D E F G
5 4 3 2 1 1 2 3 4 5
L.H.
R.H.

Puzzles

Andante

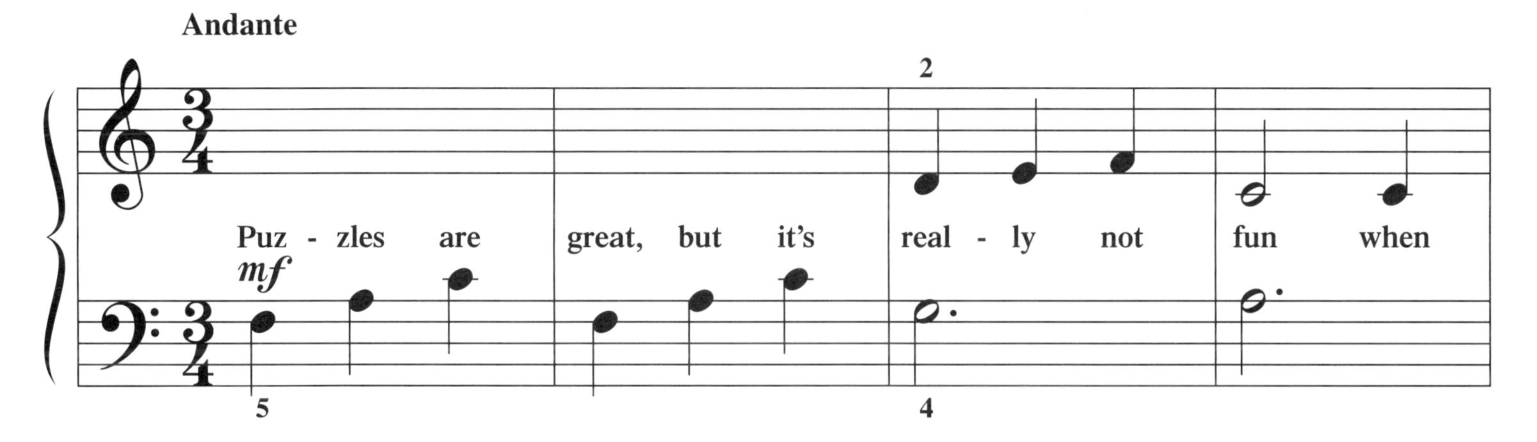
2
Puz - zles are great, but it's real - ly not fun when
mf
5
4

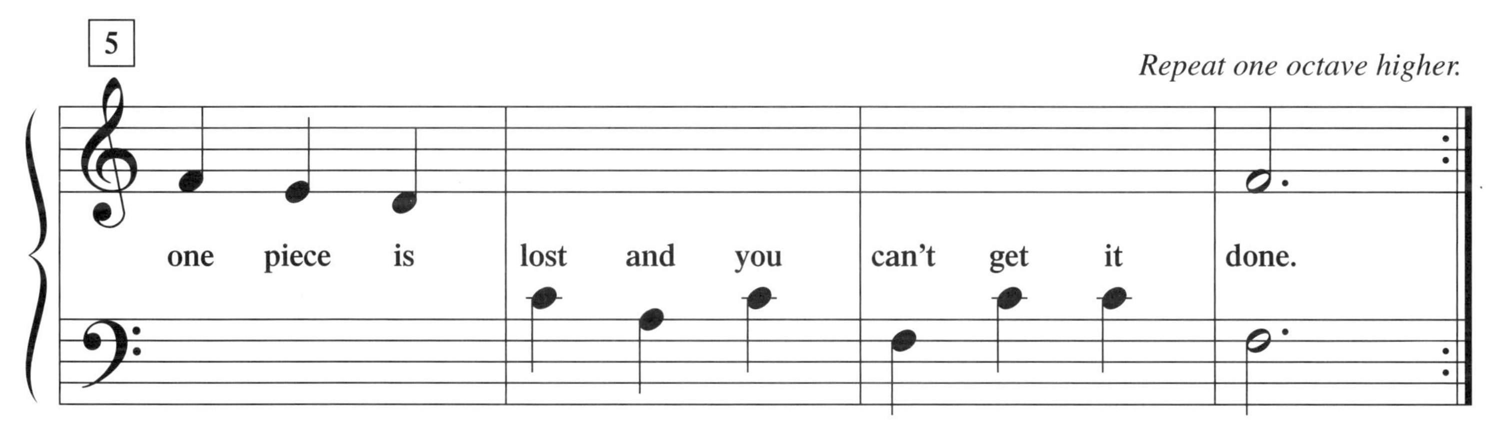
5
Repeat one octave higher.
one piece is lost and you can't get it done.

Teacher Duet: Student plays one octave higher.

5
3
R.H.
L.H.
1
mp
1
5

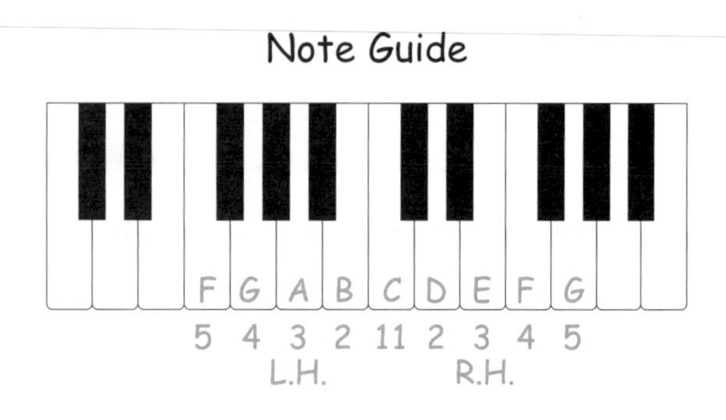
Note Guide
F G A B C D E F G
5 4 3 2 1 1 2 3 4 5
L.H.
R.H.

Mountain Man

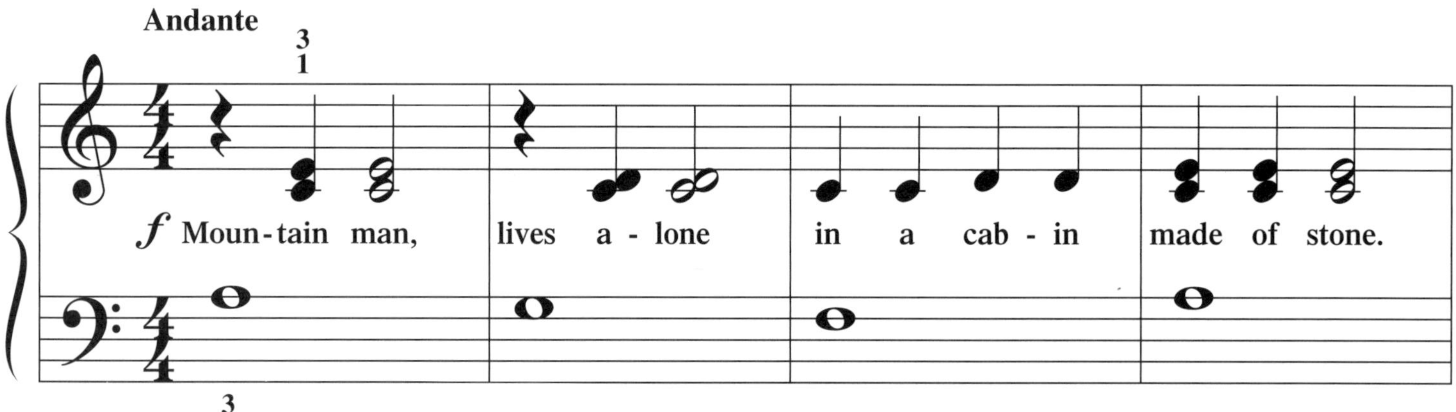
Andante
f Moun-tain man, lives a - lone in a cab - in made of stone.

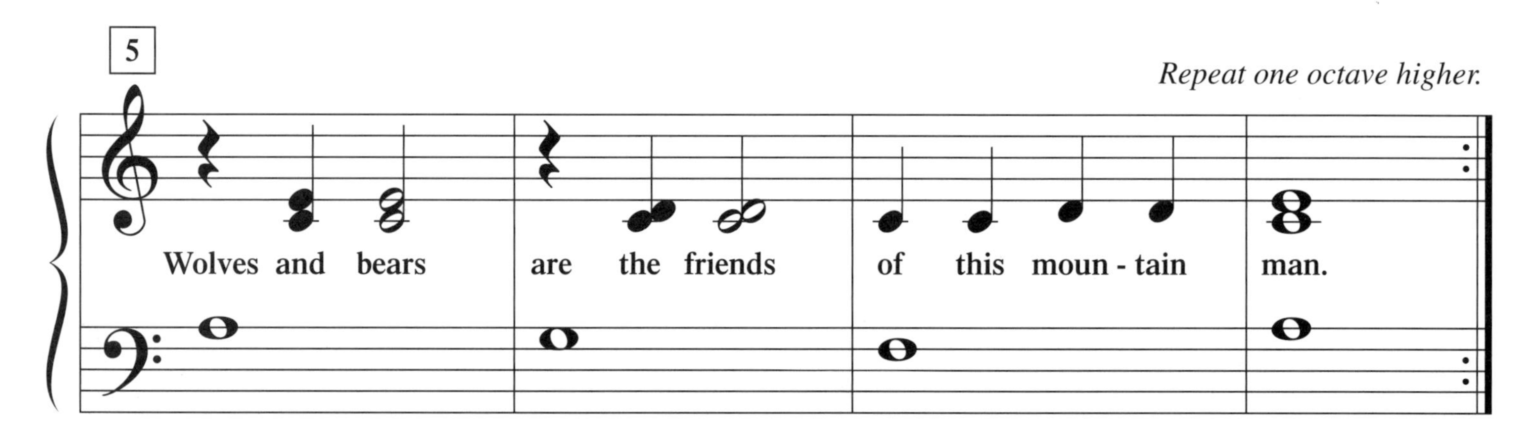
Repeat one octave higher.
Wolves and bears are the friends of this moun - tain man.

After you are comfortable with this piece, try playing with **L.H.** finger **1** on **A.**

Teacher Duet: Student plays as written.

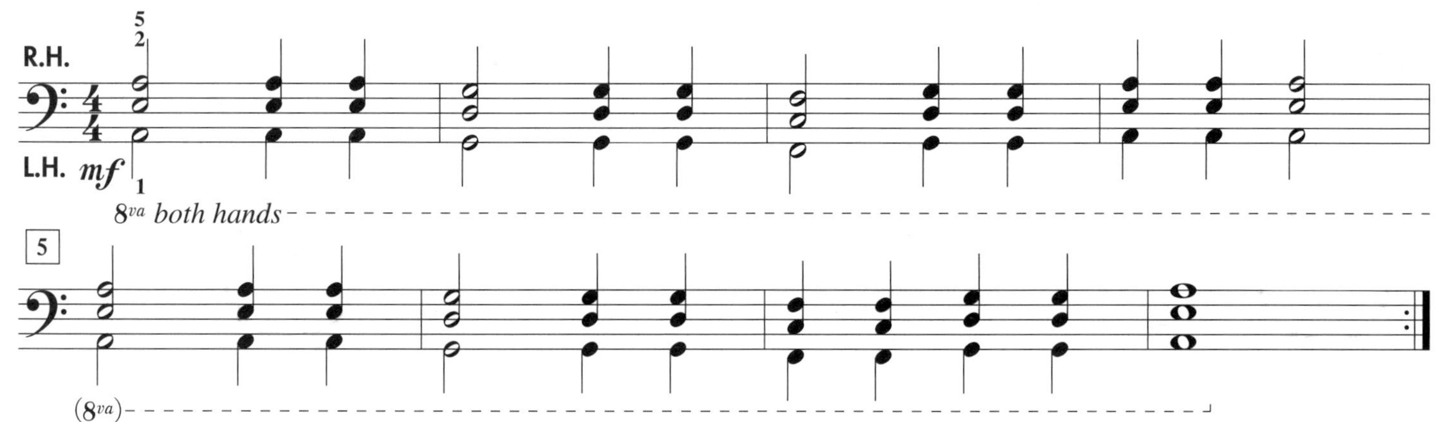
R.H.
L.H. mf
8va both hands
(8va)

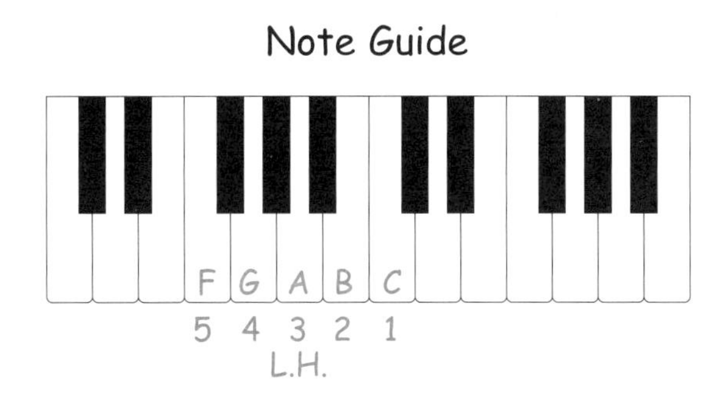
Note Guide
F G A B C
5 4 3 2 1
L.H.

Leap and Hop with C and F

C
F
5th

Andante

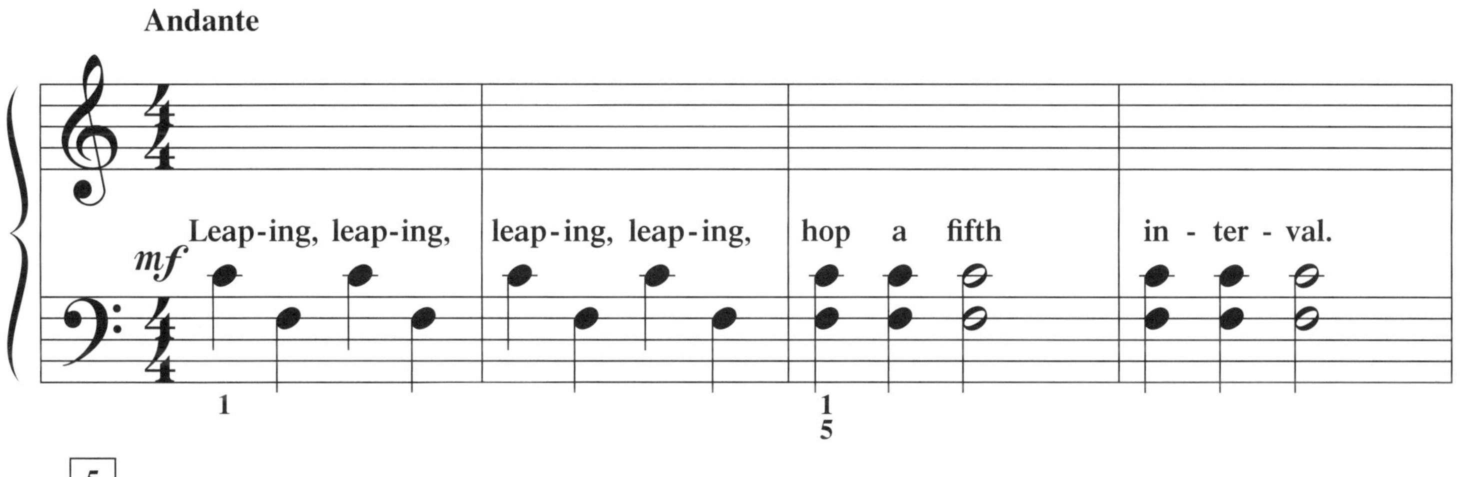
mf
Leap-ing, leap-ing, leap-ing, leap-ing, hop a fifth in - ter - val.
1
1
5

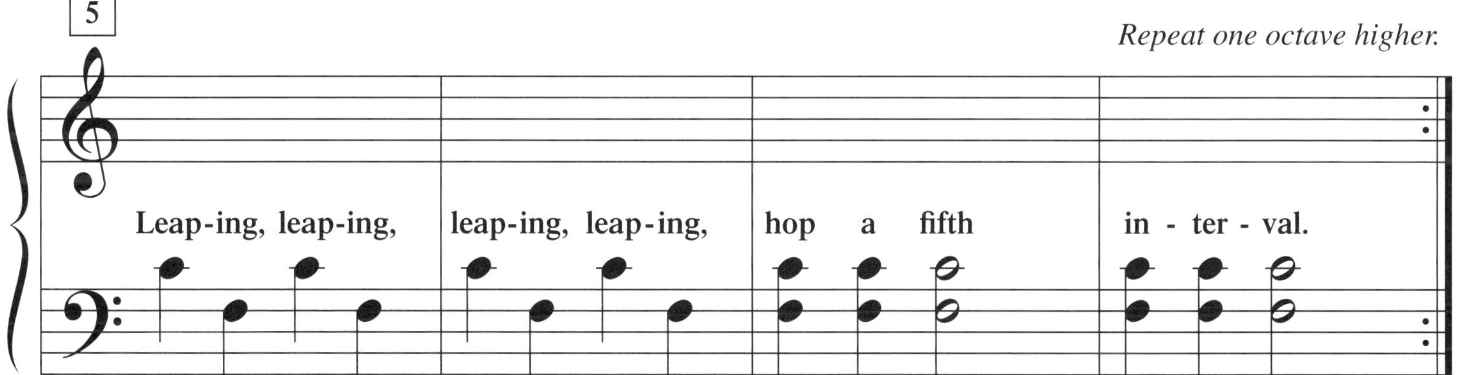
5
Repeat one octave higher.
Leap-ing, leap-ing, leap-ing, leap-ing, hop a fifth in - ter - val.

Teacher Duet: Student plays as written.

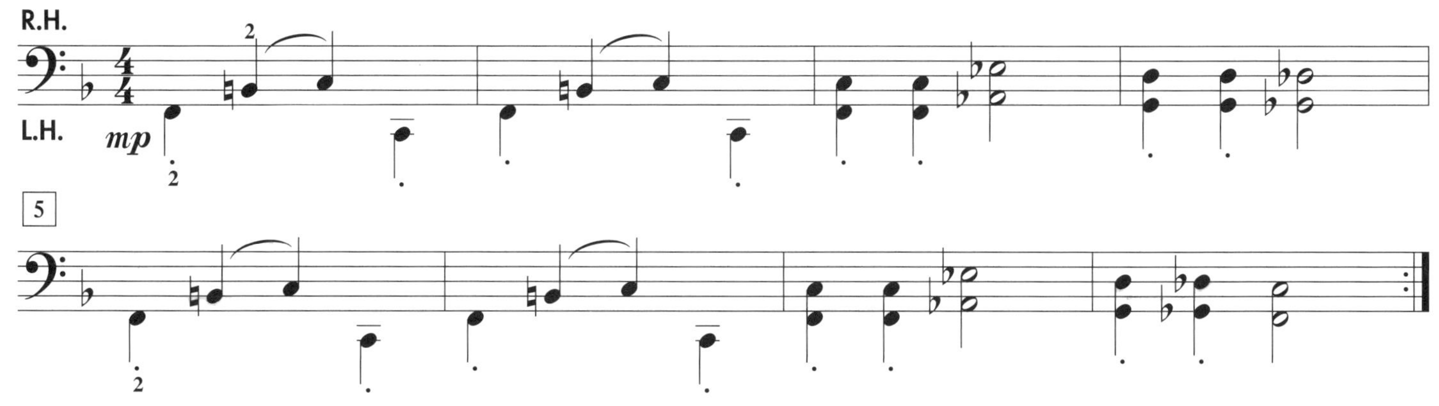
R.H.
L.H.
mp
2
2
5
2

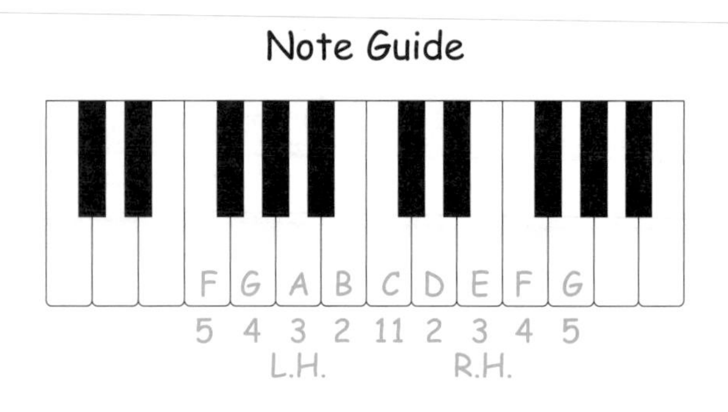
Note Guide
F G A B C D E F G
5 4 3 2 1 1 2 3 4 5
L.H.
R.H.

Church Bells

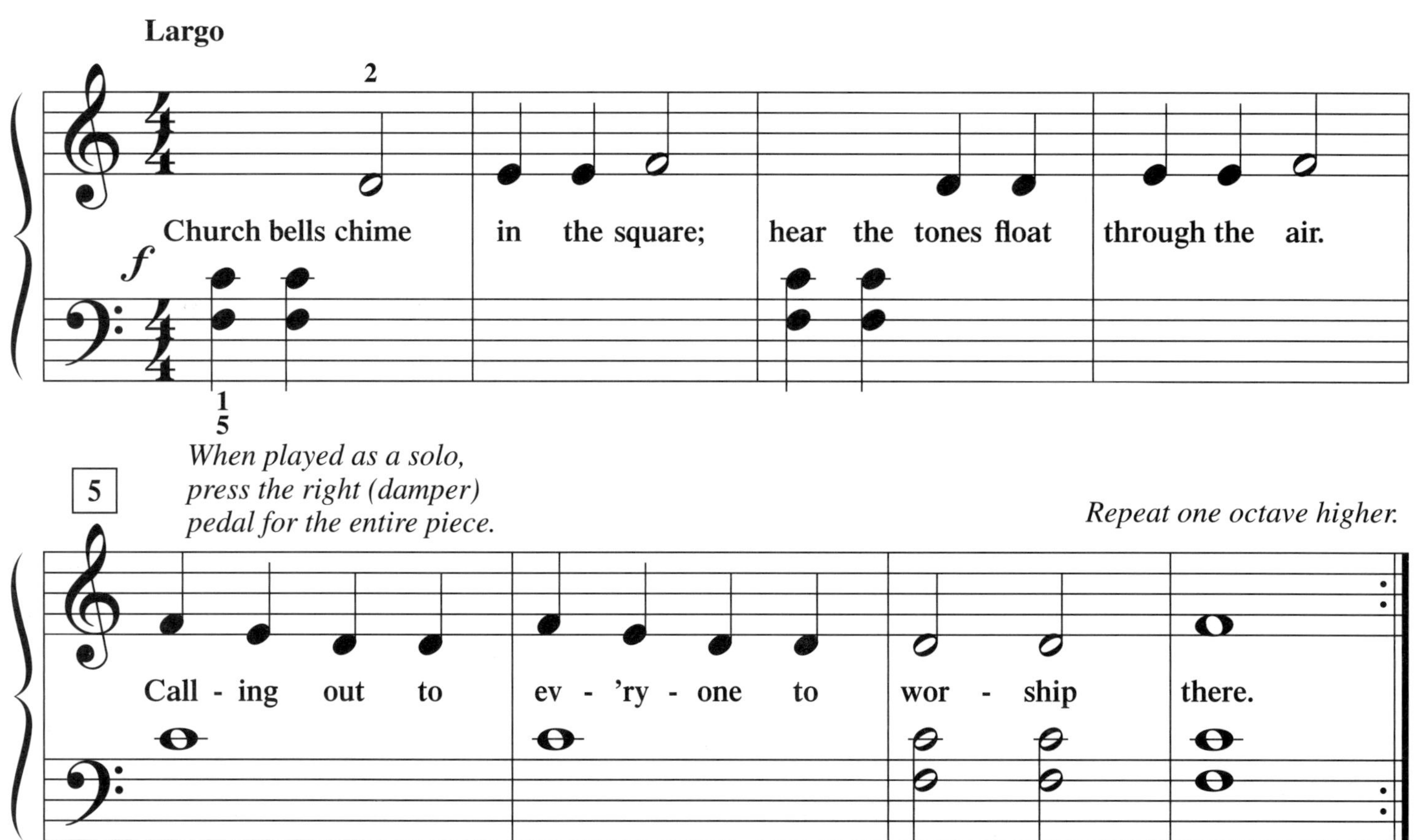
Largo
Church bells chime in the square; hear the tones float through the air.
When played as a solo, press the right (damper) pedal for the entire piece.
Repeat one octave higher.
Call - ing out to ev - 'ry - one to wor - ship there.

After you are comfortable with this piece, try playing with **R.H.** finger **1** on **D.**

Teacher Duet: Student plays one octave higher.

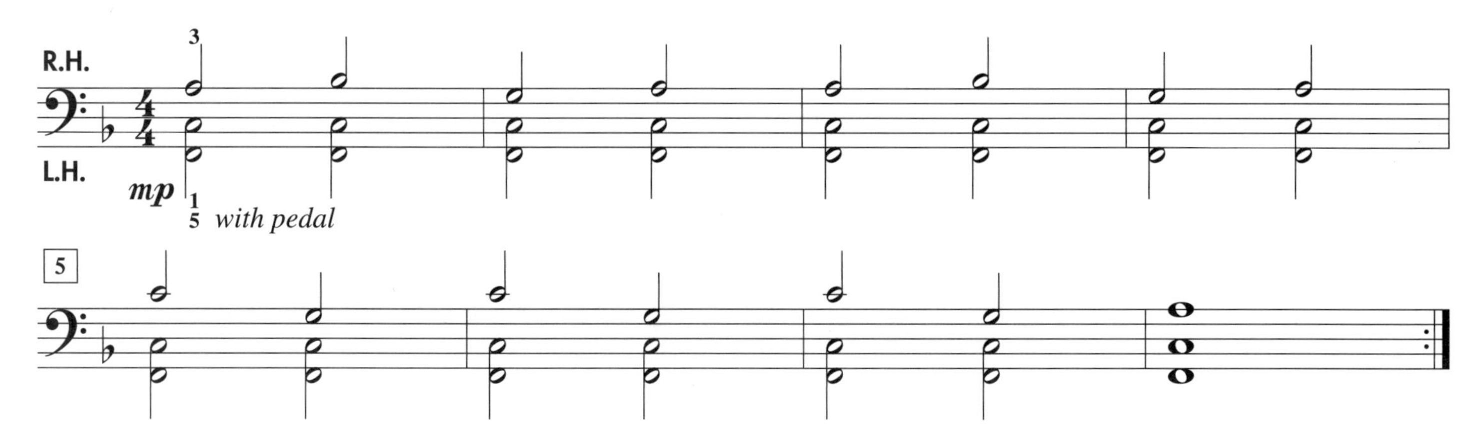
R.H.
L.H.
mp
with pedal

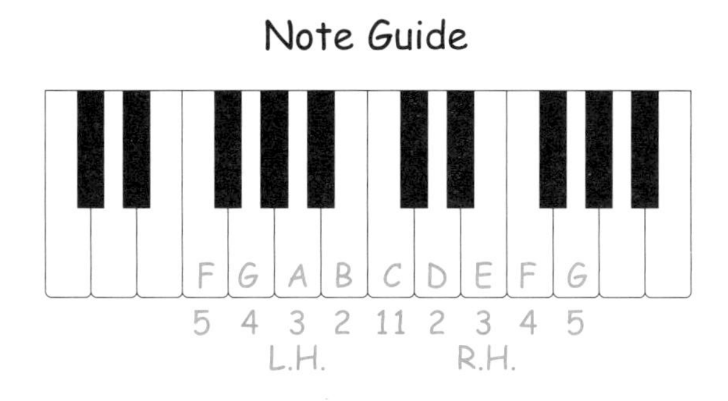
Note Guide
F G A B C D E F G
5 4 3 2 1 1 2 3 4 5
L.H.
R.H.

What's Inside That Box?

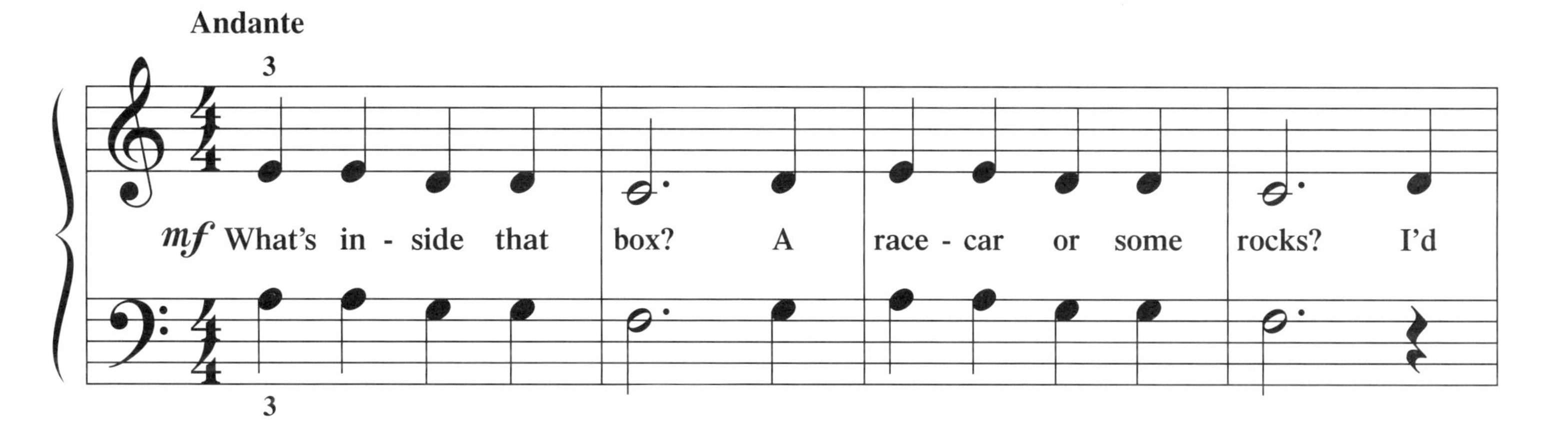
Andante
3
mf What's in - side that
box? A
race - car or some
rocks? I'd
3

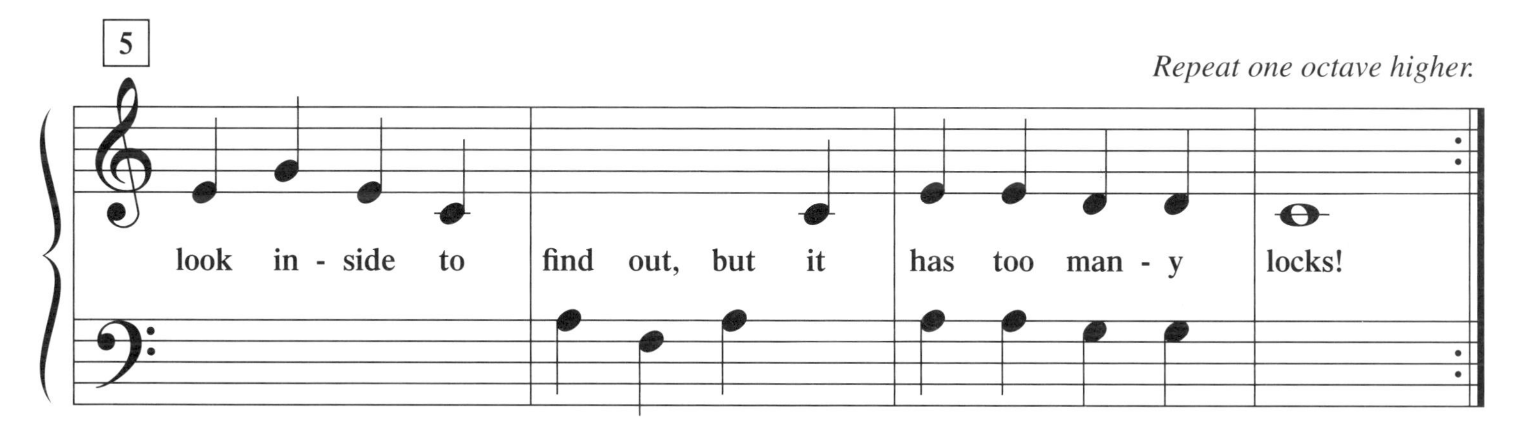
5
Repeat one octave higher.
look in - side to
find out, but it
has too man - y
locks!

Teacher Duet: Student plays one octave higher.

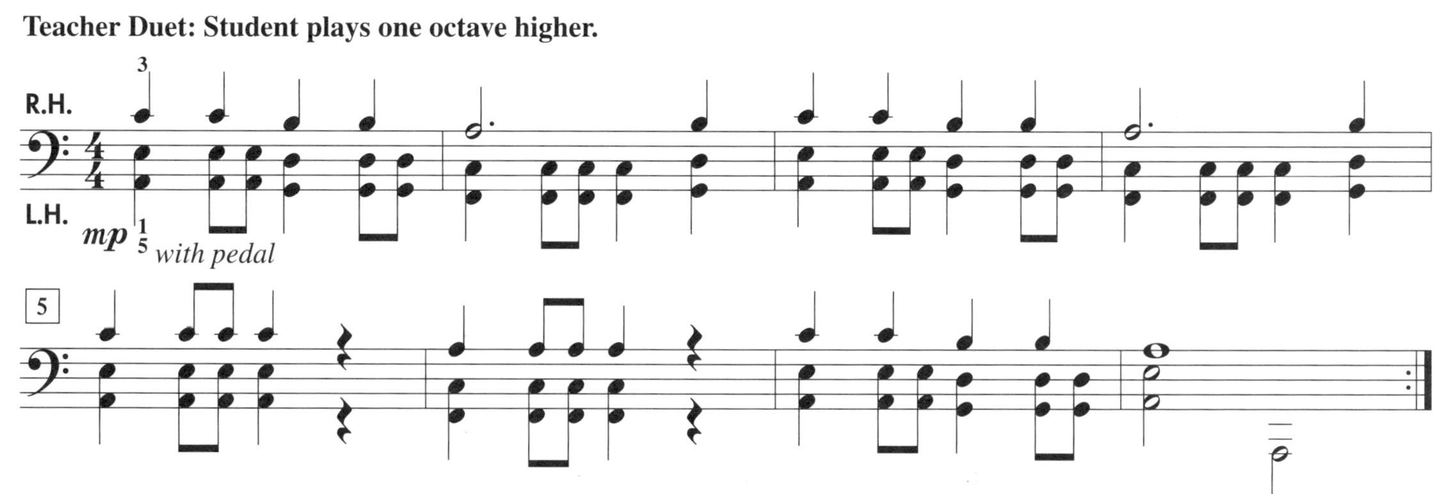
3
R.H.
L.H.
mp 1 5 with pedal
5

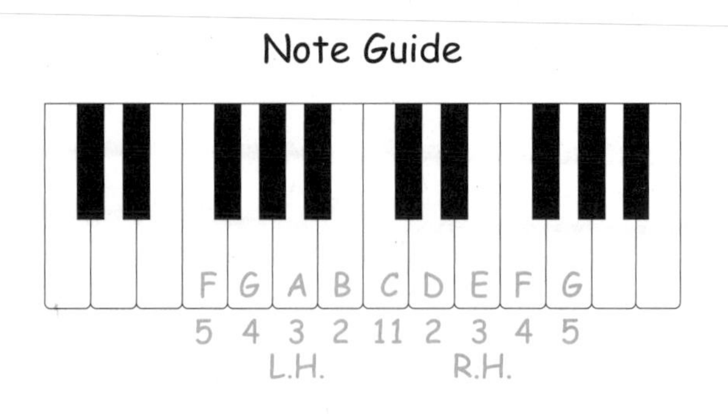
Note Guide
F G A B C D E F G
5 4 3 2 1 1 2 3 4 5
L.H. R.H.

My Dog Betty

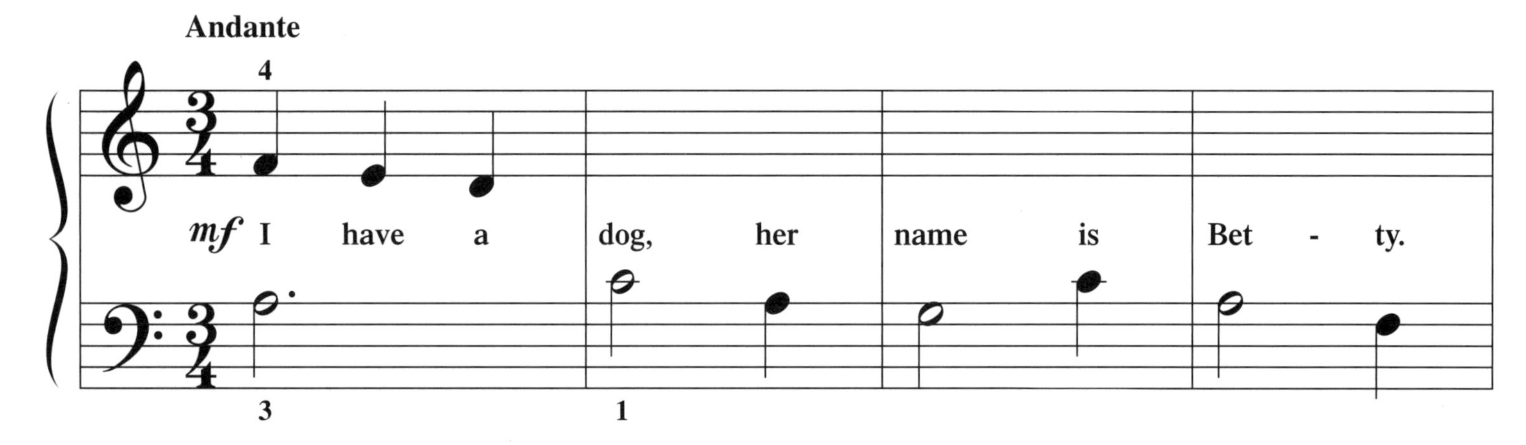
Andante
4
mf I have a dog, her name is Bet - ty.
3
1

5
Repeat one octave higher.
Her fa - v'rite food is warm spa - ghet - ti!

After you are comfortable with this piece, try playing with **R.H.** finger **3** on **F.**

Teacher Duet: Student plays one octave higher.

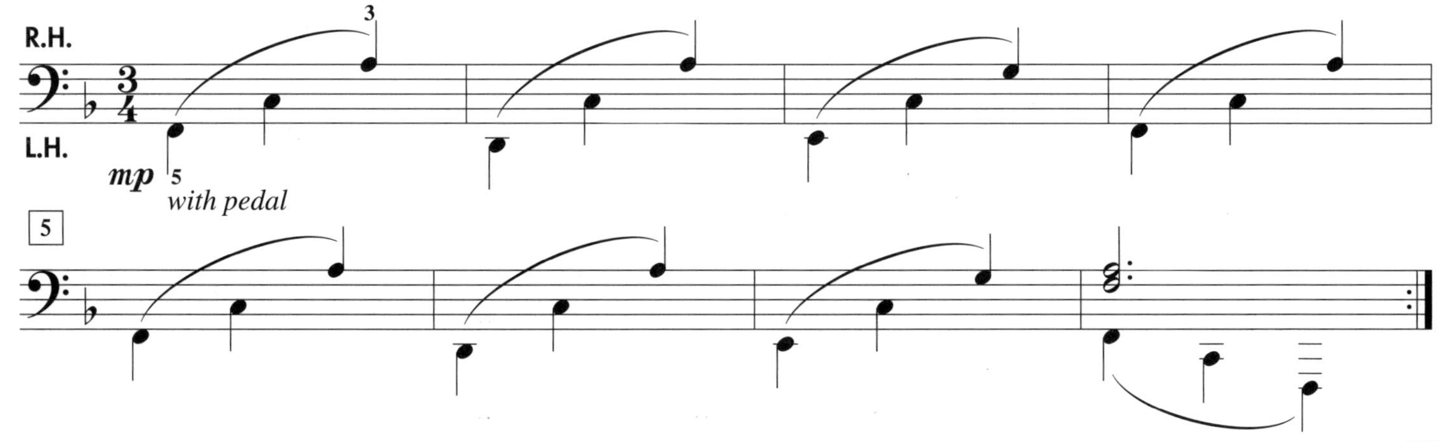
R.H.
3
L.H.
mp 5
with pedal
5

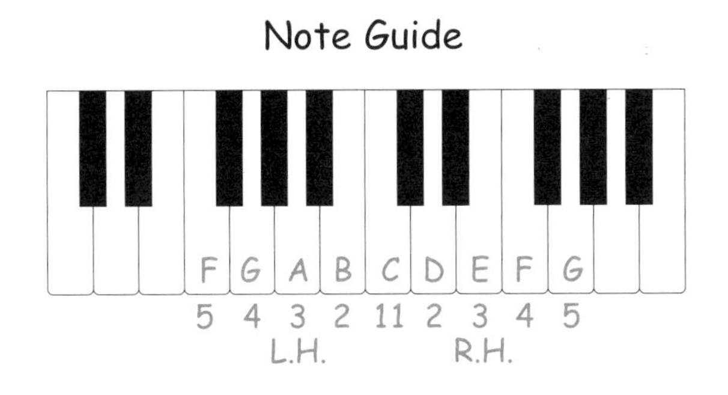
Note Guide
F G A B C D E F G
5 4 3 2 1 1 2 3 4 5
L.H. R.H.

Wink

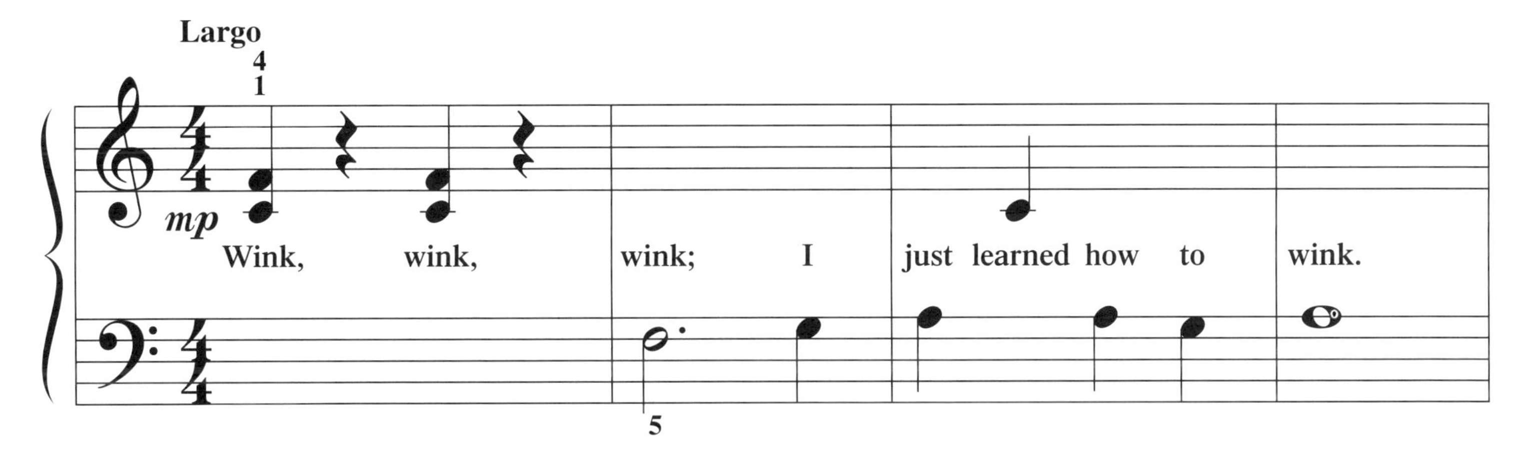
Largo
mp
Wink, wink, wink; I just learned how to wink.

5
Repeat one octave higher.
Wink, wink, wink; It's real - ly cool, I think.

After you are comfortable with this piece, try playing with **L.H.** finger **3** on **F.**

Teacher Duet: Student plays one octave higher.

R.H.
L.H.
p
5

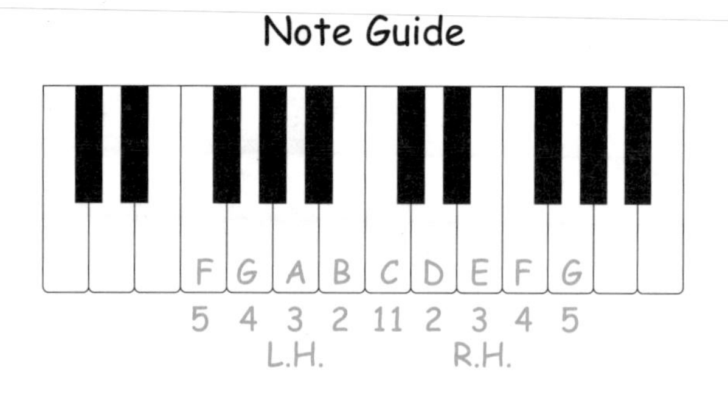
Note Guide
F G A B C D E F G
5 4 3 2 1 1 2 3 4 5
L.H.
R.H.

What Scares Me

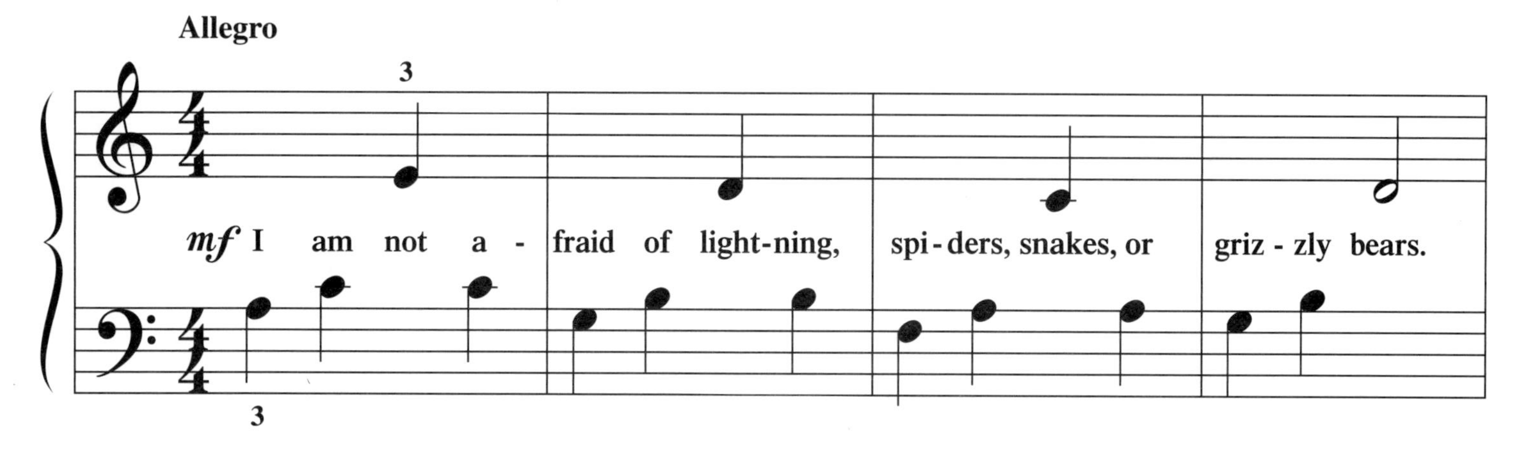
Allegro
3
mf I am not a - fraid of light-ning, spi-ders, snakes, or griz - zly bears.
3

5
Repeat one octave higher.
1
There is just one thing that scares me: it is called the den - tist's chair!
5

Teacher Duet: Student plays one octave higher.

5
R.H.
L.H. mp
5
5